Learning MATLAB® 7

How to Contact The MathWorks:

`www.mathworks.com`	Web
`comp.soft-sys.matlab`	Newsgroup

`suggest@mathworks.com`	Product enhancement suggestions
`bugs@mathworks.com`	Bug reports
`doc@mathworks.com`	Documentation error reports

ISBN 0-9755787-6-6

Revision History

August 1999	First printing	New manual
January 2001	Second printing	Revised for MATLAB 6.0 (Release 12)
November 2002	Third printing	Revised for MATLAB 6.5 (Release 13)
July 2004	Fourth printing	Revised for MATLAB 7.0 (Release 14)
December 2005	Fifth printing	Revised for MATLAB 7.1 (Release 14SP3)

Contents

1 Introducing MATLAB & Simulink Student Version

2 Installing MATLAB & Simulink Student Version

3 Introduction

4 Matrices and Arrays

5 Graphics

6 Programming

7 Creating Graphical User Interfaces

8 Desktop Tools and Development Environment

9 Introducing the Symbolic Math Toolbox

10 Using the Symbolic Math Toolbox

Index

Introducing MATLAB & Simulink Student Version

This chapter introduces MATLAB & Simulink Student Version and provides resources for using it.

Quick Start

If you need help installing the software, see Chapter 2, "Installing MATLAB & Simulink Student Version."

At the heart of MATLAB® is a programming language you must learn before you can fully exploit its power. You can learn the basics of MATLAB quickly, and mastery comes shortly after. You will be rewarded with high-productivity, high-creativity computing power that will change the way you work.

If you are new to MATLAB, you should start by reading Chapter 4, "Matrices and Arrays." The most important things to learn are how to enter matrices, how to use the : (colon) operator, and how to invoke functions. After you master the basics, you should read the rest of the MATLAB chapters in this book and run the demos:

- Chapter 3, "Introduction"

  Introduces MATLAB and the MATLAB desktop.

- Chapter 4, "Matrices and Arrays"

  Introduces matrices and arrays, how to enter and generate them, how to operate on them, and how to control Command Window input and output.

- Chapter 5, "Graphics"

  Introduces MATLAB graphic capabilities and the tools that let you customize your graphs to suit your specific needs.

- Chapter 6, "Programming"

  Describes how to use the MATLAB language to create scripts and functions, and manipulate data structures, such as cell arrays and multidimensional arrays.

About the Student Version

MATLAB and Simulink® are the premier software packages for technical computing in education and industry. MATLAB & Simulink Student Version provides all of the features of professional MATLAB, with no limitations, and the full functionality of professional Simulink, with model sizes up to 1000 blocks. The Student Version gives you immediate access to high-performance numeric computing, modeling, and simulation power.

MATLAB allows you to focus on your course work and applications rather than on programming details. It enables you to solve many numerical problems in a fraction of the time it would take you to write a program in a lower-level language such as C, C++, or Fortran. MATLAB helps you better understand and apply concepts in applications ranging from engineering and mathematics to chemistry, biology, and economics.

Simulink is an interactive tool for modeling, simulating, and analyzing dynamic systems, including controls, signal processing, communications, and other complex systems.

The Symbolic Math Toolbox, also included with the Student Version, is based on the Maple® 8 symbolic math engine and lets you perform symbolic computations and variable-precision arithmetic.

MATLAB products are used in a broad range of industries, including automotive, aerospace, electronics, environmental, telecommunications, computer peripherals, finance, and medicine. More than one million technical professionals at the world's most innovative technology companies, government research labs, financial institutions, and at more than 3500 universities, rely on MATLAB and Simulink as the fundamental tools for their engineering and scientific work.

Student Use Policy

This MATLAB & Simulink Student Version License is for use in conjunction with courses offered at degree-granting institutions. The MathWorks offers this license as a special service to the student community and asks your help in seeing that its terms are not abused.

To use this Student License, you must be a student either enrolled in a degree-granting institution or participating in a continuing education program at a degree-granting educational university.

You may not use this Student License at a company or government lab. Also, you may not use it if you are an instructor at a university, or for research, commercial, or industrial purposes. In these cases, you can acquire the appropriate professional or academic license by contacting The MathWorks.

Student Version Activation

Activation is a secure process that verifies licensed student users. This process validates the serial number and ensures that it is not used on more systems than allowed by the MathWorks End User License Agreement.

The activation technology is designed to provide an easier and more effective way for students to authenticate and use their product than prior releases of MATLAB & Simulink Student Version.

The quickest way to activate your software is to use the activation program that starts following product installation. The activation program will guide you through the activation process. Alternatively, you can activate your software on the `mathworks.com` Web site.

Activation requires completion of three activities:

- Provide registration information by creating a MathWorks Account.
- Provide your serial number and the Machine ID for the computer you will be installing the software on.
- For those students who did not provide proof of student status at the time of purchase, submission and verification of proof of student status is needed.

For more information on activation, see `www.mathworks.com/academia/student_version/activation.html`.

Obtaining Additional MathWorks Products

Many college courses recommend MATLAB and Simulink as standard instructional software. In some cases, the courses may require particular toolboxes, blocksets, or other products. Toolboxes and blocksets are add-on products that extend MATLAB and Simulink with domain-specific capabilities. Many of these products are available for MATLAB & Simulink Student Version. You may purchase and download these additional products at special student prices from the MathWorks Store at `www.mathworks.com/store`.

Some of the products you can purchase include

- Bioinformatics Toolbox
- Communications Blockset
- Control System Toolbox
- Fixed-Point Toolbox
- Fuzzy Logic Toolbox
- Image Processing Toolbox
- Neural Network Toolbox
- Optimization Toolbox
- Signal Processing Toolbox
- Statistics Toolbox
- Stateflow® (A demo version of Stateflow is included with your MATLAB & Simulink Student Version.)

For an up-to-date list of available products and their product dependencies, visit the MathWorks Store.

Note The toolboxes and blocksets that are available for MATLAB & Simulink Student Version have the same functionality as the professional versions. However, the student versions of the toolboxes and blocksets will work only with the Student Version. Likewise, the professional versions of the toolboxes and blocksets will not work with the Student Version.

Getting Started with MATLAB

What I Want	What I Should Do
I need to install and activate MATLAB.	See Chapter 2, "Installing MATLAB & Simulink Student Version."
I want to start MATLAB.	**(Microsoft Windows)** Double-click the `MATLAB` icon on your desktop. **(Macintosh OS X)** Double-click the `MATLAB` icon on your desktop. **(Linux)** Enter the `matlab` command at the command prompt.
I'm new to MATLAB and want to learn it quickly.	Start by reading Chapter 3, "Introduction," through Chapter 6, "Programming," in this book. The most important things to learn are how to enter matrices, how to use the : (colon) operator, and how to invoke functions. You will also get a brief overview of graphics and programming in MATLAB. After you master the basics, you can access the rest of the documentation through the online help facility (Help).
I want to look at some samples of what you can do with MATLAB.	There are numerous demonstrations and video tutorials included with MATLAB. You can see these by clicking **Demos** in the Help browser or selecting **Demos** from the **Help** menu. There are demonstrations of mathematics, graphics, programming, and much more. You also will find a large selection of demos at `www.mathworks.com/demos`.

Finding Reference Information

What I Want	What I Should Do
I want to know how to use a specific function.	Use the online help facility (Help). To access Help, use the command `helpbrowser` or use the **Help** menu. "MATLAB Functions: Volume 1 (A-E), Volume 2 (F-O), and Volume 3 (P-Z)" are also available in PDF format from Printing the Documentation Set on the MATLAB product page.
I want to find a function for a specific purpose, but I don't know the function name.	There are several choices: • From Help, browse the MATLAB functions by selecting **Functions — Categorical List** or **Functions — Alphabetical List**. • Use `lookfor` (e.g., `lookfor inverse`) from the command line. • Use **Index** or **Search** from Help.
I want to learn about a specific topic such as sparse matrices, ordinary differential equations, or cell arrays.	Use Help to locate the appropriate sections in the MATLAB documentation, for example, **MATLAB -> Mathematics -> Sparse Matrices**.
I want to know what functions are available in a general area.	Use Help to view **Functions — Categorical List** under MATLAB. Help provides access to the reference pages for the hundreds of functions included with MATLAB.
I want to learn about the Symbolic Math Toolbox.	See Chapter 9, "Introducing the Symbolic Math Toolbox," and Chapter 10, "Using the Symbolic Math Toolbox," in this book. For complete descriptions of the Symbolic Math Toolbox functions, use Help and select **Functions — Categorical List** or **Functions — Alphabetical List** from the Symbolic Math Toolbox documentation.

Troubleshooting

What I Want	What I Should Do
I have a specific MATLAB problem I want help with.	From Help, select **Support and Web Services** and then choose **Technical Support**.
I want to report a bug or make a suggestion.	Use Help or send e-mail to `bugs@mathworks.com` or `suggest@mathworks.com`.

Other Resources

Documentation

When you install MATLAB & Simulink Student Version on your computer, you automatically install the complete online documentation for these products. Access this documentation set from Help.

Note References to UNIX in the documentation include both Linux and Mac OS X.

Web-Based Documentation

Documentation for all MathWorks products is online and available from the Support area of the MathWorks Web site. In addition to tutorials and function reference pages, you can find PDF versions of all the manuals.

MathWorks Web Site

At `www.mathworks.com`, you'll find information about MathWorks products and how they are used in education and industry, product demos, and MATLAB and Simulink based books.

MathWorks Academia Web Site

At `www.mathworks.com/academia`, you'll find resources for students and instructors for courses in engineering, mathematics, and science.

MATLAB and Simulink Based Books

At `www.mathworks.com/support/books`, you'll find books in many disciplines that use MATLAB and Simulink for examples and assignments.

MathWorks Store

At `www.mathworks.com/store`, you can purchase add-on products and documentation.

MATLAB Central — File Exchange/Newsgroup Access

At `www.mathworks.com/matlabcentral`, you can access the MATLAB Usenet newsgroup (`comp.soft-sys.matlab`) as well as an extensive library of user-contributed files called the MATLAB Central File Exchange. MATLAB Central is also home to the Link Exchange where you can share your favorite links to various educational, personal, and commercial MATLAB Web sites.

The `comp.soft-sys.matlab` newsgroup is for professionals and students who use MATLAB and have questions or comments about it and its associated software. This is an important resource for posing questions and answering queries from other MATLAB users. MathWorks staff also participates actively in this newsgroup.

Technical Support

At `www.mathworks.com/support`, you can get technical support.

Telephone and e-mail access to our technical support staff is not available for students running MATLAB & Simulink Student Version unless you are experiencing difficulty installing or downloading MATLAB or related products. There are numerous other vehicles of technical support that you can use. The "Resources and Support" section in the CD holder identifies ways to obtain additional help.

After checking the available MathWorks sources for help, if you still cannot resolve your problem, please contact your instructor. Your instructor should be able to help you. If your instructor needs assistance doing so, telephone and e-mail technical support is available to registered instructors who have adopted MATLAB & Simulink Student Version in their courses.

Differences Between the Student and Professional Versions

MATLAB

The Student Version includes all of the features of the professional version of MATLAB.

MATLAB Differences

There are a few small differences between the Student Version and the professional version of MATLAB:

- The MATLAB prompt in the Student Version is
  `EDU>>`
- The window title bars include the words
  <Student Version>
- Printouts contain the footer
  `Student Version of MATLAB`
- The **Check for Updates** menu option on the Help menu is not available in the Student Version.

Simulink

The Student Version contains the complete Simulink product, which is used with MATLAB to model, simulate, and analyze dynamic systems.

Simulink Differences

- Models are limited to 1000 blocks.

Note You may encounter some demos that use more than 1000 blocks. In these cases, a dialog will display stating that the block limit has been exceeded and the demo will not run.

- The window title bars include the words
  <Student Version>

- Printouts contain the footer

  `Student Version of MATLAB`

Note The Using Simulink documentation, which is accessible from the Help browser, contains all of the information in the Learning Simulink book plus additional advanced information.

Symbolic Math Toolbox

The Symbolic Math Toolbox included with this Student Version lets you access all of the functions in the professional version of the Symbolic Math Toolbox except `maple`, `mapleinit`, and `mhelp`. For more information about the Symbolic Math Toolbox, see its documentation.

Installing MATLAB & Simulink Student Version

This chapter describes how to install and activate MATLAB & Simulink Student Version.

Installing on Windows

This section describes the system requirements necessary to install MATLAB & Simulink Student Version on a Windows computer. It also provides step-by-step instructions for installing and activating the software.

System Requirements

Note For more information on system requirements, visit `www.mathworks.com/academia/student_version/requirements.html`.

MATLAB and Simulink

- Windows XP® (Service Pack 1 or 2) or Windows 2000® (Service Pack 3 or 4)
- Intel® Pentium® III processor or later, Celeron® processor, or Intel® Xeon™ processor family; AMD Athlon™ / Duron™/ Opteron™; or compatible processor
- 256 MB RAM (512 MB RAM recommended)
- 500 MB disk space
- 16-, 24-, or 32-bit OpenGL® capable graphics adaptor
- CD-ROM or DVD drive (for installation)
- E-mail (required), internet access (recommended) for product activation

MEX-Files

MEX-files are dynamically linked subroutines that MATLAB can automatically load and execute. They provide a mechanism by which you can call your own C and Fortran subroutines from MATLAB as if they were built-in functions.

For More Information "External Interfaces" in the MATLAB documentation provides information on how to write MEX-files. "External Interfaces Reference" in the MATLAB documentation describes the collection of these functions. Both of these are available from Help.

If you plan to build your own MEX-files, you will need a supported compiler. For the most up-to-date information about compilers, see the support area at the MathWorks Web site (`www.mathworks.com`).

Installing and Activating the Student Version

This list summarizes the steps in the standard installation procedure. You can perform the installation and activation by simply following the instructions in the dialog boxes presented by the installation program; it walks you through this process:

1. Exit any existing copies of MATLAB you have running.
2. Insert the MATLAB & Simulink Student Version CD in your CD-ROM drive. To start the installation program, run `setup.exe` from the CD.
3. Read the **Welcome** screen, then click **Next**.
4. Enter your name and school name, then click **Next**.
5. Review the software licensing agreement and, if you agree with the terms, select **Yes** and click **Next**.
6. Review the Student Use Policy and, if you satisfy the terms, select **Yes** and click **Next**.
7. Choose your installation type. Typical installation installs all products; custom installation gives you control over the installation such as selecting which products to install. Select the installation type and click **Next**.
8. The **Folder Selection** dialog box lets you specify the name of the folder into which you want to install MATLAB. You can accept the default destination folder or specify the name of a different installation folder. If the folder doesn't exist, the installer creates it. To continue with the installation, click **Next**.
9. The **Confirmation** dialog box lets you confirm your installation options. To change a setting, click the **Back** button. To proceed with the installation, click **Install**.

Note The installation process installs the online documentation for each product you install. This does not include documentation in PDF format, which is available only at the MathWorks Web site.

---

10 When the installation successfully completes, the activation process begins by displaying the **Activation Overview**, which describes the three steps in the process. During activation, you will:

- Enter your serial number and e-mail address.
- Provide registration information by creating a MathWorks account.
- Provide proof of student status, unless previously provided.

11 As the activation process proceeds, read the screens and enter the corresponding information. At the completion of the activation process, you will be able to use your Student Version of MATLAB & Simulink. In certain cases, your software will be temporarily activated for 30 days until your proof of student status is verified. In these cases, you will be reminded that your activation is temporary and that you need to complete the activation process. Once your proof of student status is verified, your activation is complete.

Note If you encounter a problem during the activation process, check `www.mathworks.com/academia/student_version/activation.html` for more information.

---

12 To start MATLAB, double-click the MATLAB icon that the installer creates on your desktop.

13 Customize any MATLAB environment options, if desired. For example, to specify welcome messages, default definitions, or any MATLAB expressions that you want executed every time MATLAB is invoked, create a file named `startup.m` in the `$MATLAB\toolbox\local` folder, where `$MATLAB` is the name of your MATLAB installation folder. Every time you start MATLAB, it executes the commands in the `startup.m` file.

14 Perform any additional configuration by typing the appropriate command at the MATLAB command prompt. For example, to configure the MATLAB Notebook, type `notebook -setup`. To configure a compiler to work with the MATLAB External Interface, type `mex -setup`.

For More Information The Installation Guide for Windows documentation provides additional installation information. This manual is available from Help.

Installing Additional Toolboxes

To purchase additional toolboxes, visit the MathWorks Store at `www.mathworks.com/store`. Once you purchase a toolbox, the product and its online documentation are downloaded to your computer.

When you download a toolbox, you receive an installation program for the toolbox. To install the toolbox and its documentation, run the installation program by double-clicking the installer icon. After you successfully install the toolbox, all of its functionality and documentation will be available to you when you start MATLAB.

Accessing the Online Documentation (Help)

To access the online documentation (Help), select **Full Product Family Help** from the **Help** menu in the MATLAB Command Window. You can also type `helpbrowser` at the MATLAB prompt. The Help browser appears.

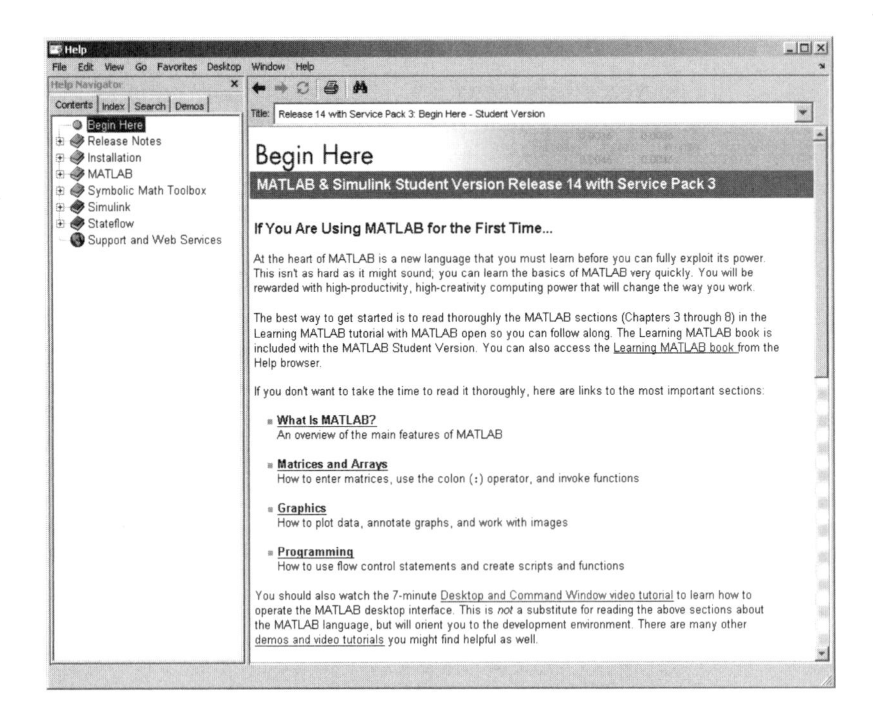

Installing on Mac OS X

This section describes the system requirements necessary to install MATLAB & Simulink Student Version on a Macintosh computer. It also provides step-by-step instructions for installing and activating the software.

System Requirements

Note For more information on system requirements, visit `www.mathworks.com/academia/student_version/requirements.html`.

MATLAB and Simulink

- Mac OS X 10.3.8, 10.3.9 (Panther™), or 10.4 (Tiger™)
- PowerPC G4 or G5 processor
- 256 MB RAM (512 MB RAM recommended)
- 500 MB disk space
- 16-bit graphics or higher adaptor and display (24-bit recommended)
- X11 (X server)
- CD-ROM or DVD drive (for installation)
- E-mail (required), internet access (recommended) for product activation

MEX-Files

MEX-files are dynamically linked subroutines that MATLAB can automatically load and execute. They provide a mechanism by which you can call your own C and Fortran subroutines from MATLAB as if they were built-in functions.

For More Information "External Interfaces" in the MATLAB documentation provides information on how to write MEX-files. "External Interfaces Reference" in the MATLAB documentation describes the collection of these functions. Both of these are available from Help.

If you plan to build your own MEX-files, you will need a supported compiler. For the most up-to-date information about compilers, see the support area at the MathWorks Web site (`www.mathworks.com`).

Installing and Activating the Student Version

The following sections describe the steps you must follow to install and activate MATLAB & Simulink Student Version on a Macintosh computer.

Note If you want to install MATLAB in a particular directory, you must have the appropriate permissions. For example, to install MATLAB in the `Applications` directory, you must have administrator status. To create symbolic links in a particular directory, you must have the appropriate permissions. For information on setting permissions (privileges), see Macintosh Help (**Command+?** from the desktop).

---

1. Insert the MATLAB & Simulink Student Version CD in the CD-ROM drive. When the CD's icon appears on the desktop, double-click the icon to display the CD's contents.
2. Double-click the `InstallForMacOSX` icon to begin the installation.

3 To install the MathWorks products, you must enter a username and password for an administrator. Enter the username and password in the **Authenticate** dialog box and then click **OK**.

Note The user account you set up when you configured your Mac is an administrator account. If you don't know the username and password for an administrator, check with the person who administers your Macintosh.

---

4 When the **Important Information** window appears, review its contents. Click **Continue** to proceed with the installation.

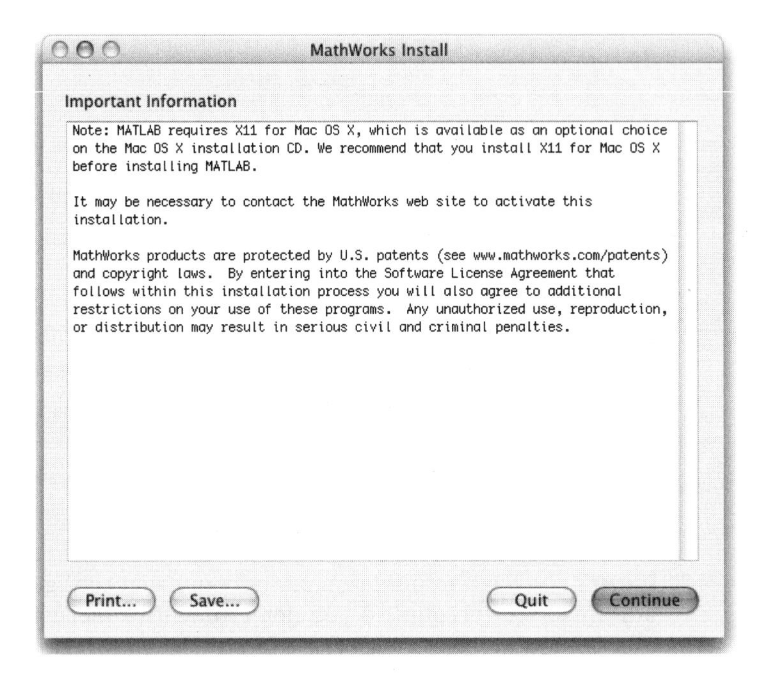

Note You will not be able to run MATLAB & Simulink Student Version until you install X11 for Mac OS X.

---

5 The Software License Agreement is displayed. If you agree to its terms, you can continue the installation.

6 The Student Use Policy is displayed. If you qualify for the student license and agree to its terms, click **Yes**.

7 The default installation location is `MATLAB_SV71` in the `Applications` folder on your system disk. To accept the default, click **Continue**. To change the location, click **Choose Folder** and then navigate to the desired location.

Note Your installation folder name cannot contain spaces, the `@` character, the `%` character, or the **$** character. You cannot install into a folder named `private`, but you can have a folder named `private` on the path. To create the installation folder in this location on your system, you must have administrator privileges. For information on setting privileges, see Macintosh Help (**Command+?** from the desktop).

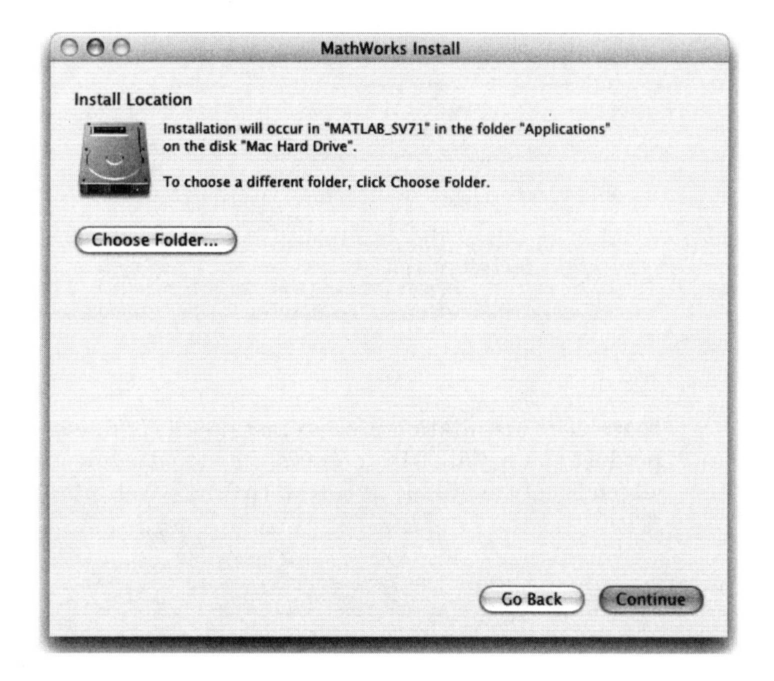

8 Select the products you want to install from the list of products available for installation and then click **Continue**.

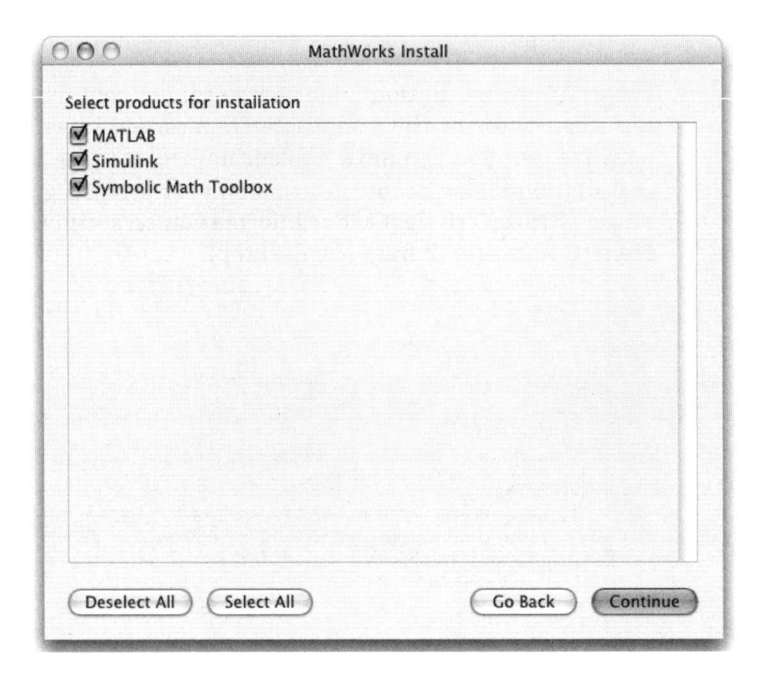

Note The installation process installs the online documentation for each product you install. This does not include documentation in PDF format, which is only available at the MathWorks Web site.

---

9 When the installation successfully completes, the installer displays the following **Installation is complete** window. This gives you options for accessing MATLAB. Check your desired options for accessing MATLAB, and click **Continue** to begin the activation process.

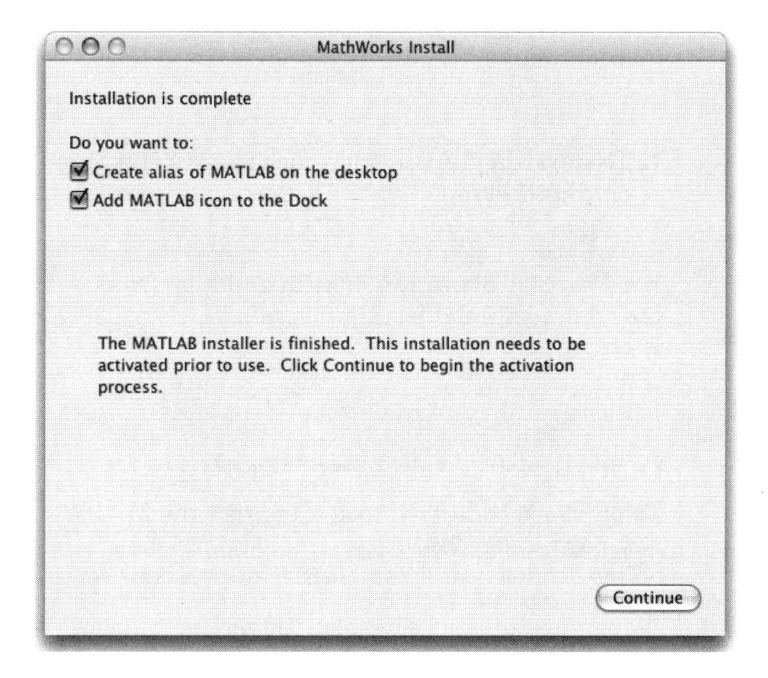

10 The activation process displays the **Activation Overview**, which describes the three steps in the process. During activation, you will:

- Enter your serial number and e-mail address.
- Provide registration information by creating a MathWorks account.
- Provide proof of student status, unless previously provided.

11 As the activation process proceeds, read the screens and enter the corresponding information. At the completion of the activation process, you will be able to use your Student Version of MATLAB & Simulink. In certain cases, your software will be temporarily activated for 30 days until your proof of student status is verified. In these cases, you will be reminded that your activation is temporary and that you need to complete the activation process. Once your proof of student status is verified, your activation is complete.

Note If you encounter a problem during the activation process, check `www.mathworks.com/academia/student_version/activation.html` for more information.

---

12 To start MATLAB, double-click the MATLAB icon that the installer creates on your desktop.

For More Information The Installation Guide for Mac OS X documentation provides additional installation information. This manual is available from Help.

Installing Additional Toolboxes

To purchase additional toolboxes, visit the MathWorks Store at `www.mathworks.com/store`. Once you purchase a toolbox, the product and its online documentation are downloaded to your computer.

When you download a toolbox, you receive a file for the toolbox. Double-clicking the downloaded file's icon creates a folder that contains the installation program for the toolbox. To install the toolbox and its documentation, run the installation program by double-clicking its icon. After you successfully install the toolbox, all of its functionality and documentation will be available to you when you start MATLAB.

Accessing the Online Documentation (Help)

To access the online documentation (Help), select **Full Product Family Help** from the **Help** menu in the MATLAB Command Window. You can also type `helpbrowser` at the MATLAB prompt. The Help browser appears.

Mac OS X Documentation

In general, the documentation for MathWorks products is not specific for individual platforms unless the product is available only on a particular platform. For the Macintosh, when you access a product's documentation either in print or online through the Help browser, make sure you refer to the UNIX platform if there is different documentation for different platforms.

Installing on Linux

This section describes the system requirements necessary to install MATLAB & Simulink Student Version on a Linux computer. It also provides step-by-step instructions for installing and activating the software.

System Requirements

Note For more information on system requirements, visit `www.mathworks.com/academia/student_version/requirements.html`.

MATLAB and Simulink

- Linux Kernel 2.4.x; glibc (glibc6) 2.3.2 and 2.2.5 or Linux 2.6.x; (glibc6) 2.3.2
- Intel® Pentium® III processor or later, Celeron® processor or Intel® Xeon™ processor family; AMD Athlon™ / Duron™/ Opteron™; or compatible processor
- 256 MB RAM (512 MB recommended)
- 500 MB disk space
- 16-bit graphics or higher adaptor and display (24-bit recommended)
- CD-ROM or DVD drive (for installation)
- E-mail (required), internet access (recommended) for product activation

MEX-Files

MEX-files are dynamically linked subroutines that MATLAB can automatically load and execute. They provide a mechanism by which you can call your own C and Fortran subroutines from MATLAB as if they were built-in functions.

For More Information "External Interfaces" in the MATLAB documentation provides information on how to write MEX-files. "External Interfaces Reference" in the MATLAB documentation describes the collection of these functions. Both of these are available from Help.

If you plan to build your own MEX-files, you will need a supported compiler. For the most up-to-date information about compilers, see the support area at the MathWorks Web site (`www.mathworks.com`).

Installing and Activating the Student Version

The following instructions describe how to install and activate MATLAB & Simulink Student Version on a Linux computer.

Note On most systems, you will need root privileges to perform certain steps in the installation procedure.

---

1 Insert the MATLAB & Simulink Student Version CD in the CD-ROM drive.

   If your CD-ROM drive is not accessible to your operating system, you will need to mount the CD-ROM drive on your system. Create a directory to be the mount point for it.

   ```
   mkdir /cdrom
   ```

   Mount a CD-ROM drive using the command

   ```
   $ mount /cdrom
   ```

   If your system requires that you have root privileges to mount a CD-ROM drive, this command should work on most systems.

   ```
   # mount -t iso9660 /dev/cdrom /cdrom
   ```

   To enable nonroot users to mount a CD-ROM drive, include the `exec` option in the entry for CD-ROM drives in your `/etc/fstab` file, as in the following example.

   ```
   /dev/cdrom /cdrom iso9660 noauto,ro,user,exec 0 0
   ```

   Note, however, that this option is often omitted from the `/etc/fstab` file for security reasons.

2 Create an installation directory and move to it, using the `cd` command. For example, if you are going to install into the location `/usr/local/matlab71_sv`, use the commands

```
cd /usr/local
mkdir matlab71_sv
cd matlab71_sv
```

Subsequent instructions in this section refer to this directory as `$MATLAB`.

3 Start the MathWorks Installer by running the install script.

```
/cdrom/install_unix.sh
```

The MathWorks Installer displays the **Welcome** dialog box. Click **OK** to proceed with the installation.

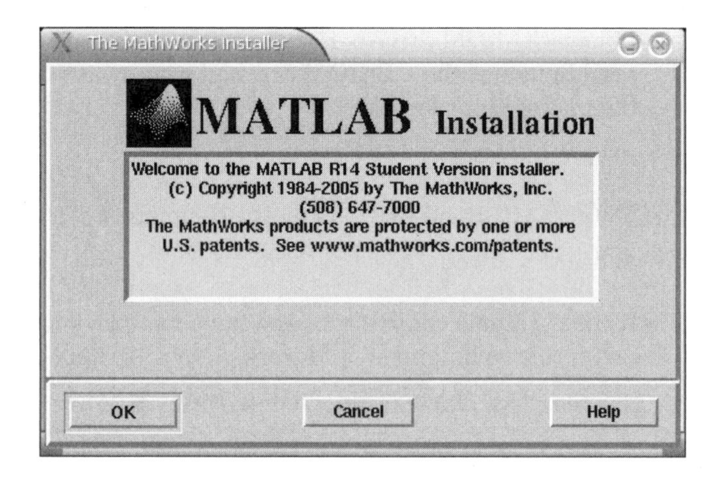

Note If you need additional help on any step during this installation process, click the **Help** button at the bottom of the dialog box.

---

4 The Software License Agreement is displayed. If you agree to its terms, you can continue the installation.

5 Verify the name of the directory in which you want to install MATLAB in the **MATLAB Root Directory** dialog box. You can edit the pathname in this dialog box. If the MATLAB root directory is correct, click **OK** to proceed with the installation.

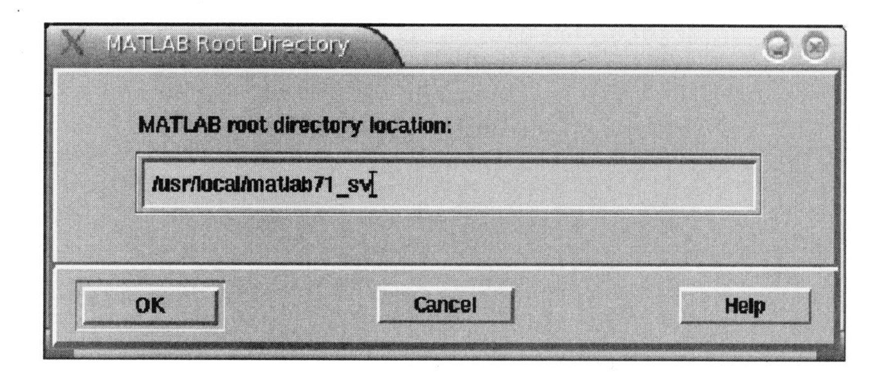

6 Select the products you want to install in the **Installation Options** dialog box.

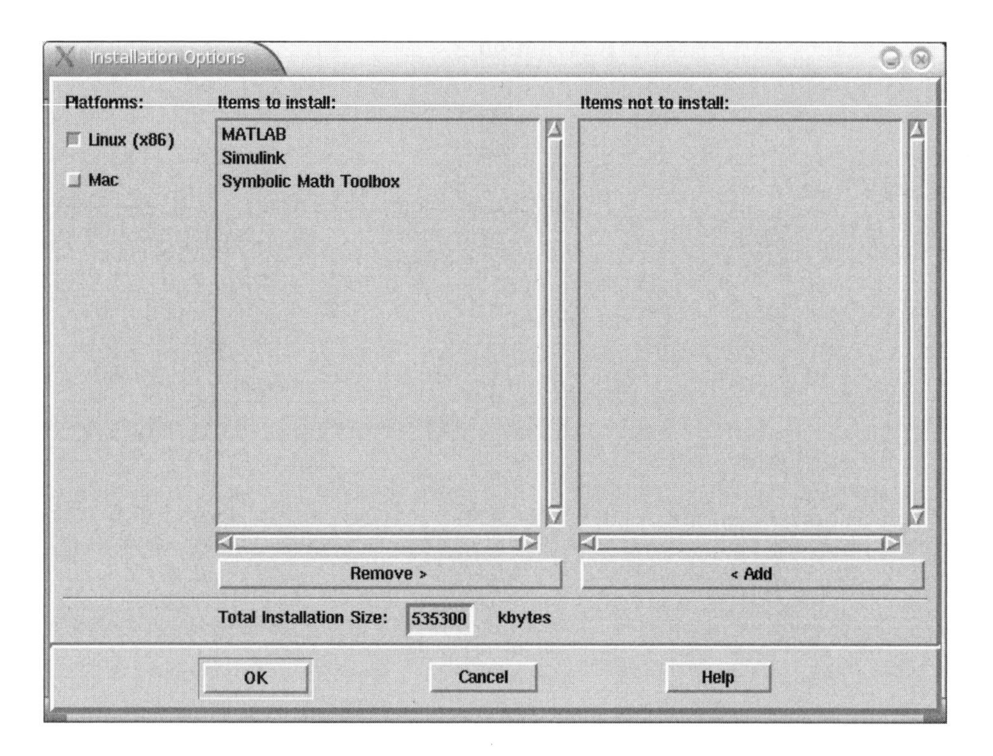

The products you are licensed to install are listed in the **Items to install** list box. If you do not want to install a product, select it in the list and click **Remove**. The installer moves the product to the **Items not to install** list.

To install the complete MATLAB & Simulink Student Version, keep all the products listed in the **Items to install** list.

After you select the products you want to install, click **OK** to proceed with the installation.

7 Specify in the **Installation Data** dialog box the directory in which you want to install symbolic links to the `matlab` and `mex` scripts. Choose a directory that is common to all users' paths, such as `/usr/local/bin`. You must be logged in as `root` to do this. If you choose not to set up these links, you can still run MATLAB; however, you must specify the full path to the MATLAB start-up script. Click **OK** to proceed with the installation.

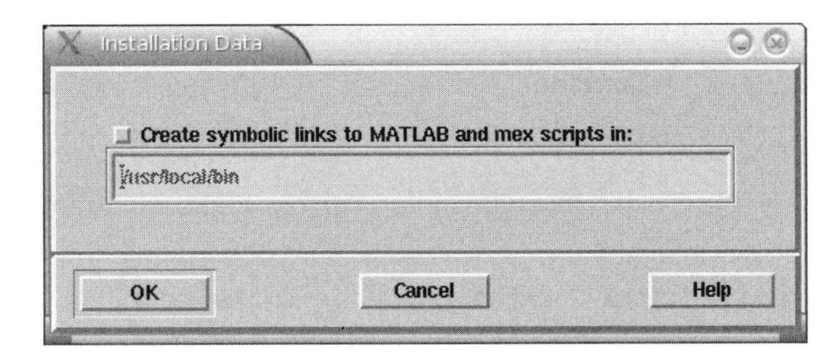

8 Start the installation by clicking **OK** in the **Begin Installation** dialog box. During the installation, the installer displays information about the status of the installation.

9 When the installation successfully completes, the activation process begins by displaying the **Activation Overview**, which describes the three steps in the process. During activation, you will:

- Enter your serial number and e-mail address.
- Provide registration information by creating a MathWorks account.
- Provide proof of student status, unless previously provided.

10 As the activation process proceeds, read the screens and enter the corresponding information. At the completion of the activation process, you will be able to use your Student Version of MATLAB & Simulink. In certain cases, your software will be temporarily activated for 30 days until your proof of student status is verified. In these cases, you will be reminded that your activation is temporary and that you need to complete the activation process. Once your proof of student status is verified, your activation is complete.

Note If you encounter a problem during the activation process, check `www.mathworks.com/academia/student_version/activation.html` for more information.

---

11 To start MATLAB, enter the `matlab` command. If you did not set up symbolic links in a directory on your path, you must provide the full pathname to the `matlab` command

```
$MATLAB/bin/matlab
```

where `$MATLAB` represents your MATLAB installation directory.

Installing Additional Toolboxes

To purchase additional toolboxes, visit the MathWorks Store at `www.mathworks.com/store`. Once you purchase a toolbox, the product and its online documentation are downloaded to your computer. When you download a toolbox on Linux, you receive a tar file (a standard, compressed archive format).

To install the toolbox and documentation, you must

1 Place the tar file in your installation directory (`$MATLAB`) and extract the files from the archive. Use the following syntax.

```
tar -xf filename
```

2 Start the MathWorks Installer.

```
install
```

After you successfully install the toolbox and documentation, all of its functionality will be available to you when you start MATLAB.

Accessing the Online Documentation (Help)

To access the online documentation (Help), select **Full Product Family Help** from the **Help** menu in the MATLAB desktop. You can also type `helpbrowser` at the MATLAB prompt.

Introduction

This chapter introduces MATLAB and Simulink, the documentation set, how to start and stop MATLAB, and the MATLAB desktop.

About MATLAB and Simulink

What Is MATLAB?

MATLAB is a high-performance language for technical computing. It integrates computation, visualization, and programming in an easy-to-use environment where problems and solutions are expressed in familiar mathematical notation. Typical uses include

- Math and computation
- Algorithm development
- Data acquisition
- Modeling, simulation, and prototyping
- Data analysis, exploration, and visualization
- Scientific and engineering graphics
- Application development, including graphical user interface building

MATLAB is an interactive system whose basic data element is an array that does not require dimensioning. This allows you to solve many technical computing problems, especially those with matrix and vector formulations, in a fraction of the time it would take to write a program in a scalar noninteractive language such as C or Fortran.

The name MATLAB stands for *matrix laboratory*. MATLAB was originally written to provide easy access to matrix software developed by the LINPACK and EISPACK projects. Today, MATLAB engines incorporate the LAPACK and BLAS libraries, embedding the state of the art in software for matrix computation.

MATLAB has evolved over a period of years with input from many users. In university environments, it is the standard instructional tool for introductory and advanced courses in mathematics, engineering, and science. In industry, MATLAB is the tool of choice for high-productivity research, development, and analysis.

Toolboxes

MATLAB features a family of add-on application-specific solutions called *toolboxes*. Very important to most users of MATLAB, toolboxes allow you to *learn* and *apply* specialized technology. Toolboxes are comprehensive collections of MATLAB functions (M-files) that extend the MATLAB environment to solve particular classes of problems. Areas in which toolboxes are available include signal processing, control systems, neural networks, fuzzy logic, wavelets, simulation, and many others.

The MATLAB System

The MATLAB system consists of five main parts:

Development Environment. This is the set of tools and facilities that help you use MATLAB functions and files. Many of these tools are graphical user interfaces. It includes the MATLAB desktop and Command Window, a command history, an editor and debugger, and browsers for viewing help, the workspace, files, and the search path.

The MATLAB Mathematical Function Library. This is a vast collection of computational algorithms ranging from elementary functions, like sum, sine, cosine, and complex arithmetic, to more sophisticated functions like matrix inverse, matrix eigenvalues, Bessel functions, and fast Fourier transforms.

The MATLAB Language. This is a high-level matrix/array language with control flow statements, functions, data structures, input/output, and object-oriented programming features. It allows both "programming in the small" to rapidly create quick and dirty throw-away programs, and "programming in the large" to create large and complex application programs.

Graphics. MATLAB has extensive facilities for displaying vectors and matrices as graphs, as well as annotating and printing these graphs. It includes high-level functions for two-dimensional and three-dimensional data visualization, image processing, animation, and presentation graphics. It also includes low-level functions that allow you to fully customize the appearance of graphics as well as to build complete graphical user interfaces on your MATLAB applications.

The MATLAB Application Program Interface (API). This is a library that allows you to write C and Fortran programs that interact with MATLAB. It includes facilities for calling routines from MATLAB (dynamic linking), calling MATLAB as a computational engine, and for reading and writing MAT-files.

What Is Simulink?

Simulink is an interactive environment for modeling, simulating, and analyzing dynamic, multidomain systems. It lets you build a block diagram, simulate the system's behavior, evaluate its performance, and refine the design. Simulink integrates seamlessly with MATLAB, providing you with immediate access to an extensive range of analysis and design tools. These benefits make Simulink the tool of choice for control system design, DSP design, communications system design, and other simulation applications.

Blocksets are collections of application-specific blocks that support multiple design areas, including electrical power-system modeling, digital signal processing, fixed-point algorithm development, and more. These blocks can be incorporated directly into your Simulink models.

Real-Time Workshop® is a program that generates optimized, portable, and customizable ANSI C code from Simulink models. Generated code can run on PC hardware, DSPs, microcontrollers on bare-board environments, and with commercial or proprietary real-time operating systems.

What Is Stateflow?

Stateflow is an interactive design tool for modeling and simulating complex reactive systems. Tightly integrated with Simulink and MATLAB, Stateflow provides Simulink users with an elegant solution for designing embedded systems by giving them an efficient way to incorporate complex control and supervisory logic within their Simulink models.

With Stateflow, you can quickly develop graphical models of event-driven systems using finite state machine theory, statechart formalisms, and flow diagram notation. Together, Stateflow and Simulink serve as an executable specification and virtual prototype of your system design.

Note Your MATLAB & Simulink Student Version includes a demo version of Stateflow.

MATLAB Documentation

MATLAB provides extensive documentation, in both printed and online format, to help you learn about and use all of its features. If you are a new user, start with the MATLAB specific sections in this book. It covers all the primary MATLAB features at a high level, including many examples.

The MATLAB online help provides task-oriented and reference information about MATLAB features. MATLAB documentation is also available in printed form and in PDF format.

MATLAB Online Help

To view the online documentation, select **MATLAB Help** from the **Help** menu in MATLAB. The MATLAB documentation is organized into these main topics:

- Desktop Tools and Development Environment — Startup and shutdown, the desktop, and other tools that help you use MATLAB
- Mathematics — Mathematical operations and data analysis
- Programming — The MATLAB language and how to develop MATLAB applications
- Graphics — Tools and techniques for plotting, graph annotation, printing, and programming with Handle Graphics®
- 3-D Visualization — Visualizing surface and volume data, transparency, and viewing and lighting techniques
- Creating Graphical User Interfaces — GUI-building tools and how to write callback functions
- External Interfaces — MEX-files, the MATLAB engine, and interfacing to Java, COM, and the serial port

MATLAB also includes reference documentation for all MATLAB functions:

- Functions — Categorical List — Lists all MATLAB functions grouped into categories
- Handle Graphics Property Browser — Provides easy access to descriptions of graphics object properties
- External Interfaces Reference — Covers those functions used by the MATLAB external interfaces, providing information on syntax in the calling language, description, arguments, return values, and examples

The MATLAB online documentation also includes

- Examples — An index of examples included in the documentation
- Release Notes — New features and known problems in the current release
- Printable Documentation — PDF versions of the documentation suitable for printing

For more information about using the Help browser, see Chapter 8, "Desktop Tools and Development Environment."

Note References to UNIX in the documentation include both Linux and Mac OS X.

Starting and Quitting MATLAB

Starting MATLAB

On Windows platforms, start MATLAB by double-clicking the MATLAB shortcut icon on your Windows desktop.

On Mac OS X platforms, start MATLAB by double-clicking the MATLAB icon on your desktop.

On Linux platforms, start MATLAB by typing `matlab` at the operating system prompt.

You can customize MATLAB startup. For example, you can change the directory in which MATLAB starts or automatically execute MATLAB statements in a script file named `startup.m`.

For More Information See "Starting MATLAB" in the Desktop Tools and Development Environment documentation.

Quitting MATLAB

To end your MATLAB session, select **File -> Exit MATLAB** in the desktop, or type `quit` in the Command Window. You can run a script file named `finish.m` each time MATLAB quits that, for example, executes functions to save the workspace, or displays a quit confirmation dialog box.

For More Information See "Quitting MATLAB" in the Desktop Tools and Development Environment documentation.

MATLAB Desktop

When you start MATLAB, the MATLAB desktop appears, containing tools (graphical user interfaces) for managing files, variables, and applications associated with MATLAB.

The following illustration shows the default desktop. You can customize the arrangement of tools and documents to suit your needs. For more information about the desktop tools, see Chapter 8, “Desktop Tools and Development Environment.”

Enter MATLAB functions at the Command Window prompt.

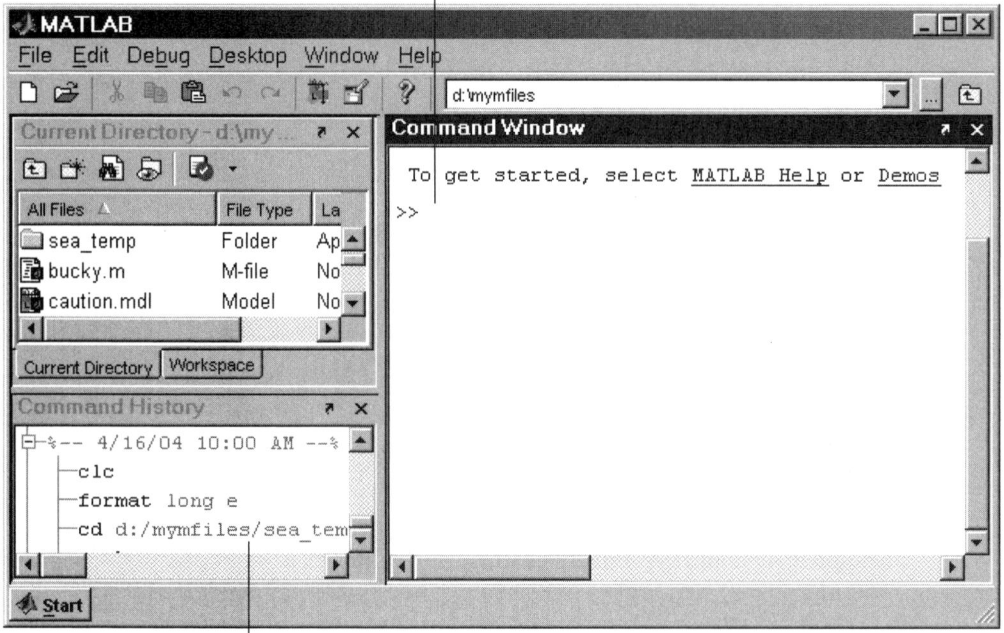

The Command History maintains a record of the MATLAB functions you ran.

4

Matrices and Arrays

This chapter introduces you to MATLAB by teaching you how to handle matrices.

Matrices and Magic Squares

In MATLAB, a matrix is a rectangular array of numbers. Special meaning is sometimes attached to 1-by-1 matrices, which are scalars, and to matrices with only one row or column, which are vectors. MATLAB has other ways of storing both numeric and nonnumeric data, but in the beginning, it is usually best to think of everything as a matrix. The operations in MATLAB are designed to be as natural as possible. Where other programming languages work with numbers one at a time, MATLAB allows you to work with entire matrices quickly and easily. A good example matrix, used throughout this book, appears in the Renaissance engraving Melencolia I by the German artist and amateur mathematician Albrecht Dürer.

This image is filled with mathematical symbolism, and if you look carefully, you will see a matrix in the upper right corner. This matrix is known as a magic square and was believed by many in Dürer's time to have genuinely magical properties. It does turn out to have some fascinating characteristics worth exploring.

Entering Matrices

The best way for you to get started with MATLAB is to learn how to handle matrices. Start MATLAB and follow along with each example.

You can enter matrices into MATLAB in several different ways:

- Enter an explicit list of elements.
- Load matrices from external data files.
- Generate matrices using built-in functions.
- Create matrices with your own functions in M-files.

Start by entering Dürer's matrix as a list of its elements. You only have to follow a few basic conventions:

- Separate the elements of a row with blanks or commas.
- Use a semicolon, `;` , to indicate the end of each row.
- Surround the entire list of elements with square brackets, `[ ]`.

To enter Dürer's matrix, simply type in the Command Window

```
A = [16 3 2 13; 5 10 11 8; 9 6 7 12; 4 15 14 1]
```

MATLAB displays the matrix you just entered.

```
A =
    16     3     2    13
     5    10    11     8
     9     6     7    12
     4    15    14     1
```

This matrix matches the numbers in the engraving. Once you have entered the matrix, it is automatically remembered in the MATLAB workspace. You can refer to it simply as A. Now that you have A in the workspace, take a look at what makes it so interesting. Why is it magic?

sum, transpose, and diag

You are probably already aware that the special properties of a magic square have to do with the various ways of summing its elements. If you take the sum along any row or column, or along either of the two main diagonals, you will always get the same number. Let us verify that using MATLAB. The first statement to try is

```
sum(A)
```

MATLAB replies with

```
ans =
    34    34    34    34
```

When you do not specify an output variable, MATLAB uses the variable ans, short for *answer*, to store the results of a calculation. You have computed a row vector containing the sums of the columns of A. Sure enough, each of the columns has the same sum, the *magic* sum, 34.

How about the row sums? MATLAB has a preference for working with the columns of a matrix, so the easiest way to get the row sums is to transpose the matrix, compute the column sums of the transpose, and then transpose the result.

MATLAB has two transpose operators. The apostrophe operator (e.g., A') performs a complex conjugate transposition. It flips a matrix about its main diagonal, and also changes the sign of the imaginary component of any complex elements of the matrix. The apostrophe-dot operator (e.g., `A'.`), transposes without affecting the sign of complex elements. For matrices containing all real elements, the two operators return the same result.

So

```
A'
```

produces

```
ans =
    16     5     9     4
     3    10     6    15
     2    11     7    14
    13     8    12     1
```

and

```
sum(A')'
```

produces a column vector containing the row sums

```
ans =
    34
    34
    34
    34
```

The sum of the elements on the main diagonal is obtained with the `sum` and the `diag` functions.

```
diag(A)
```

produces

```
ans =
    16
    10
     7
     1
```

and

```
sum(diag(A))
```

produces

```
ans =
    34
```

The other diagonal, the so-called *antidiagonal,* is not so important mathematically, so MATLAB does not have a ready-made function for it. But a function originally intended for use in graphics, `fliplr`, flips a matrix from left to right.

```
sum(diag(fliplr(A)))
```

```
ans =
    34
```

You have verified that the matrix in Dürer's engraving is indeed a magic square and, in the process, have sampled a few MATLAB matrix operations. The following sections continue to use this matrix to illustrate additional MATLAB capabilities.

Subscripts

The element in row `i` and column `j` of `A` is denoted by `A(i,j)`. For example, `A(4,2)` is the number in the fourth row and second column. For our magic square, `A(4,2)` is `15`. So to compute the sum of the elements in the fourth column of `A`, type

```
A(1,4) + A(2,4) + A(3,4) + A(4,4)
```

This produces

```
ans =
     34
```

but is not the most elegant way of summing a single column.

It is also possible to refer to the elements of a matrix with a single subscript, `A(k)`. This is the usual way of referencing row and column vectors. But it can also apply to a fully two-dimensional matrix, in which case the array is regarded as one long column vector formed from the columns of the original matrix. So, for our magic square, `A(8)` is another way of referring to the value `15` stored in `A(4,2)`.

If you try to use the value of an element outside of the matrix, it is an error.

```
t = A(4,5)
```

```
Index exceeds matrix dimensions.
```

On the other hand, if you store a value in an element outside of the matrix, the size increases to accommodate the newcomer.

```
X = A;
X(4,5) = 17

X =
    16     3     2    13     0
     5    10    11     8     0
     9     6     7    12     0
     4    15    14     1    17
```

The Colon Operator

The colon, :, is one of the most important MATLAB operators. It occurs in several different forms. The expression

```
1:10
```

is a row vector containing the integers from 1 to 10,

```
1     2     3     4     5     6     7     8     9    10
```

To obtain nonunit spacing, specify an increment. For example,

```
100:-7:50
```

is

```
100    93    86    79    72    65    58    51
```

and

```
0:pi/4:pi
```

is

```
0    0.7854    1.5708    2.3562    3.1416
```

Subscript expressions involving colons refer to portions of a matrix.

```
A(1:k,j)
```

is the first `k` elements of the `j`th column of `A`. So

```
sum(A(1:4,4))
```

computes the sum of the fourth column. But there is a better way. The colon by itself refers to *all* the elements in a row or column of a matrix and the keyword `end` refers to the *last* row or column. So

```
sum(A(:,end))
```

computes the sum of the elements in the last column of `A`.

```
ans =
      34
```

Why is the magic sum for a 4-by-4 square equal to 34? If the integers from 1 to 16 are sorted into four groups with equal sums, that sum must be

```
sum(1:16)/4
```

which, of course, is

```
ans =
      34
```

The magic Function

MATLAB actually has a built-in function that creates magic squares of almost any size. Not surprisingly, this function is named `magic`.

```
B = magic(4)

B =
    16     2     3    13
     5    11    10     8
     9     7     6    12
     4    14    15     1
```

This matrix is almost the same as the one in the Dürer engraving and has all the same "magic" properties; the only difference is that the two middle columns are exchanged.

To make this `B` into Dürer's `A`, swap the two middle columns.

```
A = B(:,[1 3 2 4])
```

This says, for each of the rows of matrix B, reorder the elements in the order 1, 3, 2, 4. It produces

```
A =
    16     3     2    13
     5    10    11     8
     9     6     7    12
     4    15    14     1
```

Why would Dürer go to the trouble of rearranging the columns when he could have used MATLAB ordering? No doubt he wanted to include the date of the engraving, 1514, at the bottom of his magic square.

Expressions

Like most other programming languages, MATLAB provides mathematical *expressions*, but unlike most programming languages, these expressions involve entire matrices. The building blocks of expressions are

- "Variables" on page 4-10
- "Numbers" on page 4-11
- "Operators" on page 4-11
- "Functions" on page 4-12

See also "Examples of Expressions" on page 4-13.

Variables

MATLAB does not require any type declarations or dimension statements. When MATLAB encounters a new variable name, it automatically creates the variable and allocates the appropriate amount of storage. If the variable already exists, MATLAB changes its contents and, if necessary, allocates new storage. For example,

```
num_students = 25
```

creates a 1-by-1 matrix named `num_students` and stores the value 25 in its single element. To view the matrix assigned to any variable, simply enter the variable name.

Variable names consist of a letter, followed by any number of letters, digits, or underscores. MATLAB is case sensitive; it distinguishes between uppercase and lowercase letters. `A` and `a` are *not* the same variable.

Although variable names can be of any length, MATLAB uses only the first `N` characters of the name, (where `N` is the number returned by the function `namelengthmax`), and ignores the rest. Hence, it is important to make each variable name unique in the first `N` characters to enable MATLAB to distinguish variables.

```
N = namelengthmax
N =
    63
```

The `genvarname` function can be useful in creating variable names that are both valid and unique.

Numbers

MATLAB uses conventional decimal notation, with an optional decimal point and leading plus or minus sign, for numbers. *Scientific notation* uses the letter `e` to specify a power-of-ten scale factor. *Imaginary numbers* use either `i` or `j` as a suffix. Some examples of legal numbers are

```
3              -99            0.0001
9.6397238      1.60210e-20    6.02252e23
1i             -3.14159j      3e5i
```

All numbers are stored internally using the *long* format specified by the IEEE floating-point standard. Floating-point numbers have a finite *precision* of roughly 16 significant decimal digits and a finite *range* of roughly 10^{-308} to 10^{+308}.

Operators

Expressions use familiar arithmetic operators and precedence rules.

+	Addition
-	Subtraction
*	Multiplication
/	Division
\	Left division (described in "Matrices and Linear Algebra" in the MATLAB documentation)
^	Power
'	Complex conjugate transpose
( )	Specify evaluation order

Functions

MATLAB provides a large number of standard elementary mathematical functions, including `abs`, `sqrt`, `exp`, and `sin`. Taking the square root or logarithm of a negative number is not an error; the appropriate complex result is produced automatically. MATLAB also provides many more advanced mathematical functions, including Bessel and gamma functions. Most of these functions accept complex arguments. For a list of the elementary mathematical functions, type

```
help elfun
```

For a list of more advanced mathematical and matrix functions, type

```
help specfun
help elmat
```

Some of the functions, like `sqrt` and `sin`, are *built in*. Built-in functions are part of the MATLAB core so they are very efficient, but the computational details are not readily accessible. Other functions, like `gamma` and `sinh`, are implemented in M-files.

There are some differences between built-in functions and other functions. For example, for built-in functions, you cannot see the code. For other functions, you can see the code and even modify it if you want.

Several special functions provide values of useful constants.

`pi`	3.14159265...
`i`	Imaginary unit, $\sqrt{-1}$
`j`	Same as `i`
`eps`	Floating-point relative precision, $\varepsilon = 2^{-52}$
`realmin`	Smallest floating-point number, 2^{-1022}
`realmax`	Largest floating-point number, $(2-\varepsilon)2^{1023}$
`Inf`	Infinity
`NaN`	Not-a-number

Infinity is generated by dividing a nonzero value by zero, or by evaluating well defined mathematical expressions that *overflow*, i.e., exceed `realmax`. Not-a-number is generated by trying to evaluate expressions like `0/0` or `Inf-Inf` that do not have well defined mathematical values.

The function names are not reserved. It is possible to overwrite any of them with a new variable, such as

```
eps = 1.e-6
```

and then use that value in subsequent calculations. The original function can be restored with

```
clear eps
```

Examples of Expressions

You have already seen several examples of MATLAB expressions. Here are a few more examples, and the resulting values.

```
rho = (1+sqrt(5))/2
rho =
    1.6180

a = abs(3+4i)
a =
     5

z = sqrt(besselk(4/3,rho-i))
z =
   0.3730+ 0.3214i

huge = exp(log(realmax))
huge =
  1.7977e+308

toobig = pi*huge
toobig =
   Inf
```

Working with Matrices

This section introduces you to other ways of creating matrices:

- "Generating Matrices" on page 4-14
- "The load Function" on page 4-15
- "M-Files" on page 4-15
- "Concatenation" on page 4-16
- "Deleting Rows and Columns" on page 4-17

Generating Matrices

MATLAB provides four functions that generate basic matrices.

`zeros`	All zeros
`ones`	All ones
`rand`	Uniformly distributed random elements
`randn`	Normally distributed random elements

Here are some examples.

```
Z = zeros(2,4)
Z =
     0     0     0     0
     0     0     0     0

F = 5*ones(3,3)
F =
     5     5     5
     5     5     5
     5     5     5

N = fix(10*rand(1,10))
N =
     9     2     6     4     8     7     4     0     8     4

R = randn(4,4)
```

```
R =
    0.6353    0.0860   -0.3210   -1.2316
   -0.6014   -2.0046    1.2366    1.0556
    0.5512   -0.4931   -0.6313   -0.1132
   -1.0998    0.4620   -2.3252    0.3792
```

The load Function

The `load` function reads binary files containing matrices generated by earlier MATLAB sessions, or reads text files containing numeric data. The text file should be organized as a rectangular table of numbers, separated by blanks, with one row per line, and an equal number of elements in each row. For example, outside of MATLAB, create a text file containing these four lines.

```
16.0     3.0     2.0    13.0
 5.0    10.0    11.0     8.0
 9.0     6.0     7.0    12.0
 4.0    15.0    14.0     1.0
```

Store the file under the name `magik.dat`. Then the statement

```
load magik.dat
```

reads the file and creates a variable, `magik`, containing our example matrix.

An easy way to read data into MATLAB in many text or binary formats is to use Import Wizard.

M-Files

You can create your own matrices using *M-files*, which are text files containing MATLAB code. Use the MATLAB Editor or another text editor to create a file containing the same statements you would type at the MATLAB command line. Save the file under a name that ends in `.m`.

For example, create a file containing these five lines.

```
A = [ ...
16.0     3.0     2.0    13.0
 5.0    10.0    11.0     8.0
 9.0     6.0     7.0    12.0
 4.0    15.0    14.0     1.0 ];
```

Store the file under the name magik.m. Then the statement

```
magik
```

reads the file and creates a variable, A, containing our example matrix.

Concatenation

Concatenation is the process of joining small matrices to make bigger ones. In fact, you made your first matrix by concatenating its individual elements. The pair of square brackets, [ ], is the concatenation operator. For an example, start with the 4-by-4 magic square, A, and form

```
B = [A  A+32; A+48  A+16]
```

The result is an 8-by-8 matrix, obtained by joining the four submatrices.

```
B =

    16     3     2    13    48    35    34    45
     5    10    11     8    37    42    43    40
     9     6     7    12    41    38    39    44
     4    15    14     1    36    47    46    33
    64    51    50    61    32    19    18    29
    53    58    59    56    21    26    27    24
    57    54    55    60    25    22    23    28
    52    63    62    49    20    31    30    17
```

This matrix is halfway to being another magic square. Its elements are a rearrangement of the integers 1:64. Its column sums are the correct value for an 8-by-8 magic square.

```
sum(B)

ans =
   260   260   260   260   260   260   260   260
```

But its row sums, sum(B')', are not all the same. Further manipulation is necessary to make this a valid 8-by-8 magic square.

Deleting Rows and Columns

You can delete rows and columns from a matrix using just a pair of square brackets. Start with

```
X = A;
```

Then, to delete the second column of X, use

```
X(:,2) = []
```

This changes X to

```
X =
    16     2    13
     5    11     8
     9     7    12
     4    14     1
```

If you delete a single element from a matrix, the result is not a matrix anymore. So, expressions like

```
X(1,2) = []
```

result in an error. However, using a single subscript deletes a single element, or sequence of elements, and reshapes the remaining elements into a row vector. So

```
X(2:2:10) = []
```

results in

```
X =
    16     9     2     7    13    12     1
```

More About Matrices and Arrays

This section shows you more about working with matrices and arrays, focusing on

Linear Algebra

Informally, the terms *matrix* and *array* are often used interchangeably. More precisely, a *matrix* is a two-dimensional numeric array that represents a *linear transformation*. The mathematical operations defined on matrices are the subject of *linear algebra*.

Dürer's magic square

```
A = [16     3     2    13
      5    10    11     8
      9     6     7    12
      4    15    14     1 ]
```

provides several examples that give a taste of MATLAB matrix operations. You have already seen the matrix transpose, `A'`. Adding a matrix to its transpose produces a *symmetric* matrix.

```
A + A'

ans =
    32     8    11    17
     8    20    17    23
    11    17    14    26
    17    23    26     2
```

The multiplication symbol, `*`, denotes the *matrix* multiplication involving inner products between rows and columns. Multiplying the transpose of a matrix by the original matrix also produces a symmetric matrix.

```
A'*A

ans =
   378   212   206   360
   212   370   368   206
   206   368   370   212
   360   206   212   378
```

The determinant of this particular matrix happens to be zero, indicating that the matrix is *singular*.

```
d = det(A)

d =
     0
```

The reduced row echelon form of `A` is not the identity.

```
R = rref(A)

R =
     1     0     0     1
     0     1     0    -3
     0     0     1     3
     0     0     0     0
```

Since the matrix is singular, it does not have an inverse. If you try to compute the inverse with

```
X = inv(A)
```

you will get a warning message

```
Warning: Matrix is close to singular or badly scaled.
         Results may be inaccurate. RCOND = 9.796086e-018.
```

Roundoff error has prevented the matrix inversion algorithm from detecting exact singularity. But the value of `rcond`, which stands for *reciprocal condition estimate*, is on the order of `eps`, the floating-point relative precision, so the computed inverse is unlikely to be of much use.

The eigenvalues of the magic square are interesting.

```
e = eig(A)

e =
   34.0000
    8.0000
    0.0000
   -8.0000
```

One of the eigenvalues is zero, which is another consequence of singularity. The largest eigenvalue is 34, the magic sum. That is because the vector of all ones is an eigenvector.

```
v = ones(4,1)

v =
     1
     1
     1
     1

A*v

ans =
    34
    34
    34
    34
```

When a magic square is scaled by its magic sum,

```
P = A/34
```

the result is a *doubly stochastic* matrix whose row and column sums are all 1.

```
P =
    0.4706    0.0882    0.0588    0.3824
    0.1471    0.2941    0.3235    0.2353
    0.2647    0.1765    0.2059    0.3529
    0.1176    0.4412    0.4118    0.0294
```

Such matrices represent the transition probabilities in a *Markov process*. Repeated powers of the matrix represent repeated steps of the process. For our example, the fifth power

```
P^5
```

is

```
0.2507    0.2495    0.2494    0.2504
0.2497    0.2501    0.2502    0.2500
0.2500    0.2498    0.2499    0.2503
0.2496    0.2506    0.2505    0.2493
```

This shows that as k approaches infinity, all the elements in the k th power, p^k, approach $1/4$.

Finally, the coefficients in the characteristic polynomial

```
poly(A)
```

are

```
1    -34    -64    2176      0
```

This indicates that the characteristic polynomial

$$\det(A - \lambda I)$$

is

$$\lambda^4 - 34\lambda^3 - 64\lambda^2 + 2176\lambda$$

The constant term is zero, because the matrix is singular, and the coefficient of the cubic term is -34, because the matrix is magic!

Arrays

When they are taken away from the world of linear algebra, matrices become two-dimensional numeric arrays. Arithmetic operations on arrays are done element by element. This means that addition and subtraction are the same for arrays and matrices, but that multiplicative operations are different. MATLAB uses a dot, or decimal point, as part of the notation for multiplicative array operations.

The list of operators includes

+	Addition
-	Subtraction
.*	Element-by-element multiplication
./	Element-by-element division
.\	Element-by-element left division
.^	Element-by-element power
.'	Unconjugated array transpose

If the Dürer magic square is multiplied by itself with array multiplication

```
A.*A
```

the result is an array containing the squares of the integers from 1 to 16, in an unusual order.

```
ans =
   256     9     4   169
    25   100   121    64
    81    36    49   144
    16   225   196     1
```

Building Tables

Array operations are useful for building tables. Suppose n is the column vector

```
n = (0:9)';
```

Then

```
pows = [n  n.^2  2.^n]
```

builds a table of squares and powers of 2.

```
pows =
     0     0     1
     1     1     2
     2     4     4
     3     9     8
     4    16    16
     5    25    32
     6    36    64
     7    49   128
     8    64   256
     9    81   512
```

The elementary math functions operate on arrays element by element. So

```
format short g
x = (1:0.1:2)';
logs = [x log10(x)]
```

builds a table of logarithms.

```
logs =
     1.0           0
     1.1     0.04139
     1.2     0.07918
     1.3     0.11394
     1.4     0.14613
     1.5     0.17609
     1.6     0.20412
     1.7     0.23045
     1.8     0.25527
     1.9     0.27875
     2.0     0.30103
```

Multivariate Data

MATLAB uses column-oriented analysis for multivariate statistical data. Each column in a data set represents a variable and each row an observation. The `(i,j)`th element is the `i`th observation of the `j`th variable.

As an example, consider a data set with three variables:

- Heart rate
- Weight
- Hours of exercise per week

For five observations, the resulting array might look like

```
D = [ 72          134          3.2
      81          201          3.5
      69          156          7.1
      82          148          2.4
      75          170          1.2 ]
```

The first row contains the heart rate, weight, and exercise hours for patient 1, the second row contains the data for patient 2, and so on. Now you can apply many MATLAB data analysis functions to this data set. For example, to obtain the mean and standard deviation of each column, use

```
mu = mean(D), sigma = std(D)

mu =
      75.8        161.8          3.48

sigma =
    5.6303       25.499        2.2107
```

For a list of the data analysis functions available in MATLAB, type

```
help datafun
```

If you have access to the Statistics Toolbox, type

```
help stats
```

Scalar Expansion

Matrices and scalars can be combined in several different ways. For example, a scalar is subtracted from a matrix by subtracting it from each element. The average value of the elements in our magic square is 8.5, so

```
B = A - 8.5
```

forms a matrix whose column sums are zero.

```
B =
        7.5     -5.5     -6.5      4.5
       -3.5      1.5      2.5     -0.5
        0.5     -2.5     -1.5      3.5
       -4.5      6.5      5.5     -7.5

sum(B)

ans =
     0     0     0     0
```

With scalar expansion, MATLAB assigns a specified scalar to all indices in a range. For example,

```
B(1:2,2:3) = 0
```

zeroes out a portion of B.

```
B =
        7.5        0        0      4.5
       -3.5        0        0     -0.5
        0.5     -2.5     -1.5      3.5
       -4.5      6.5      5.5     -7.5
```

Logical Subscripting

The logical vectors created from logical and relational operations can be used to reference subarrays. Suppose `X` is an ordinary matrix and `L` is a matrix of the same size that is the result of some logical operation. Then `X(L)` specifies the elements of `X` where the elements of `L` are nonzero.

This kind of subscripting can be done in one step by specifying the logical operation as the subscripting expression. Suppose you have the following set of data.

```
x = [2.1 1.7 1.6 1.5 NaN 1.9 1.8 1.5 5.1 1.8 1.4 2.2 1.6 1.8];
```

The `NaN` is a marker for a missing observation, such as a failure to respond to an item on a questionnaire. To remove the missing data with logical indexing, use `isfinite(x)`, which is true for all finite numerical values and false for `NaN` and `Inf`.

```
x = x(isfinite(x))
x =
  2.1 1.7 1.6 1.5 1.9 1.8 1.5 5.1 1.8 1.4 2.2 1.6 1.8
```

Now there is one observation, `5.1`, which seems to be very different from the others. It is an *outlier*. The following statement removes outliers, in this case those elements more than three standard deviations from the mean.

```
x = x(abs(x-mean(x)) <= 3*std(x))
x =
  2.1 1.7 1.6 1.5 1.9 1.8 1.5 1.8 1.4 2.2 1.6 1.8
```

For another example, highlight the location of the prime numbers in Dürer's magic square by using logical indexing and scalar expansion to set the nonprimes to 0. (See "The magic Function" on page 4-8.)

```
A(~isprime(A)) = 0

A =
     0     3     2    13
     5     0    11     0
     0     0     7     0
     0     0     0     0
```

The find Function

The `find` function determines the indices of array elements that meet a given logical condition. In its simplest form, `find` returns a column vector of indices. Transpose that vector to obtain a row vector of indices. For example, start again with Dürer's magic square. (See "The magic Function" on page 4-8.)

```
k = find(isprime(A))'
```

picks out the locations, using one-dimensional indexing, of the primes in the magic square.

```
k =
     2     5     9    10    11    13
```

Display those primes, as a row vector in the order determined by `k`, with

```
A(k)

ans =
     5     3     2    11     7    13
```

When you use `k` as a left-hand-side index in an assignment statement, the matrix structure is preserved.

```
A(k) = NaN

A =
    16   NaN   NaN   NaN
   NaN    10   NaN     8
     9     6   NaN    12
     4    15    14     1
```

Controlling Command Window Input and Output

So far, you have been using the MATLAB command line, typing functions and expressions, and seeing the results printed in the Command Window. This section describes

- "The format Function" on page 4-28
- "Suppressing Output" on page 4-30
- "Entering Long Statements" on page 4-30
- "Command Line Editing" on page 4-30

The format Function

The `format` function controls the numeric format of the values displayed by MATLAB. The function affects only how numbers are displayed, not how MATLAB computes or saves them. Here are the different formats, together with the resulting output produced from a vector `x` with components of different magnitudes.

Note To ensure proper spacing, use a fixed-width font, such as Courier.

```
x = [4/3 1.2345e-6]

format short

   1.3333    0.0000

format short e

   1.3333e+000  1.2345e-006

format short g

   1.3333  1.2345e-006
```

```
format long

   1.33333333333333    0.00000123450000

format long e

   1.333333333333333e+000    1.234500000000000e-006

format long g

   1.33333333333333                  1.2345e-006

format bank

   1.33           0.00

format rat

   4/3            1/810045

format hex

   3ff5555555555555    3eb4b6231abfd271
```

If the largest element of a matrix is larger than 10^3 or smaller than 10^{-3}, MATLAB applies a common scale factor for the short and long formats.

In addition to the `format` functions shown above

```
format compact
```

suppresses many of the blank lines that appear in the output. This lets you view more information on a screen or window. If you want more control over the output format, use the `sprintf` and `fprintf` functions.

Suppressing Output

If you simply type a statement and press **Return** or **Enter**, MATLAB automatically displays the results on screen. However, if you end the line with a semicolon, MATLAB performs the computation but does not display any output. This is particularly useful when you generate large matrices. For example,

```
A = magic(100);
```

Entering Long Statements

If a statement does not fit on one line, use an ellipsis (three periods), `...`, followed by **Return** or **Enter** to indicate that the statement continues on the next line. For example,

```
s = 1 -1/2 + 1/3 -1/4 + 1/5 - 1/6 + 1/7 ...
      - 1/8 + 1/9 - 1/10 + 1/11 - 1/12;
```

Blank spaces around the `=`, `+`, and `-` signs are optional, but they improve readability.

Command Line Editing

Various arrow and control keys on your keyboard allow you to recall, edit, and reuse statements you have typed earlier. For example, suppose you mistakenly enter

```
rho = (1 + sqt(5))/2
```

You have misspelled `sqrt`. MATLAB responds with

```
Undefined function or variable 'sqt'.
```

Instead of retyping the entire line, simply press the ↑ key. The statement you typed is redisplayed. Use the ← key to move the cursor over and insert the missing `r`. Repeated use of the ↑ key recalls earlier lines. Typing a few characters and then the ↑ key finds a previous line that begins with those characters. You can also copy previously executed statements from the Command History. For more information, see "Command History" on page 8-5.

Following is the list of arrow and control keys you can use in the Command Window. If the preference you select for **Command line key bindings** is **Emacs (MATLAB standard)**, you can also use the **Ctrl**+key combinations shown. See also general keyboard shortcuts for desktop tools in the Desktop Tools and Development Environment documentation.

Key	Control Key for Emacs (MATLAB standard) Preference	Operation
↑	**Ctrl+P**	Recall *p*revious line. Works only at command line.
↓	**Ctrl+N**	Recall *n*ext line. Works only at command line if you previously used the up arrow or **Ctrl+P**.
←	**Ctrl+B**	Move *b*ack one character.
→	**Ctrl+F**	Move *f*orward one character.
Ctrl+ →		Move *r*ight one word.
Ctrl+ ←		Move *l*eft one word.
Home	**Ctrl+A**	Move to beginning of command line.
End	**Ctrl+E**	Move to *e*nd of command line.
Ctrl+Home		Move to top of Command Window.
Ctrl+End		Move to end of Command Window.
Esc	**Ctrl+U**	Clear command line.
Delete	**Ctrl+D**	Delete character at cursor in command line.
Backspace	**Ctrl+H**	Delete character before cursor in command line.
	Ctrl+K	Cut contents (*k*ill) to end of command line.
Shift+Home		Highlight to beginning of command line.
Shift+End		Highlight to end of last line. Can start at any line in the Command Window.

5

Graphics

This chapter provides an introduction to plotting data in MATLAB.

Overview of MATLAB Plotting

MATLAB provides a wide variety of techniques to display data graphically. Interactive tools enable you to manipulate graphs to achieve results that reveal the most information about your data. You can also annotate and print graphs for presentations, or export graphs to standard graphics formats for presentation in web browsers or other media.

For More Information "Graphics" and "3-D Visualization" in the MATLAB documentation provide in-depth coverage of MATLAB graphics and visualization tools. Access these topics from the Help browser.

The Plotting Process

The process of visualizing data typically involves a series of operations. This section provides a "big picture" view of the plotting process and contains links to sections that have examples and specific details about performing each operation.

Creating a Graph

The type of graph you choose to create depends on the nature of your data and what you want to reveal about the data. MATLAB predefines many graph types, such as line, bar, histogram, and pie graphs. There are also 3-D graphs, such as surfaces, slice planes, and streamlines.

There are two basic ways to create graphs in MATLAB:

- Use plotting tools to create graphs interactively.

  See "Examples — Using MATLAB Plotting Tools" on page 5-20.
- Use the command interface to enter commands in the Command Window or create plotting programs.

  See "Basic Plotting Functions" on page 5-38.

You might find it useful to combine both approaches. For example, you might issue a plotting command to create a graph and then modify the graph using one of the interactive tools.

Exploring Data

Once you create a graph, you can extract specific information about the data, such as the numeric value of a peak in a plot, the average value of a series of data, or you can perform data fitting.

For More Information See "Data Exploration Tools" and "Basic Fitting Options" in the MATLAB documentation.

Editing the Graph Components

Graphs are composed of objects, which have properties you can change. These properties affect the way the various graph components look and behave.

For example, the axes used to define the coordinate system of the graph has properties that define the limits of each axis, the scale, color, etc. The line used to create a line graph has properties such as color, type of marker used at each data point (if any), line style, etc.

Note that the data used to create a line graph are properties of the line. You can, therefore, change the data without actually creating a new graph.

See "Editing Plots" on page 5-16.

Annotating Graphs

Annotations are the text, arrows, callouts, and other labels added to graphs to help viewers see what is important about the data. You typically add annotations to graphs when you want to show them to other people or when you want to save them for later reference.

For More Information See "Annotating Graphs" in the MATLAB documentation or select **Annotating Graphs** from the figure **Help** menu.

Printing and Exporting Graphs

You can print your graph on any printer connected to your computer. The print previewer enables you to view how your graph will look when printed. It enables you to add headers, footers, a date, and so on. The page setup dialog lets you control the size, layout, and other characteristics of the graph (select **Page Setup** from the figure **File** menu).

Exporting a graph means creating a copy of it in a standard graphics file format, such as TIF, JPEG, or EPS. You can then import the file into a word processor, include it in an HTML document, or edit it in a drawing package select **Export Setup** from the figure **File** menu).

For More Information See the `print` command reference page and "Printing and Exporting" in the MATLAB documentation or select **Printing and Exporting** from the figure **Help** menu.

Saving Graphs to Reload into MATLAB

There are two ways to save graphs that enable you to save the work you have invested in their preparation:

- Save the graph as a FIG-file (select **Save** from the figure **File** menu).
- Generate MATLAB code that can recreate the graph (select **Generate M-File** from the figure **File** menu).

FIG-Files. FIG-files are a binary format that saves a figure in its current state. This means that all graphics objects and property settings are stored in the file when you create it. You can reload the file into a different MATLAB session, even if you are running MATLAB on a different type of computer. When you load a FIG-file, MATLAB creates a new figure in the same state as the one you saved.

Note that the states of any figure tools (i.e., any items on the toolbars) are not saved in a FIG-file; only the contents of the graph are saved.

Generated Code. You can use the MATLAB M-code generator to create code that recreates the graph. Unlike a FIG-file, the generated code does not contain any data. You must pass the data to the generated function when you run the code.

Note that studying the generating code for a graph is a good way to learn how to program with MATLAB.

For More Information See the `print` command reference page and "Saving Your Work" in the MATLAB documentation.

Graph Components

MATLAB displays graphs in a special window known as a figure. To create a graph, you need to define a coordinate system. Therefore every graph is placed within axes, which are contained by the figure.

The actual visual representation of the data is achieved with graphics objects like lines and surfaces. These objects are drawn within the coordinate system defined by the axes, which MATLAB automatically creates specifically to accommodate the range of the data. The actual data is stored as properties of the graphics objects.

See "Handle Graphics" on page 5-62 for more information about graphics object properties.

The following picture shows the basic components of a typical graph.

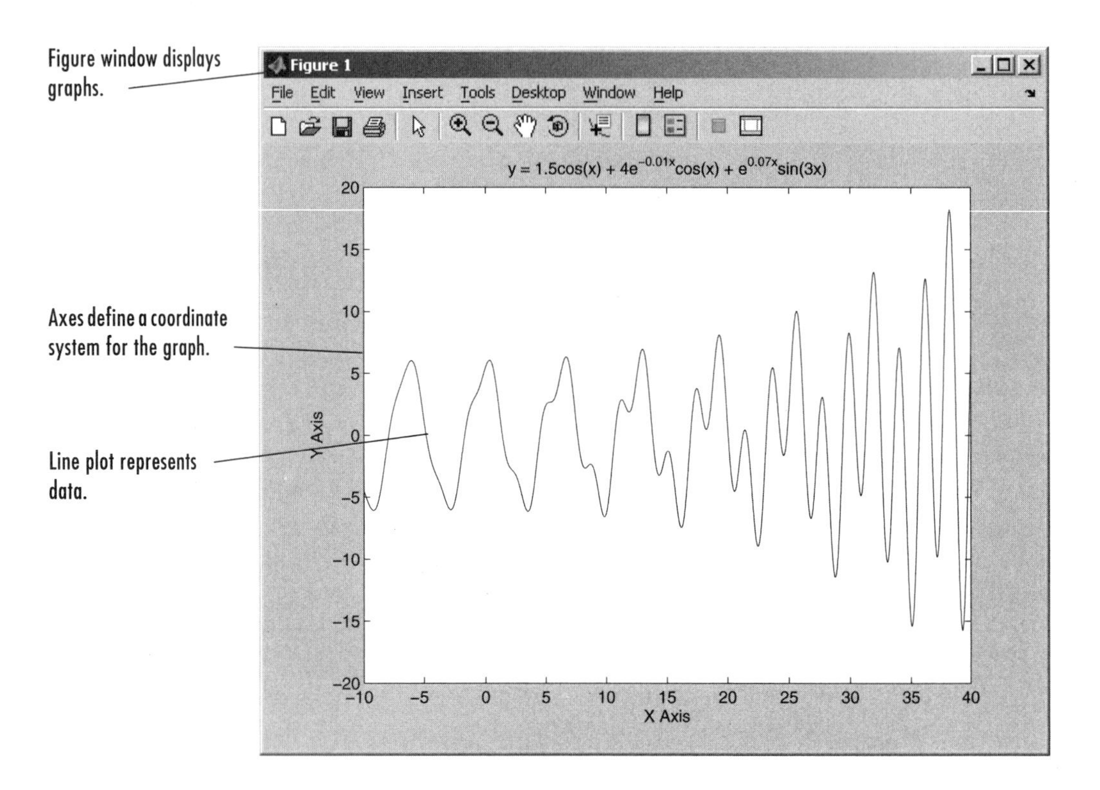
Figure window displays graphs.
Axes define a coordinate system for the graph.
Line plot represents data.
Figure 1
File Edit View Insert Tools Desktop Window Help
y = 1.5cos(x) + 4e^{−0.01x}cos(x) + e^{0.07x}sin(3x)
Y Axis
X Axis
20
15
10
5
0
−5
−10
−15
−20
−10
−5
0
5
10
15
20
25
30
35
40

Figure Tools

The figure is equipped with sets of tools that operate on graphs. The figure **Tools** menu provides access to many graph tools.

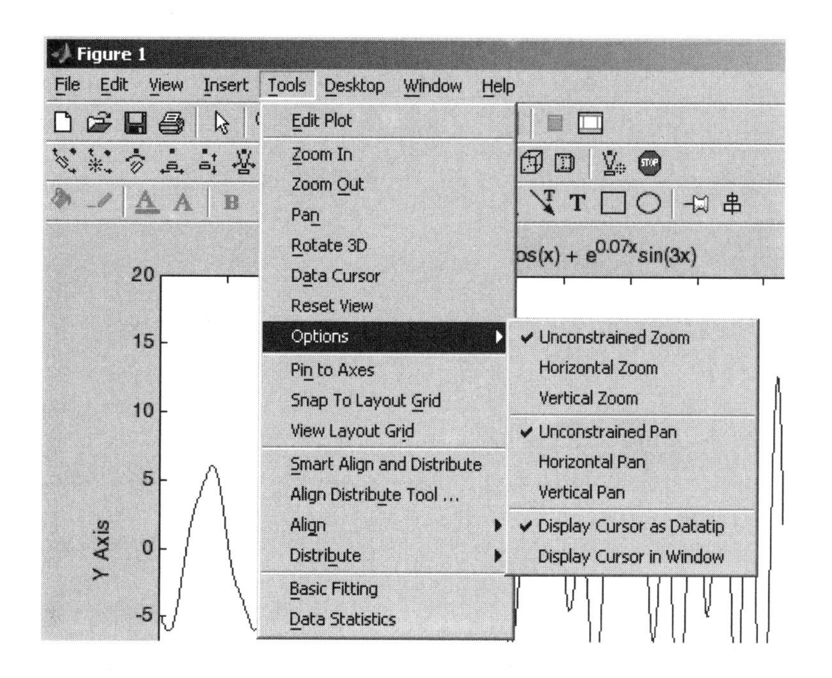

For More Information See "MATLAB Plotting Tools" in the MATLAB documentation or select **Plotting Tools** from the figure **Help** menu.

Access to Tools

You can access the figure toolbars and the plotting tools from the **View** menu, as shown in the following picture.

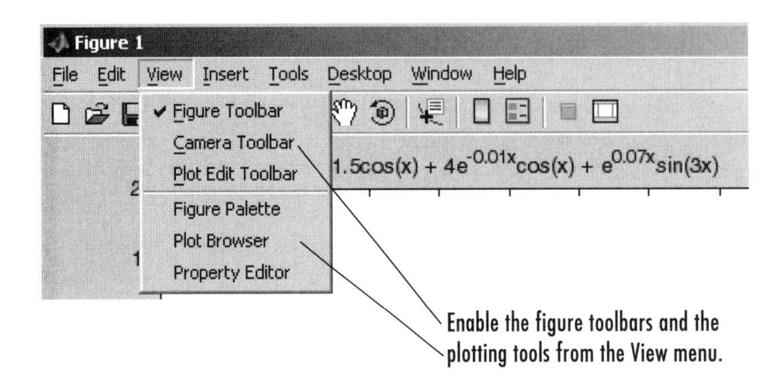

Figure Toolbars

Figure toolbars provide easy access to many graph modification features. There are three toolbars. When you place the cursor over a particular tool, a text box pops up with the tool name. The following picture shows the three toolbars displayed with the cursor over the Data Cursor tool.

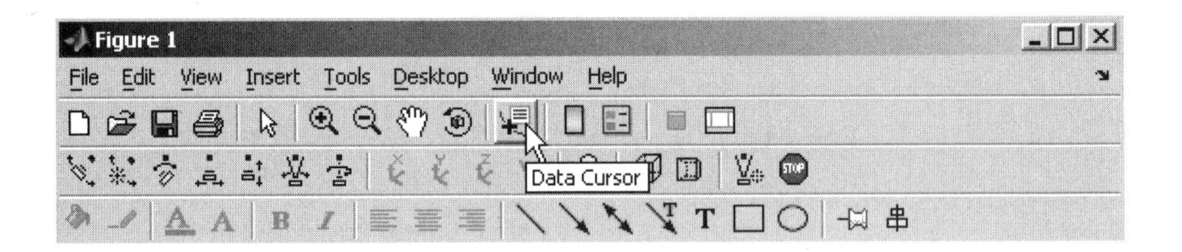

For More Information See "Figure Toolbars" in the MATLAB documentation.

Plotting Tools

Plotting tools are attached to figures and create an environment for creating graphs. These tools enable you to do the following:

- Select from a wide variety of graph types
- Set the properties of graphics objects
- Annotate graphs with text, arrows, etc.
- Create and arrange subplots in the figure
- Drag and drop data into graphs

Display the plotting tools from the **View** menu or by clicking in the figure toolbar, as shown in the following picture.

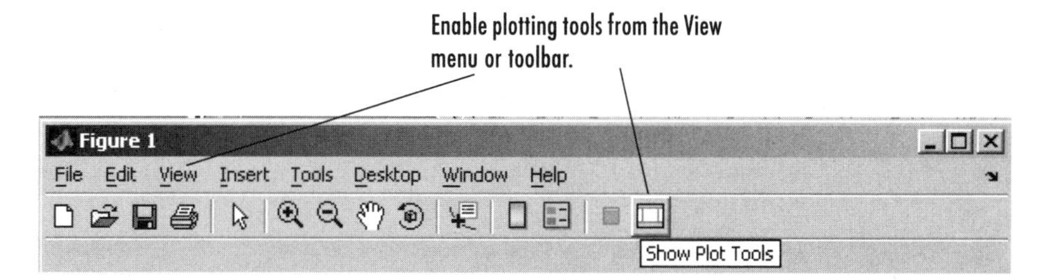

There are three components to the plotting tools:

- Figure Palette — Specify and arrange subplots, access workspace variables for plotting or editing, and add annotations.
- Plot Browser — Select objects in the graphics hierarchy, control visibility, and add data to axes.
- Property Editor — Change key properties of the selected object. Click **Inspector** for access to all object properties.

The following picture shows a figure with the plotting tools enabled.

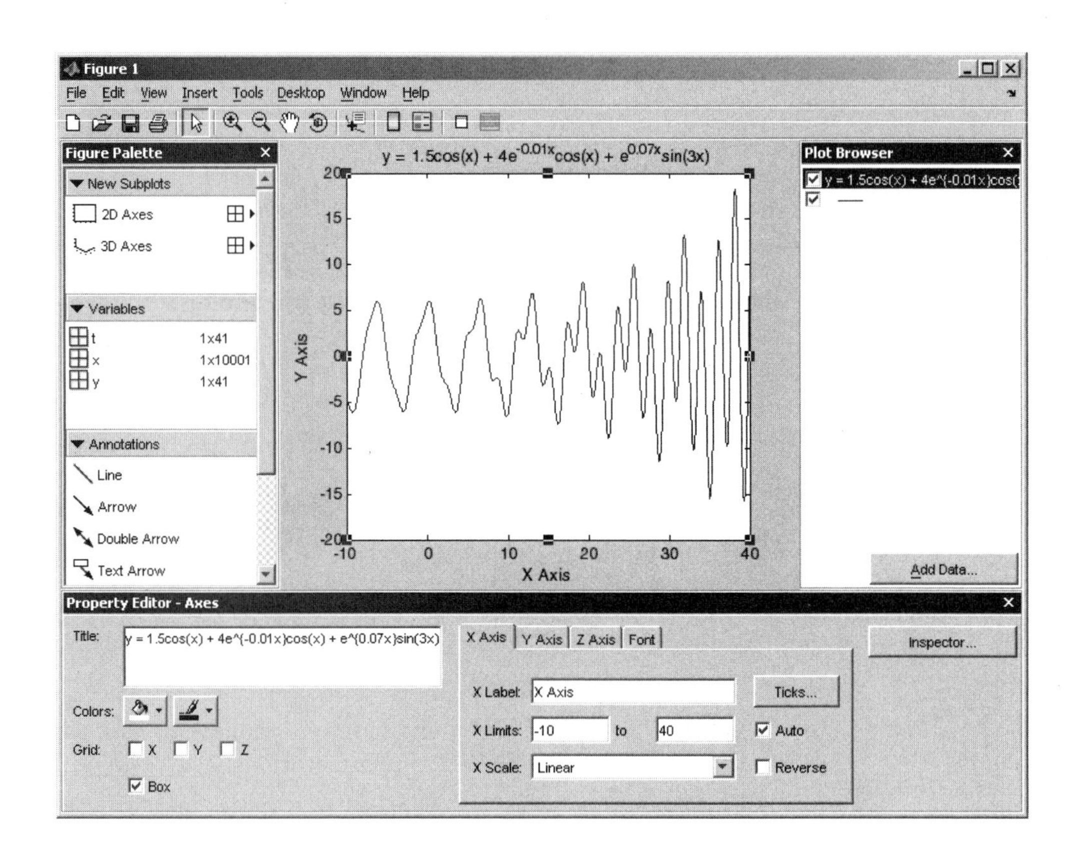

Plotting Tools and MATLAB Commands

You can enable the plotting tools on any graph, even if you created it using MATLAB commands. For example, suppose you create the following graph.

```
t = 0:pi/20:2*pi;
y = exp(sin(t));
plotyy(t,y,t,y,'plot','stem')
xlabel('X Axis')
ylabel('Plot Y Axis')
title('Two Y Axes')
```

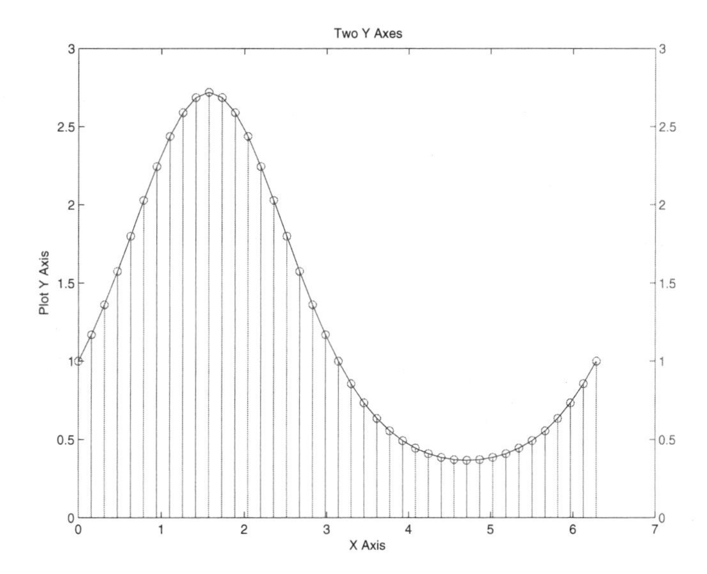

This graph contains two y-axes, one for each plot type (lineseries and stem graphs). The plotting tools make it easy to select any of the objects that the graph contains and set their properties.

For example, adding a label for the *y*-axis that corresponds to the stem plot is easily accomplished by selecting that axes in the Plot Browser and setting the **YLabel** property in the Property Editor.

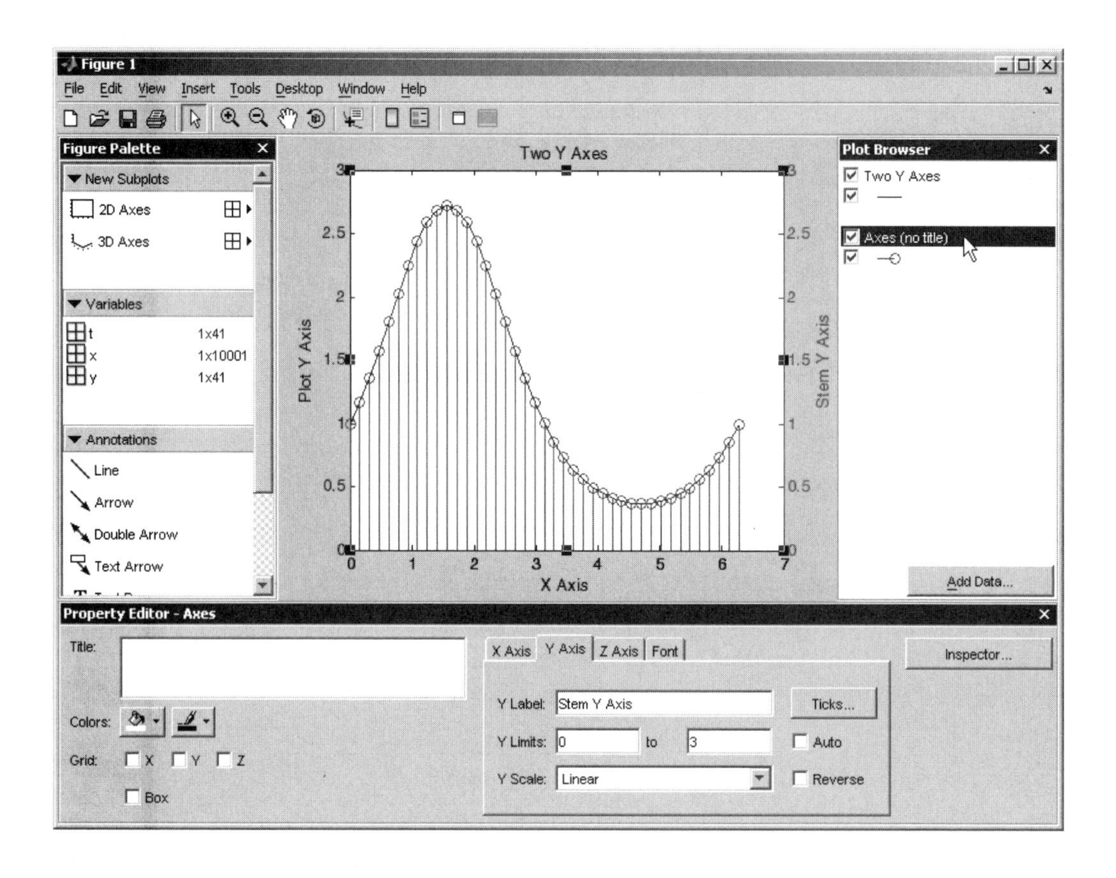

Arranging Graphs Within a Figure

You can place a number of axes within a figure by selecting the layout you want from the Figure Palette. For example, the following picture shows how to specify four 2-D axes in the figure.

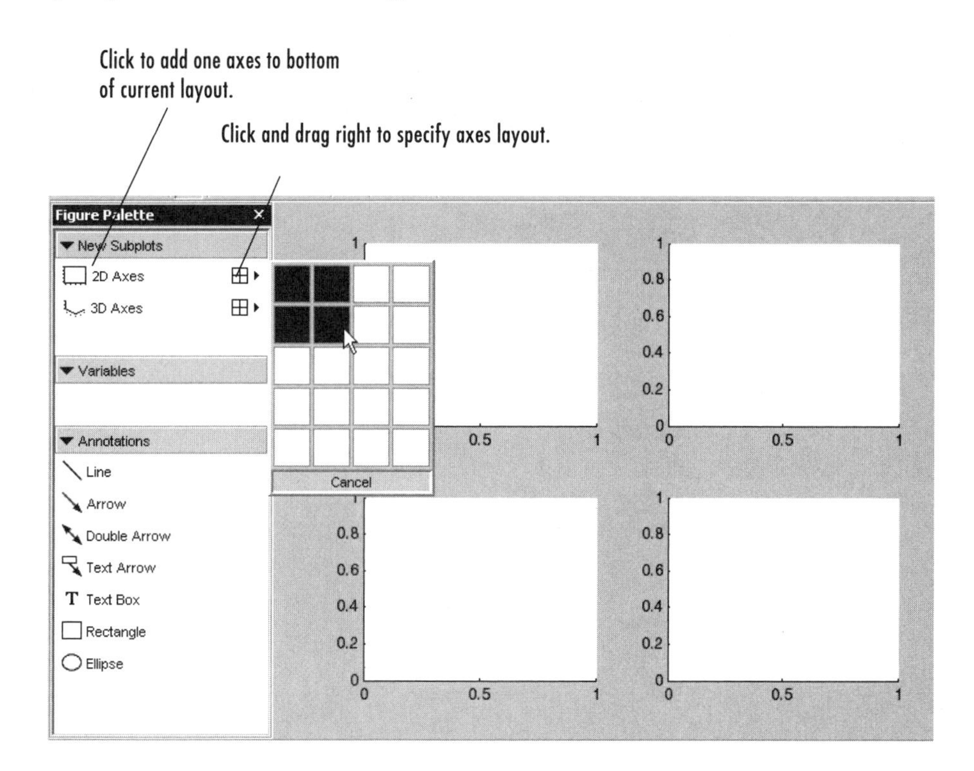

Select the axes you want to target for plotting. You can also use the `subplot` command to create multiple axes.

Selecting Plot Types

You can use the Plot Catalog to select from a variety of techniques for plotting data. To access the Plot Catalog,

1 Select the variables you want to plot in the Figure Palette.

2 Right-click to display the context menu.

3 Select **More Plots** to display the catalog.

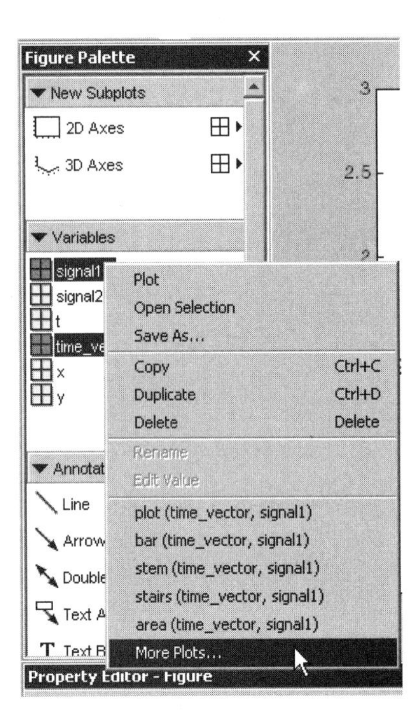

MATLAB displays the Plot Catalog with the selected variables ready to plot, once you select a plot type.

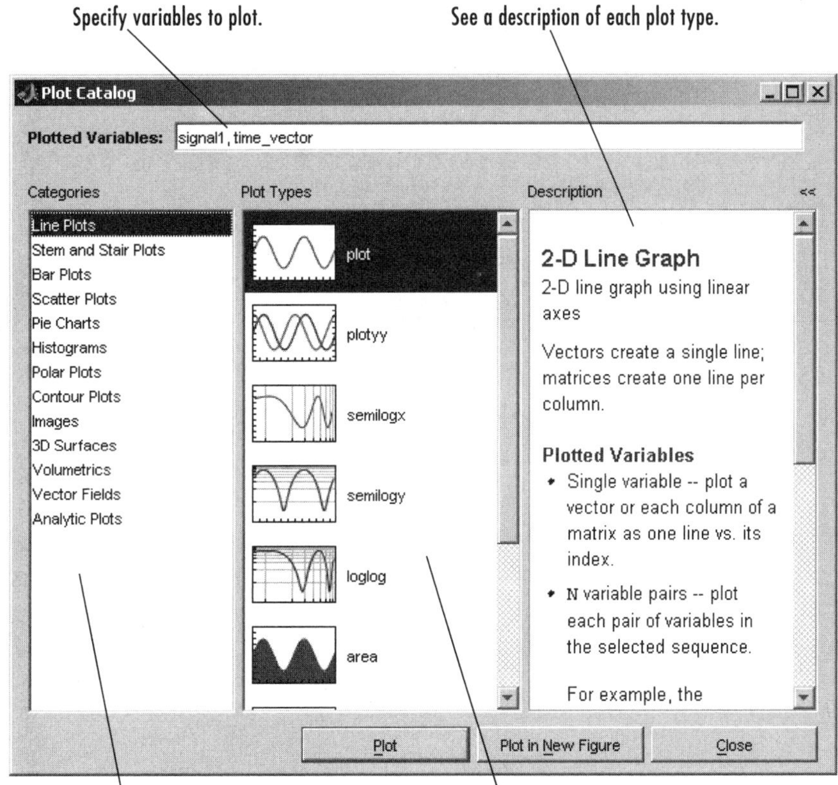

Editing Plots

MATLAB automatically formats graphs by setting the scale of the axes, adding tick marks along axes, and using colors and line styles to distinguish the data plotted in the graph. However, if you are creating graphics for presentation, you can change the default formatting or add descriptive labels, titles, legends and other annotations to help explain your data.

Plot Editing Mode

Plot editing mode enables you to perform point-and-click editing of the graphics objects in your graph.

Enabling Plot Edit Mode

To enable plot edit mode, click the arrowhead in the figure toolbar:

Enable plot edit mode.

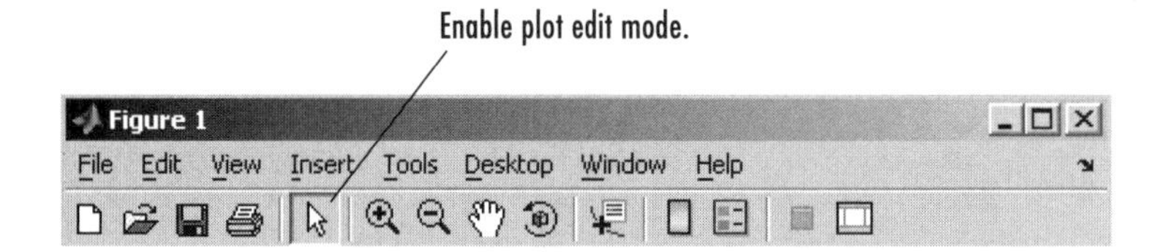

You can also select **Edit Plot** from the figure **Tools** menu.

Setting Object Properties

Once you have enabled plot edit mode, you can select objects by clicking on them in the graph. Selection handles appear and indicate that the object is selected. Select multiple objects using **Shift+click**.

Right-click with the pointer over the selected object to display the object's context menu:

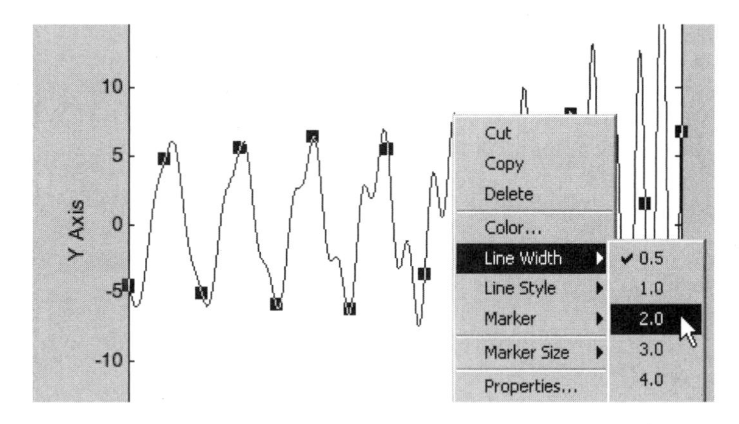

The context menu provides quick access to the most commonly used operations and properties.

Using the Property Editor

In plot edit mode, double-clicking on an object in a graph starts the Property Editor with that object's major properties displayed. The Property Editor provides access to the most used object properties. It is updated to display the properties of whatever object you select.

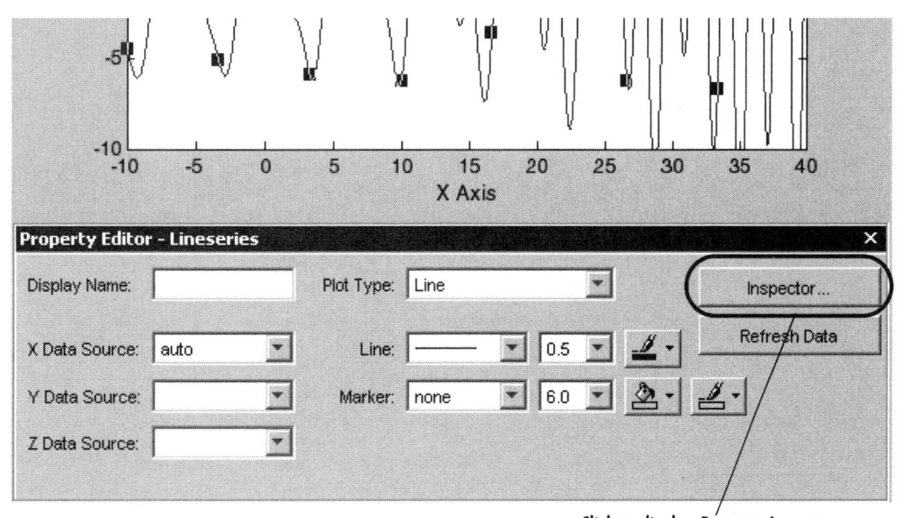

Click to display Property Inspector.

Accessing All Properties — Property Inspector

The Property Inspector is a tool that enables you to access all object properties. If you do not find the property you want to set in the Property Editor, click the **Inspector** button to display the Property Inspector. You can also use the `inspect` command to start the Property Inspector.

The following picture shows the Property Inspector displaying the properties of a graph's axes. It lists each property and provides a text field or other appropriate device (such as a color picker) from which you can set the value of the property.

As you select different objects, the Property Inspector is updated to display the properties of the current object.

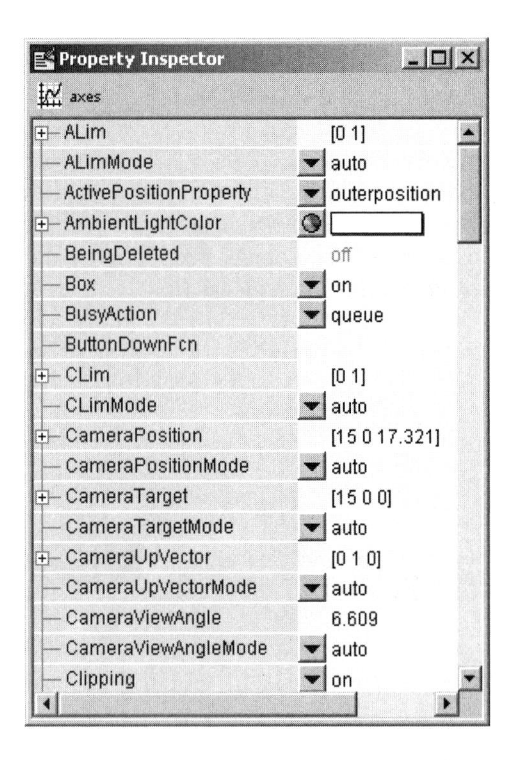

Using Functions to Edit Graphs

If you prefer to work from the MATLAB command line, or if you are creating an M-file, you can use MATLAB commands to edit the graphs you create. You can use the `set` and `get` commands to change the properties of the objects in a graph. For more information about using graphics commands, see "Handle Graphics" on page 5-62.

Examples — Using MATLAB Plotting Tools

Suppose you want to graph the function $y = x^3$ over the x domain -1 to 1. The first step is to generate the data to plot.

It is simple to evaluate a function because MATLAB can distribute arithmetic operations over all elements of a multivalued variable.

For example, the following statement creates a variable x that contains values ranging from -1 to 1 in increments of 0.1 (you could also use the linspace function to generate data for x). The second statement raises each value in x to the third power and stores these values in y.

```
x = -1:.1:1; % Define the range of x
y = x.^3;    % Raise each element in x to the third power
```

Now that you have generated some data, you can plot it using the MATLAB plotting tools. To start the plotting tools, type

```
plottools
```

MATLAB displays a figure with plotting tools attached.

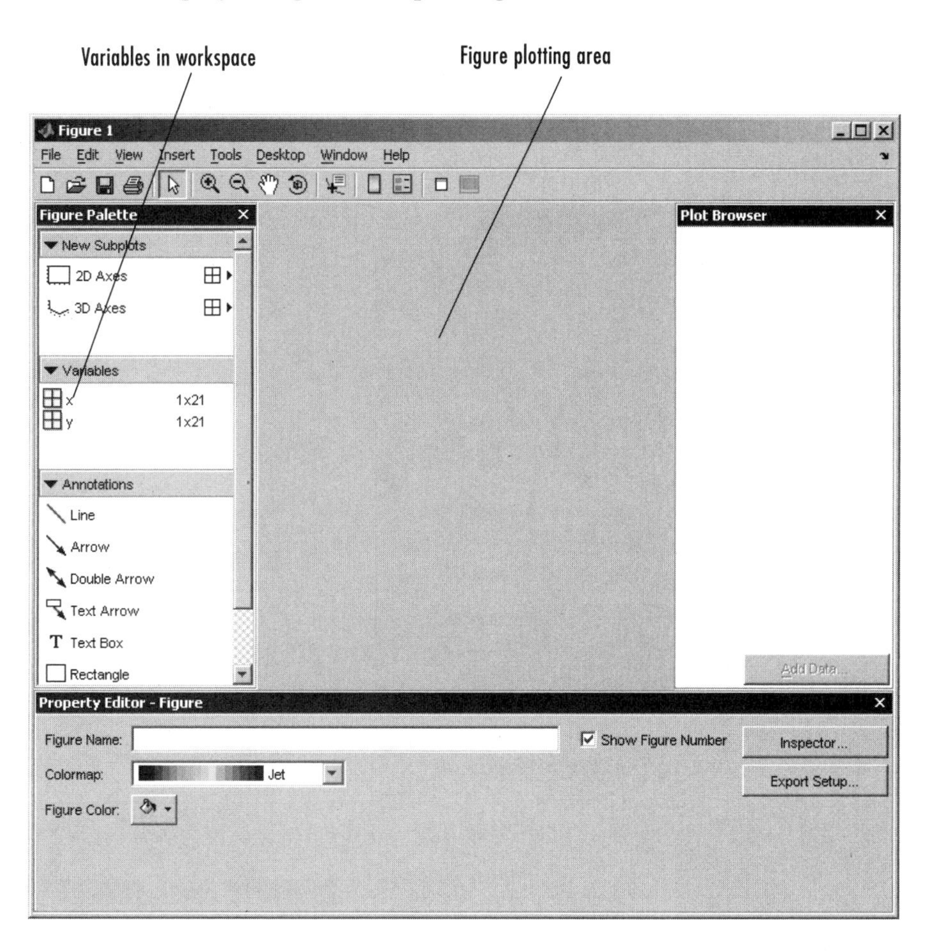

Plotting Two Variables

A simple line graph is a suitable way to display x as the independent variable and y as the dependent variable. To do this, select both variables (click to select, then **Shift-click** to select again), then right-click to display the context menu.

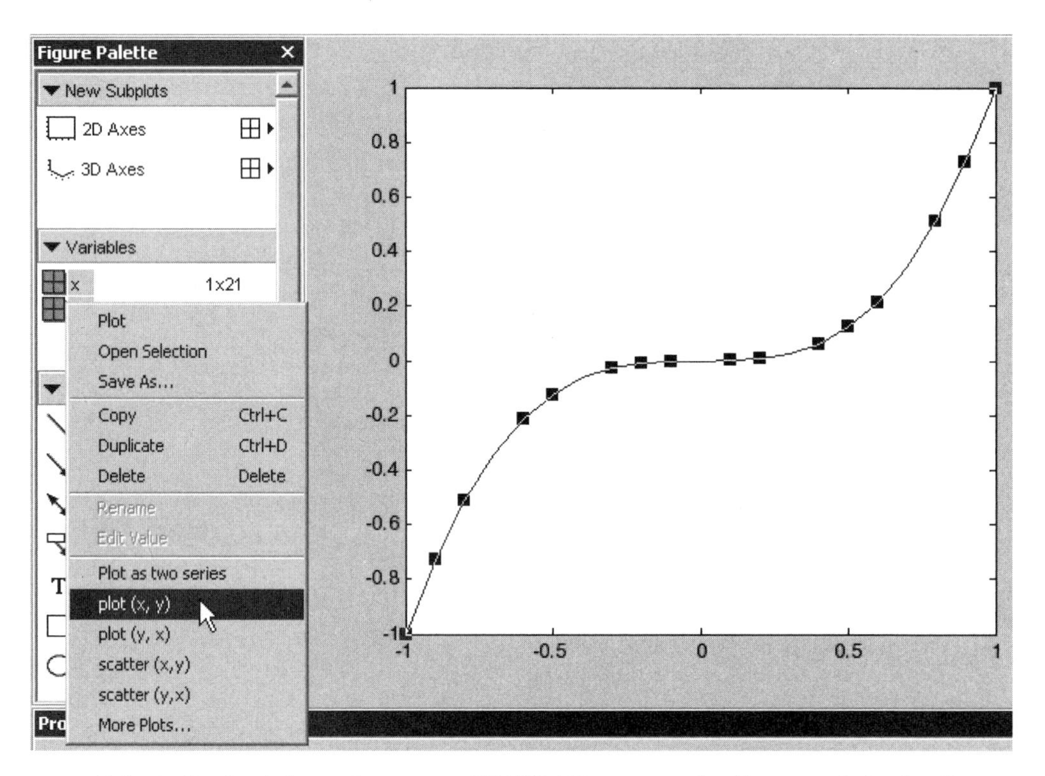

Select **plot(x,y)** from the menu. MATLAB creates the line graph in the figure area. The black squares indicate that the line is selected and you can edit its properties with the Property Editor.

Changing the Appearance

Next change the line properties so that the graph displays only the data point. Use the Property Editor to set following properties:

- Line to no line
- Marker to o
- Marker size to 4.0
- Marker fill color to red

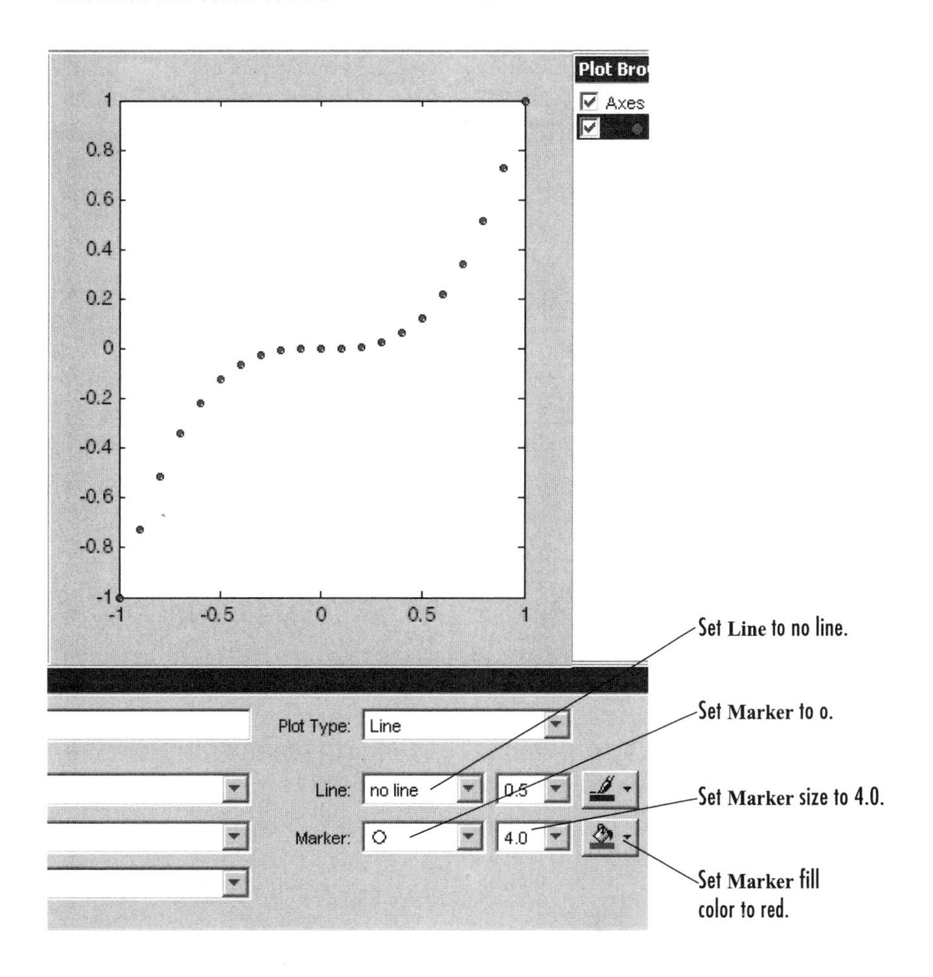

Adding More Data to the Graph

You can add more data to the graph by defining more variables or by specifying an expression that MATLAB uses to generate data for the plot. This second approach makes it easy to explore variations of the data already plotted.

To add data to the graph, select the axes in the Plot Browser and click the **Add Data** button. When you are using the plotting tools, MATLAB always adds data to the existing graph, instead of replacing the graph, as it would if you issued repeated plotting commands. That is, the plotting tools are in a `hold on` state.

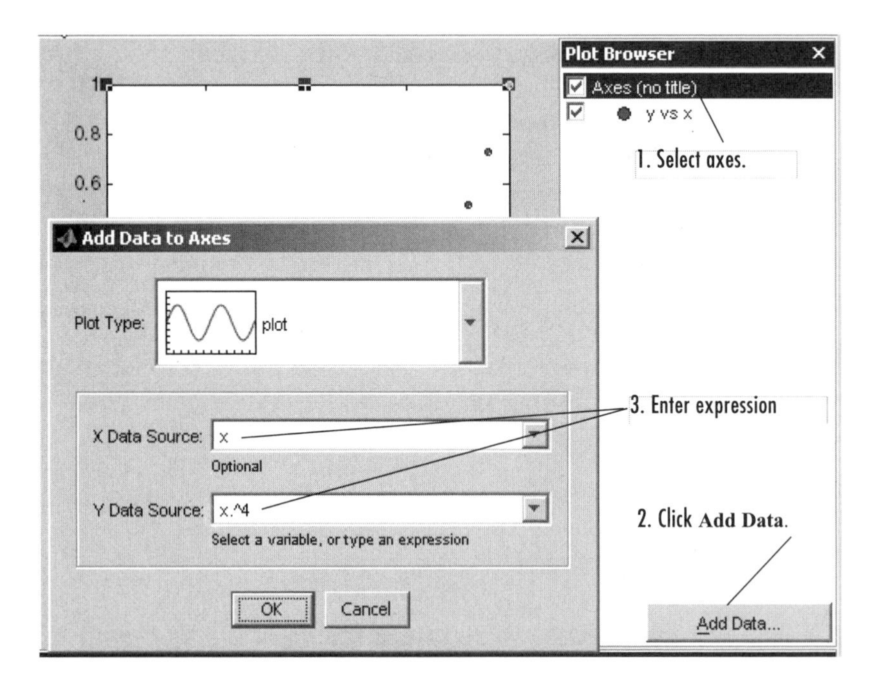

The picture above shows how to configure the **Add Data to Axes** dialog to create a line plot of $y = x^4$, which is added to the existing plot of $y = x^3$.

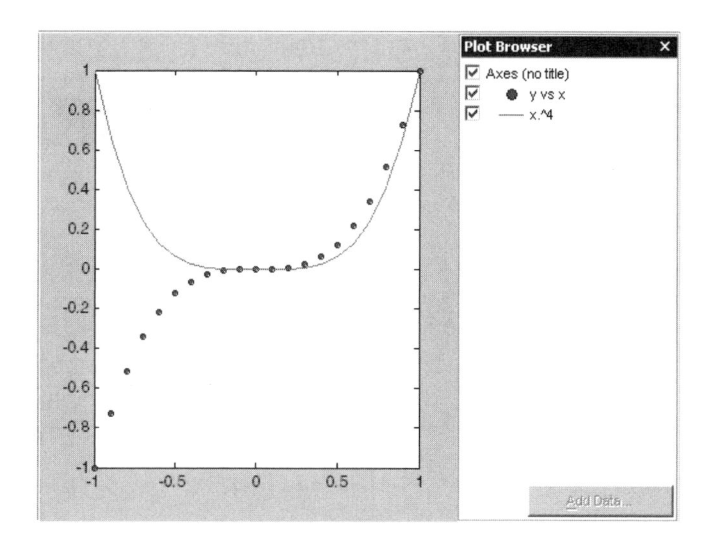

Changing the Type of Graph

The plotting tools enable you to easily view your data with a variety of plot types. The following picture shows the same data as above converted to stem plots. To change the plot type,

1 Select the plotted data in the Plot Browser.

2 Select **Stem** in the **Plot Type** menu.

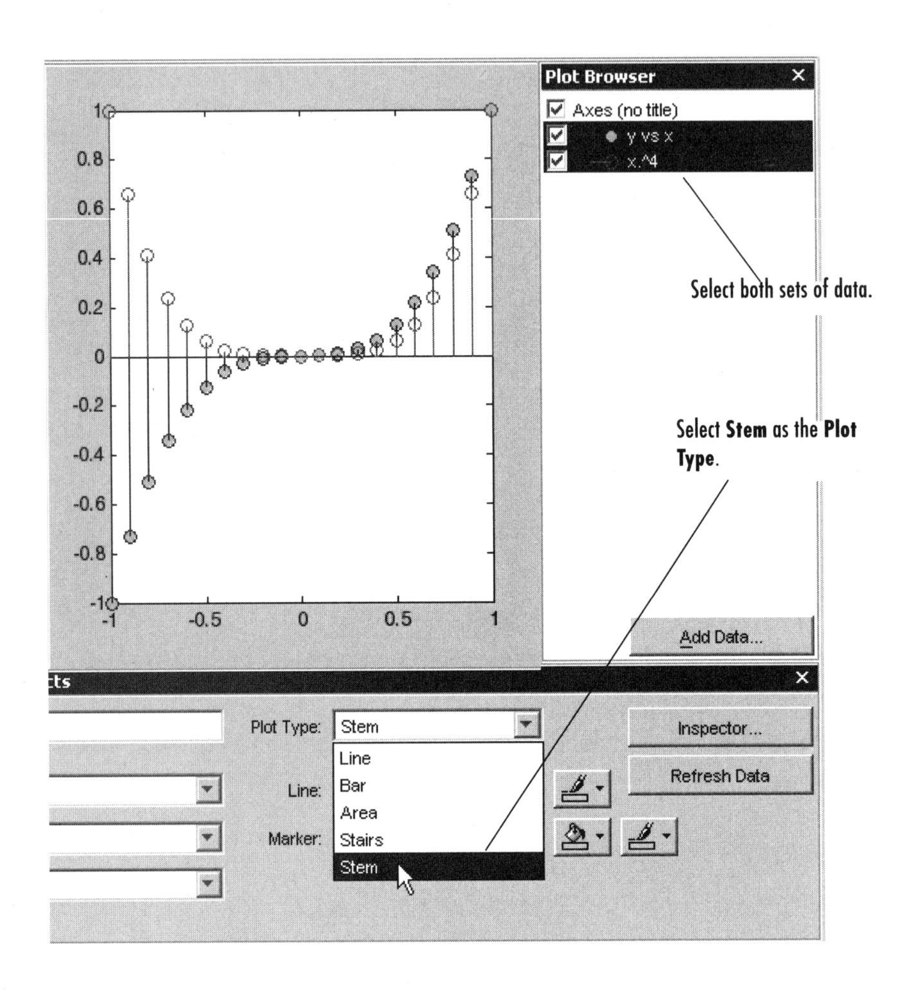

Plot Browser
Axes (no title)
y vs x
x.^4
Add Data...
Select both sets of data.
Select Stem as the Plot Type.
Plot Type:
Stem
Line
Bar
Area
Stairs
Stem
Line:
Marker:
Inspector...
Refresh Data

Modifying the Graph Data Source

You can link graph data to variables in your workspace. When you change the values contained in the variables, you can then update the graph to use the new data without having to create a new graph. (See also the `refresh` function.)

Suppose you have the following data:

```
x = linspace(-pi,pi,25); % 25 points between -π and π
y = sin(x);
```

Using the plotting tools, create a graph of $y = sin(x)$.

```
plottools
```

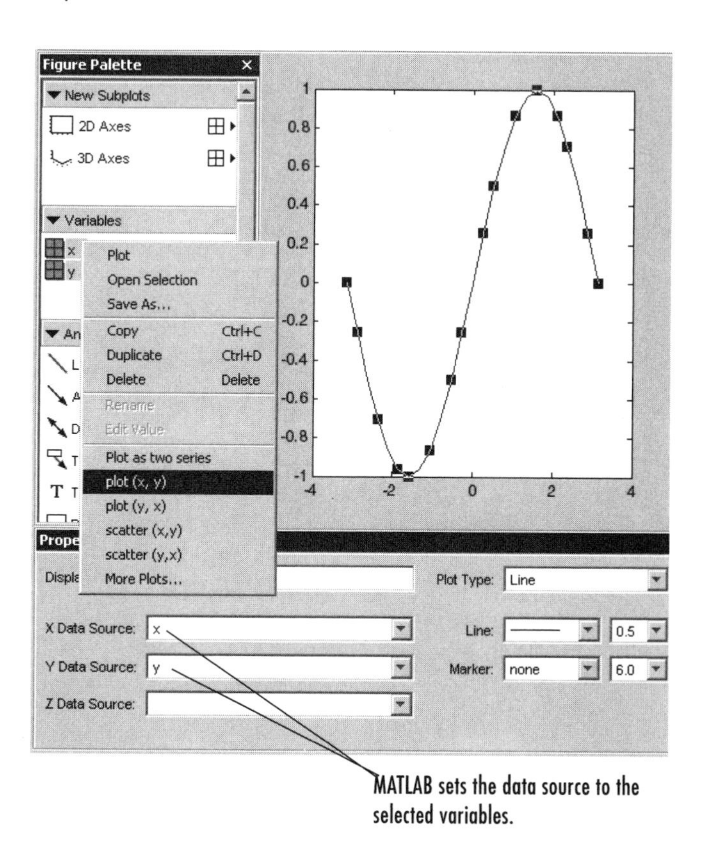

MATLAB sets the data source to the selected variables.

New Values for the Data Source

The data that defines the graph is linked to the x and y variables in the base workspace. If you assign new values to these variables and click the **Refresh Data** button, MATLAB updates the graph to use the new data.

```
x = linspace(-2*pi,2*pi,25); % 25 points between -2pi and 2pi
y = sin(x); % Recalculate y based on the new x values
```

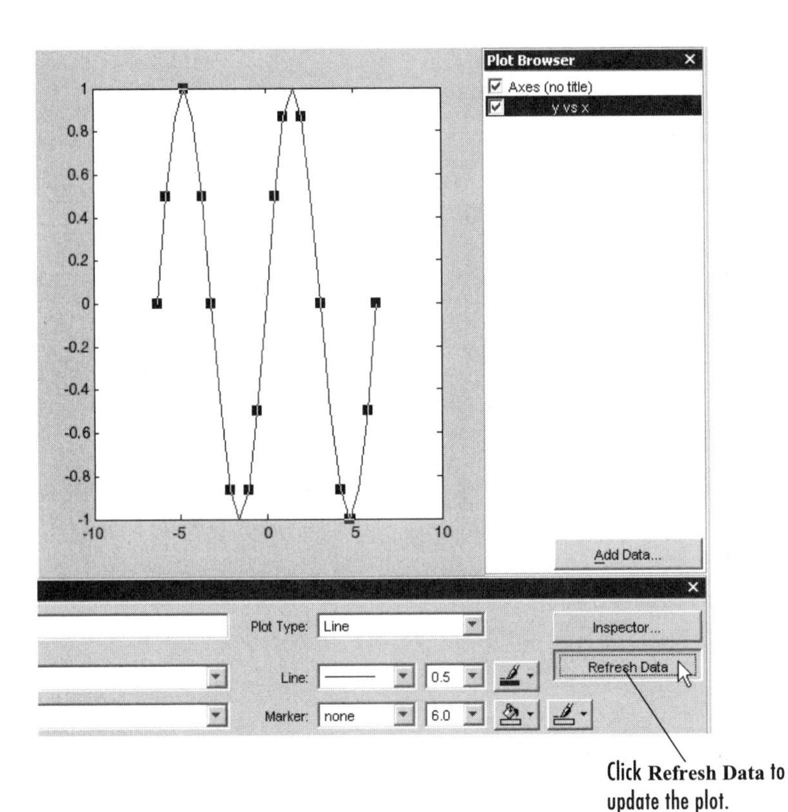

Click **Refresh Data** to update the plot.

Preparing Graphs for Presentation

Suppose you plot the following data and want to create a graph that presents certain information about the data.

```
x = -10:.005:40;
y = [1.5*cos(x)+4*exp(-.01*x).*cos(x)+exp(.07*x).*sin(3*x)];
plot(x,y)
```

This picture shows the graph created by the code above.

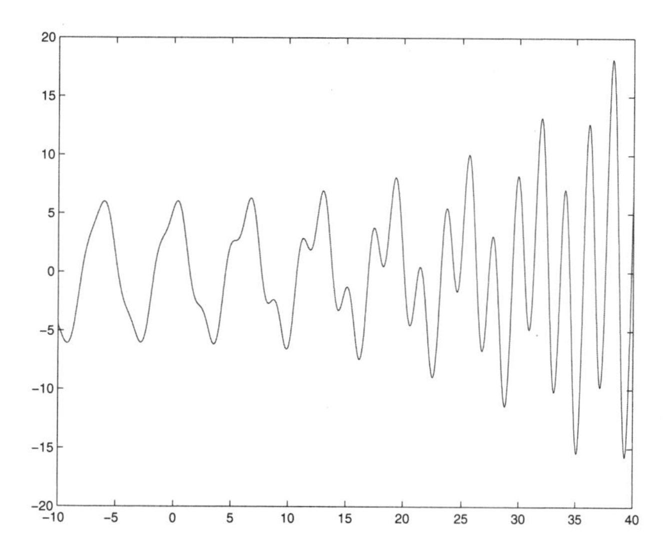

Now suppose you want to save copies of the graph by

- Printing the graph on a local printer so you have a copy for your notebook
- Exporting the graph to an Encapsulated PostScript (EPS) file to incorporate into a word processor document

Modify the Graph to Enhance the Presentation

To obtain a better view, zoom in on the graph using horizontal zoom.

After enabling zoom mode from the figure toolbar, right-click to display the context menu. Select **Horizontal Zoom (2-D Plots Only)** from the **Zoom Options**.

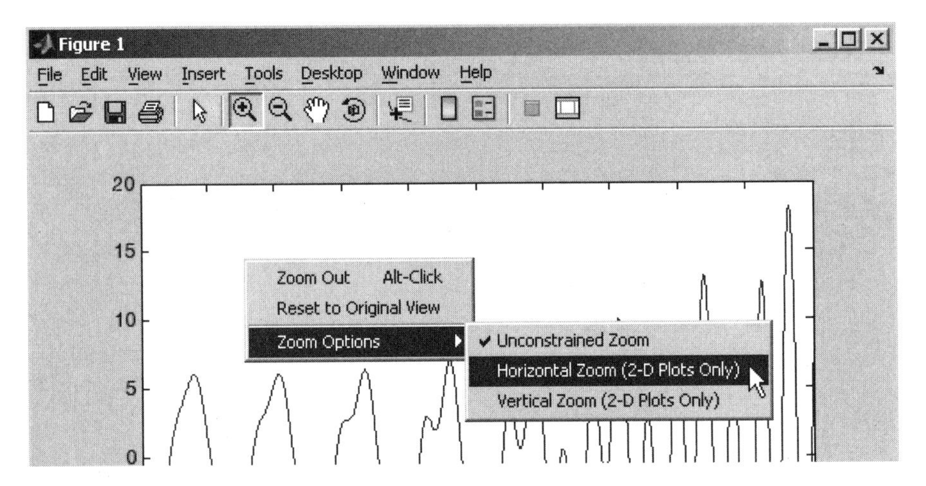

Left-click to zoom in on a region of the graph and use the panning tool to position the points of interest where you want them on the graph.

Label some key points using data tips.

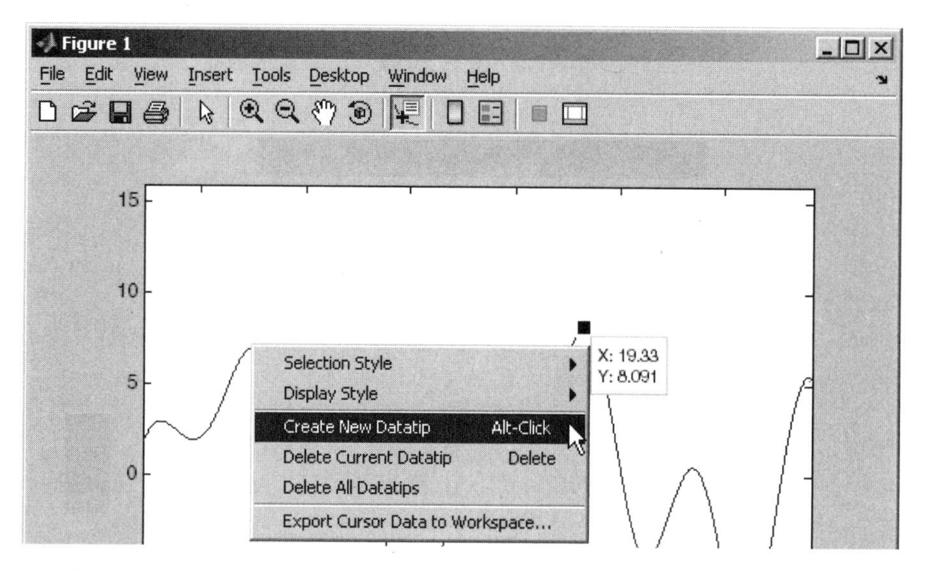

Finally, add text annotations, axis labels, and a title. You can add the title and axis labels using the following commands:

```
title ('y = 1.5cos(x) + 4e^{-0.01x}cos(x) + e^{0.07x}sin(3x)')
xlabel('X Axis')
ylabel('Y Axis')
```

Note that the text string passed to the `title` command uses $\TeX$ syntax to produce the exponents. See the text `String` property for more information on using $\TeX$ syntax to produce mathematical symbols.

The graph is now ready to print and export.

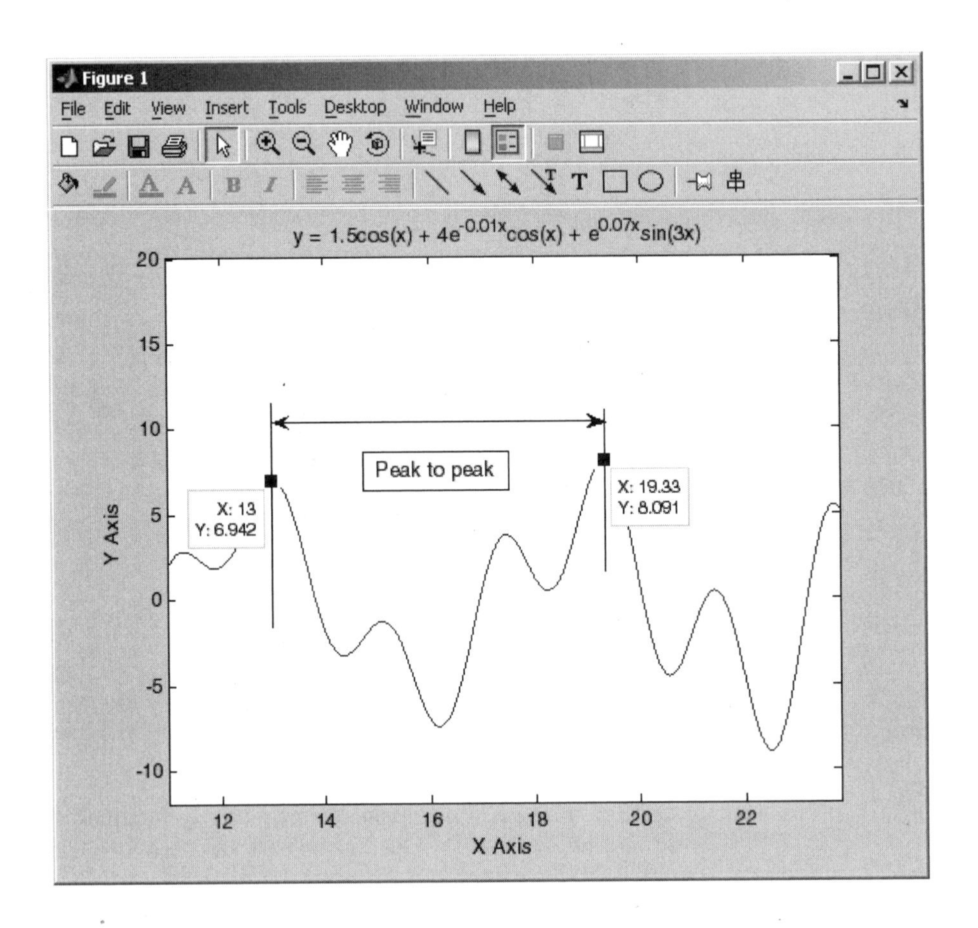
Figure 1
File Edit View Insert Tools Desktop Window Help
y = 1.5cos(x) + 4e-0.01xcos(x) + e0.07xsin(3x)
Peak to peak
X: 13
Y: 6.942
X: 19.33
Y: 8.091
Y Axis
X Axis
20
15
10
5
0
-5
-10
12
14
16
18
20
22

Printing the Graph

Before printing the graph, use the print previewer to see how the graph will be laid out on the page. Display the graph in the print previewer by selecting **Print Preview** from the figure **File** menu.

- Click the **Header** button to add some descriptive text to the top of the page.

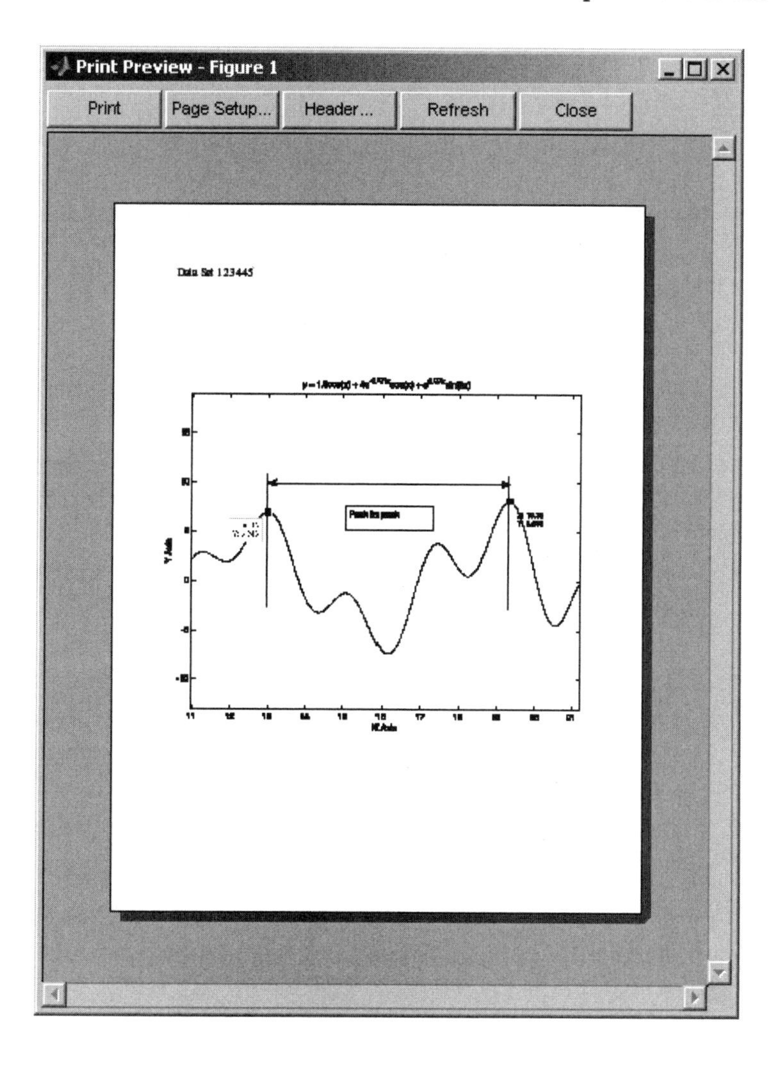

- Next click the **Page Setup** button. The **Page Setup** dialog enables you to set a number of properties that control how the page is printed.

  Note that MATLAB recalculates the values of the axes tick marks because the printed graph is larger than the one displayed on the computer screen. To force MATLAB to use the same tick marks and limits, select **Keep screen limits and ticks** from the **Axes and Figure** tab in the **Page Setup** dialog.
- Click **OK** to accept the setting and dismiss the dialog.

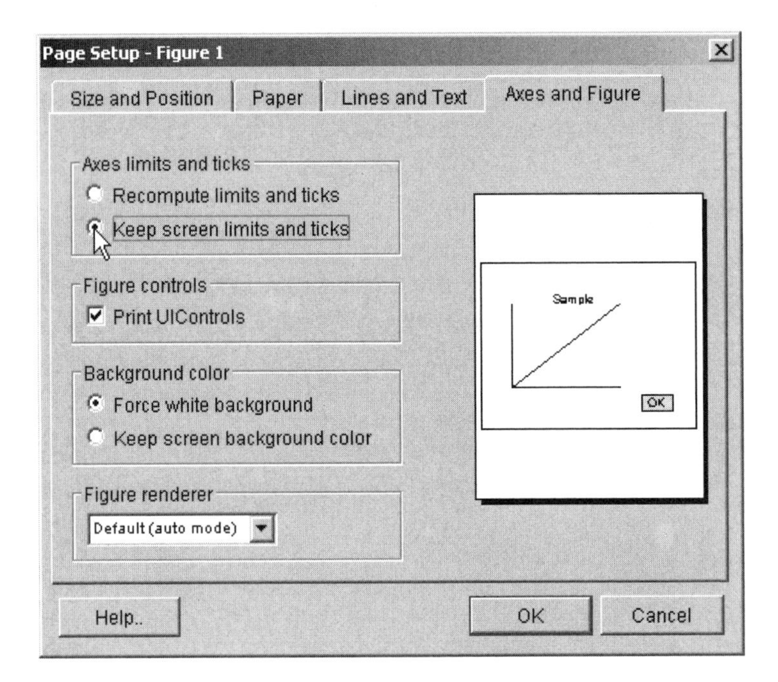

- Click **Print** on the print previewer to send the graph to your default printer.

The **Page Setup** dialog provides many other options for controlling how printed graphs look. Click **Help** for more information.

Exporting the Graph

Exporting a graph is the process of creating a standard graphics file format of the graph (such as EPS or TIFF), which you can then import into other applications like word processors, drawing packages, etc.

This example exports the graph as an EPS file with the following requirements:

- The size of the picture when imported into the word processor document should be four inches wide and three inches high.
- All the text in the figure should have a size of 8 points.

Specifying the Size of the Graph

To set the size, select **Export Setup** from the figure **File** menu.

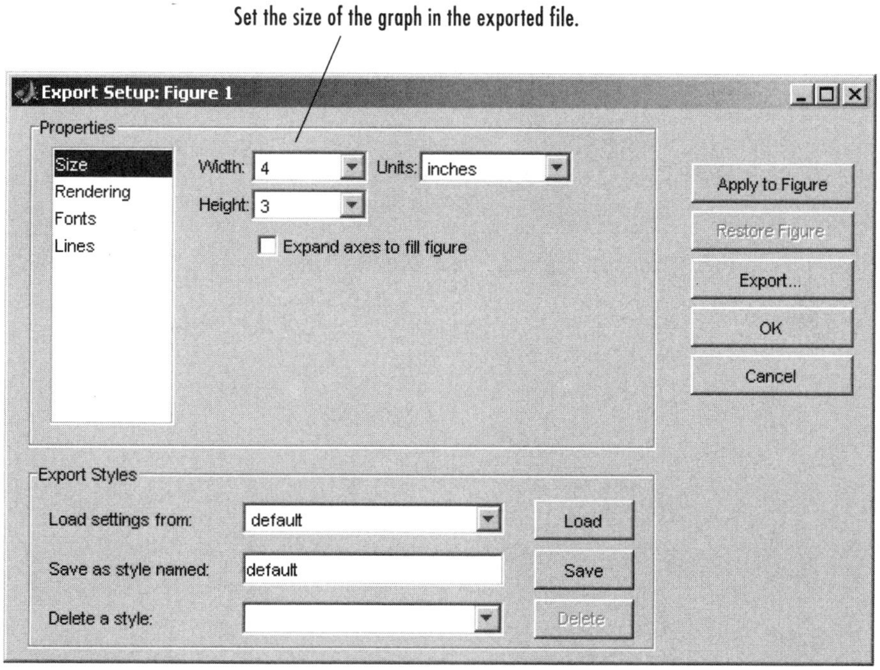

Set the size of the graph in the exported file.

Specifying the Font Size

To set the font size of all the text in the graph, select **Fonts** in the **Export Setup** dialog's **Properties** selector. Then select **Use fixed font size** and enter 8 in the text box.

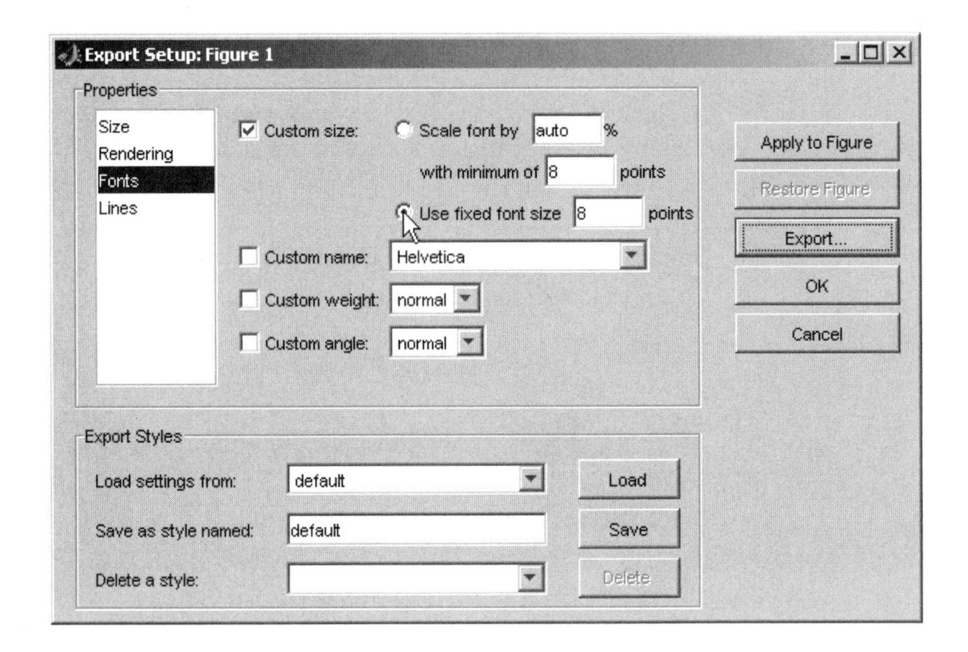

Selecting the File Format

Once you finish setting options for the exported graph, click the **Export** button. MATLAB displays a **Save As** dialog that enables you to specify a name for the file as well as select the type of file format you want to use.

For this example, select EPS, as shown in the following picture.

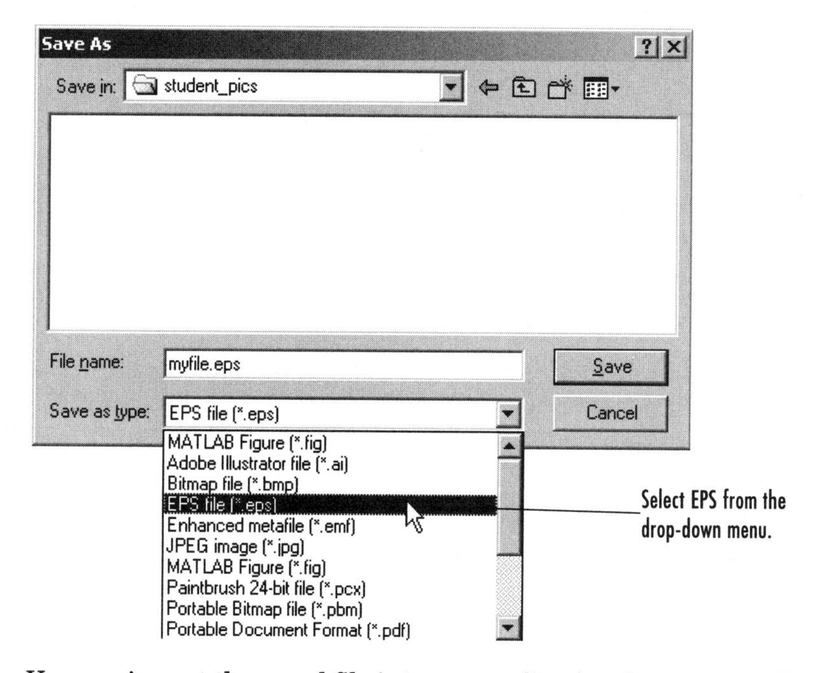

You can import the saved file into any application that supports EPS files. The **Save as type** drop-down menu lists other options for file types.

You can also use the `print` command to print figures on your local printer or to export graphs to standard file types.

For More Information See the `print` command reference page and "Printing and Exporting" in the MATLAB documentation or select **Printing and Exporting** from the figure **Help** menu.

Basic Plotting Functions

This section describes important graphics functions and provides examples of some typical applications. The plotting tools, described in previous sections, make use of MATLAB plotting functions and use these functions to generate code for graphs.

Creating a Plot

The `plot` function has different forms, depending on the input arguments. If `y` is a vector, `plot(y)` produces a piecewise linear graph of the elements of `y` versus the index of the elements of `y`. If you specify two vectors as arguments, `plot(x,y)` produces a graph of `y` versus `x`.

For example, these statements use the `colon` operator to create a vector of `x` values ranging from 0 to 2π, compute the sine of these values, and plot the result.

```
x = 0:pi/100:2*pi;
y = sin(x);
plot(x,y)
```

Now label the axes and add a title. The characters `\pi` create the symbol π. See the text string property for more symbols.

```
xlabel('x = 0:2\pi')
ylabel('Sine of x')
title('Plot of the Sine Function','FontSize',12)
```

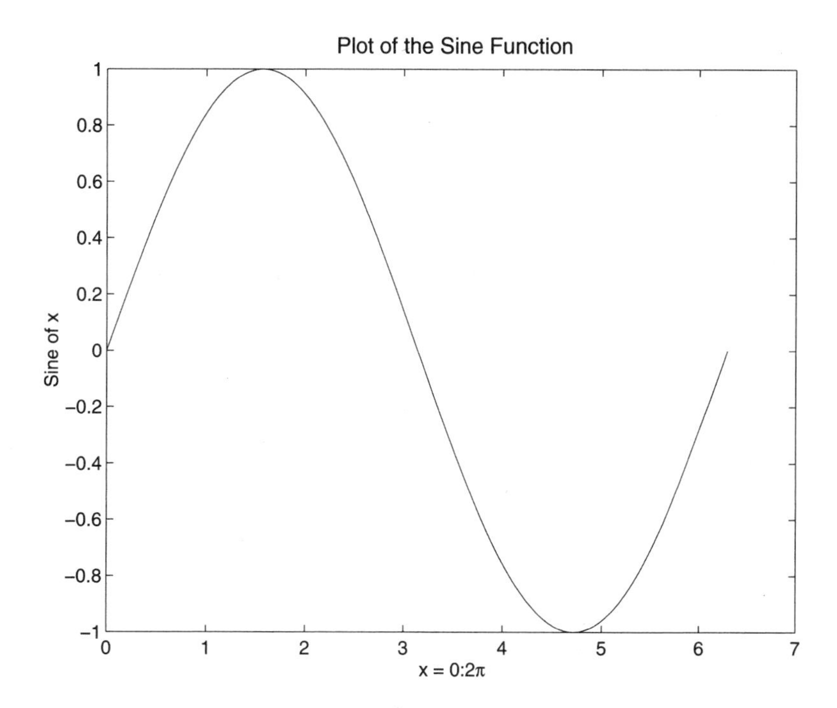

Multiple Data Sets in One Graph

Multiple x-y pair arguments create multiple graphs with a single call to plot. MATLAB automatically cycles through a predefined (but user settable) list of colors to allow discrimination among sets of data. See the axes ColorOrder and LineStyleOrder properties.

For example, these statements plot three related functions of x, with each curve in a separate distinguishing color.

```
x = 0:pi/100:2*pi;
y = sin(x);
y2 = sin(x-.25);
y3 = sin(x-.5);
plot(x,y,x,y2,x,y3)
```

The legend command provides an easy way to identify the individual plots.

```
legend('sin(x)','sin(x-.25)','sin(x-.5)')
```

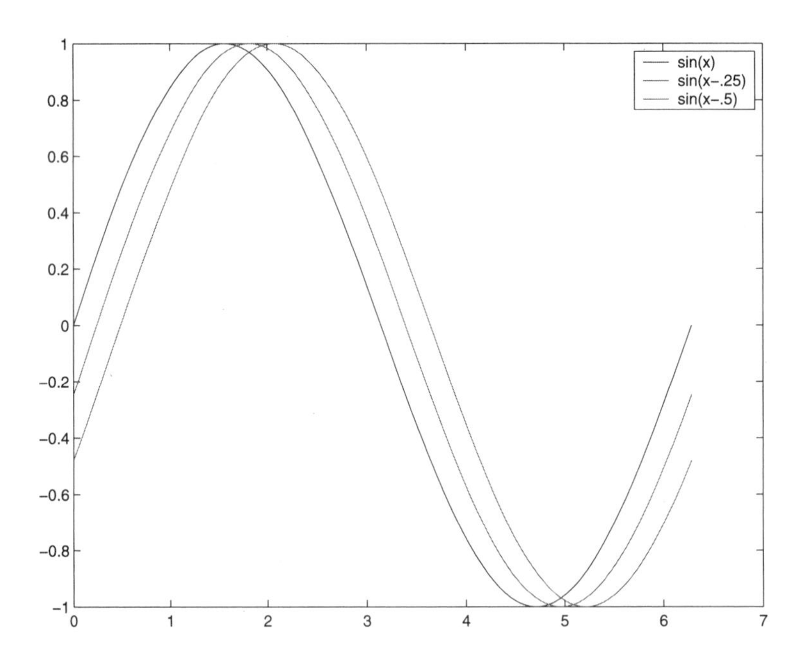

For More Information See "Defining the Color of Lines for Plotting" in "Axes Properties" in the MATLAB documentation.

Specifying Line Styles and Colors

It is possible to specify color, line styles, and markers (such as plus signs or circles) when you plot your data using the `plot` command.

```
plot(x,y,'color_style_marker')
```

`color_style_marker` is a string containing from one to four characters (enclosed in single quotation marks) constructed from a color, a line style, and a marker type:

- Color strings are `'c'`, `'m'`, `'y'`, `'r'`, `'g'`, `'b'`, `'w'`, and `'k'`. These correspond to cyan, magenta, yellow, red, green, blue, white, and black.
- Line style strings are `'-'` for solid, `'--'` for dashed, `':'` for dotted, `'-.'` for dash-dot. Omit the line style for no line.
- The marker types are `'+'`, `'o'`, `'*'`, and `'x'`, and the filled marker types are `'s'` for square, `'d'` for diamond, `'^'` for up triangle, `'v'` for down triangle, `'>'` for right triangle, `'<'` for left triangle, `'p'` for pentagram, `'h'` for hexagram, and `none` for no marker.

You can also edit color, line style, and markers interactively. See "Editing Plots" on page 5-16 for more information.

Plotting Lines and Markers

If you specify a marker type but not a line style, MATLAB draws only the marker. For example,

```
plot(x,y,'ks')
```

plots black squares at each data point, but does not connect the markers with a line.

The statement

```
plot(x,y,'r:+')
```

plots a red dotted line and places plus sign markers at each data point.

Placing Markers at Every Tenth Data Point

You might want to use fewer data points to plot the markers than you use to plot the lines. This example plots the data twice using a different number of points for the dotted line and marker plots.

```
x1 = 0:pi/100:2*pi;
x2 = 0:pi/10:2*pi;
plot(x1,sin(x1),'r:',x2,sin(x2),'r+')
```

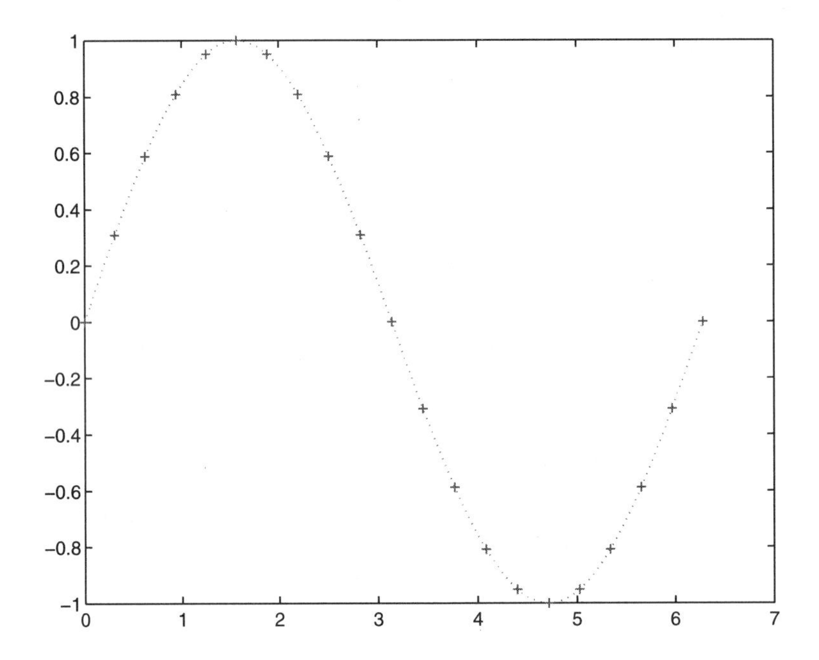

Imaginary and Complex Data

When the arguments to `plot` are complex, the imaginary part is ignored *except* when you pass `plot` a single complex argument. For this special case, the command is a shortcut for a graph of the real part versus the imaginary part. Therefore,

```
plot(Z)
```

where `Z` is a complex vector or matrix, is equivalent to

```
plot(real(Z),imag(Z))
```

For example,

```
t = 0:pi/10:2*pi;
plot(exp(i*t),'-o')
axis equal
```

draws a 20-sided polygon with little circles at the vertices. The command `axis equal` makes the individual tick-mark increments on the *x*- and *y*-axes the same length, which makes this plot more circular in appearance.

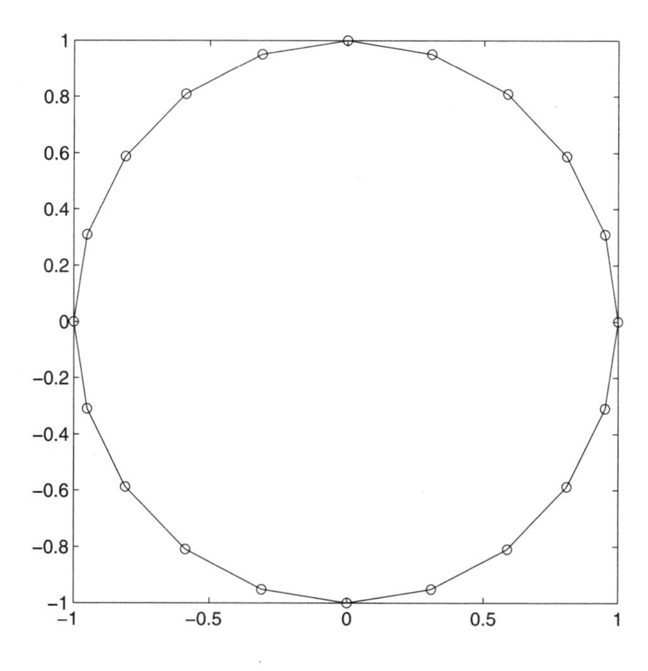

Adding Plots to an Existing Graph

The hold command enables you to add plots to an existing graph. When you type

```
hold on
```

MATLAB does not replace the existing graph when you issue another plotting command; it adds the new data to the current graph, rescaling the axes if necessary.

For example, these statements first create a contour plot of the peaks function, then superimpose a pseudocolor plot of the same function.

```
[x,y,z] = peaks;
pcolor(x,y,z)
shading interp
hold on
contour(x,y,z,20,'k')
hold off
```

The hold on command causes the pcolor plot to be combined with the contour plot in one figure.

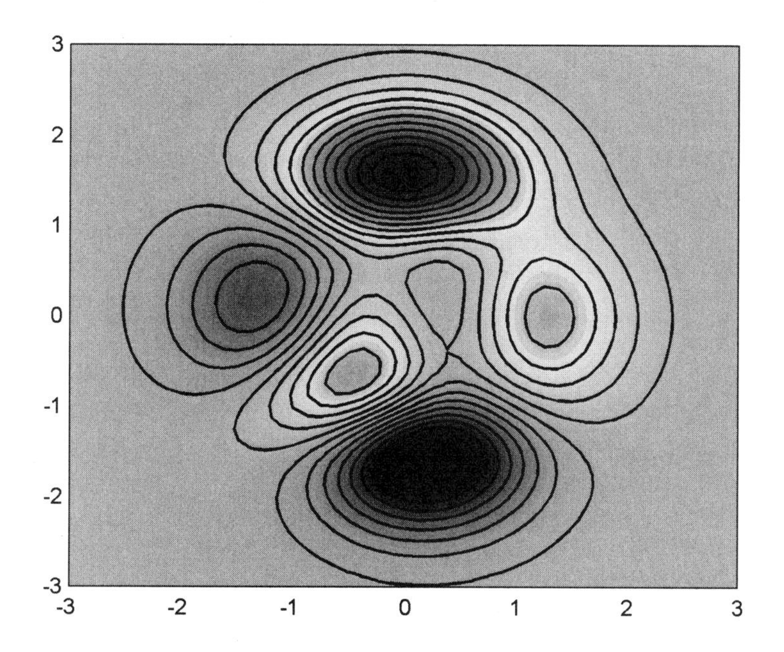

For More Information See “Creating Specialized Plots” in the MATLAB documentation for information on a variety of graph types.

Figure Windows

Graphing functions automatically open a new figure window if there are no figure windows already on the screen. If a figure window exists, MATLAB uses that window for graphics output. If there are multiple figure windows open, MATLAB targets the one that is designated the "current figure" (the last figure used or clicked in).

To make an existing figure window the current figure, you can click the mouse while the pointer is in that window or you can type

```
figure(n)
```

where `n` is the number in the figure title bar. The results of subsequent graphics commands are displayed in this window.

To open a new figure window and make it the current figure, type

```
figure
```

Clearing the Figure for a New Plot

When a figure already exists, most plotting commands clear the axes and use this figure to create the new plot. However, these commands do not reset figure properties, such as the background color or the colormap. If you have set any figure properties in the previous plot, you might want to use the `clf` command with the `reset` option,

```
clf reset
```

before creating your new plot to restore the figure's properties to their defaults.

For More Information See "Figure Properties" and "Graphics Window — the Figure" in the MATLAB documentation for information on figures.

Multiple Plots in One Figure

The `subplot` command enables you to display multiple plots in the same window or print them on the same piece of paper. Typing

```
subplot(m,n,p)
```

partitions the figure window into an m-by-n matrix of small subplots and selects the pth subplot for the current plot. The plots are numbered along first the top row of the figure window, then the second row, and so on. For example, these statements plot data in four different subregions of the figure window.

```
t = 0:pi/10:2*pi;
[X,Y,Z] = cylinder(4*cos(t));
subplot(2,2,1); mesh(X)
subplot(2,2,2); mesh(Y)
subplot(2,2,3); mesh(Z)
subplot(2,2,4); mesh(X,Y,Z)
```

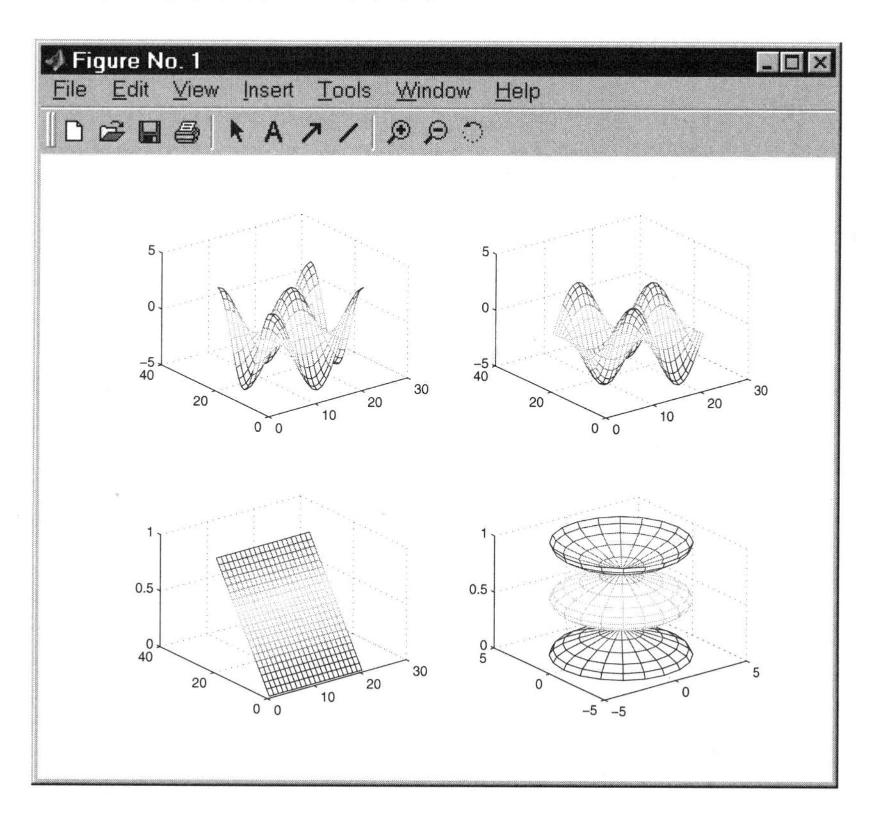

Controlling the Axes

The `axis` command provides a number of options for setting the scaling, orientation, and aspect ratio of graphs. You can also set these options interactively. See "Editing Plots" on page 5-16 for more information.

Setting Axis Limits

By default, MATLAB finds the maxima and minima of the data and chooses the axis limits to span this range. The `axis` command enables you to specify your own limits:

```
axis([xmin xmax ymin ymax])
```

or for three-dimensional graphs,

```
axis([xmin xmax ymin ymax zmin zmax])
```

Use the command

```
axis auto
```

to reenable MATLAB automatic limit selection.

Setting Axis Aspect Ratio

`axis` also enables you to specify a number of predefined modes. For example,

```
axis square
```

makes the x-axis and y-axis the same length.

```
axis equal
```

makes the individual tick mark increments on the x-axes and y-axes the same length. This means

```
plot(exp(i*[0:pi/10:2*pi]))
```

followed by either `axis square` or `axis equal` turns the oval into a proper circle.

```
axis auto normal
```

returns the axis scaling to its default automatic mode.

Setting Axis Visibility

You can use the `axis` command to make the axis visible or invisible.

```
axis on
```

makes the axes visible. This is the default.

```
axis off
```

makes the axes invisible.

Setting Grid Lines

The `grid` command toggles grid lines on and off. The statement

```
grid on
```

turns the grid lines on, and

```
grid off
```

turns them back off again.

For More Information See the `axis` and `axes` reference pages and "Axes Properties" in the MATLAB documentation.

Axis Labels and Titles

The `xlabel`, `ylabel`, and `zlabel` commands add x-, y-, and z-axis labels. The `title` command adds a title at the top of the figure and the `text` function inserts text anywhere in the figure.

You can produce mathematical symbols using LaTeX notation in the text string, as the following example illustrates.

```
t = -pi:pi/100:pi;
y = sin(t);
plot(t,y)
axis([-pi pi -1 1])
xlabel('-\pi \leq {\itt} \leq \pi')
ylabel('sin(t)')
title('Graph of the sine function')
text(1,-1/3,'{\itNote the odd symmetry.}')
```

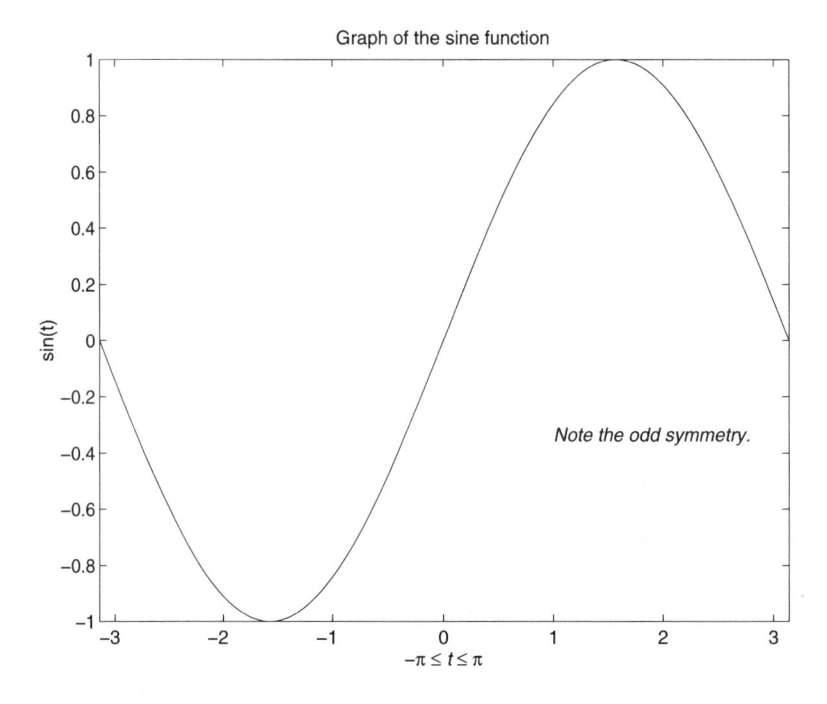

You can also set these options interactively. See "Editing Plots" on page 5-16 for more information.

Note that the location of the text string is defined in axes units (i.e., the same units as the data). See the `annotation` function for a way to place text in normalized figure units.

Saving Figures

Save a figure by selecting **Save** from the **File** menu to display a file save dialog. MATLAB saves the data it needs to recreate the figure and its contents (i.e., the entire graph) in a file with a `.fig` extension.

To save a figure using a standard graphics format, such as TIFF, for use with other applications, select **Export Setup** from the **File** menu. You can also save from the command line — use the `saveas` command, including any options to save the figure in a different format.

See "Exporting the Graph" on page 5-35 for an example.

Saving Workspace Data

You can save the variables in your workspace using the **Save Workspace As** item in the figure **File** menu. You can reload saved data using the **Import Data** item in the figure **File** menu. MATLAB supports a variety of data file formats, including MATLAB data files, which have a `.mat` extension.

Generating M-Code to Recreate a Figure

You can generate MATLAB code that recreates a figure and the graph it contains by selecting the **Generate M-File** item from the figure **File** menu. This option is particularly useful if you have developed a graph using plotting tools and want to create a similar graph using the same or different data.

Saving Figures That Are Compatible with Previous Version of MATLAB

Create backward-compatible FIG-files by following these two steps.

- Ensure that any plotting functions used to create the contents of the figure are called with the `'v6'` argument, where applicable.
- Use the `'-v6'` option with the `hgsave` command.

For More Information See "Plot Objects and Backward Compatibility" in the MATLAB documentation more information.

Mesh and Surface Plots

MATLAB defines a surface by the z-coordinates of points above a grid in the x-y plane, using straight lines to connect adjacent points. The `mesh` and `surf` plotting functions display surfaces in three dimensions. `mesh` produces wireframe surfaces that color only the lines connecting the defining points. `surf` displays both the connecting lines and the faces of the surface in color.

The figure colormap and figure properties determine how MATLAB colors the surface.

Visualizing Functions of Two Variables

To display a function of two variables, $z = f(x,y)$,

- Generate `X` and `Y` matrices consisting of repeated rows and columns, respectively, over the domain of the function.
- Use `X` and `Y` to evaluate and graph the function.

The `meshgrid` function transforms the domain specified by a single vector or two vectors `x` and `y` into matrices `X` and `Y` for use in evaluating functions of two variables. The rows of `X` are copies of the vector `x` and the columns of `Y` are copies of the vector `y`.

Example — Graphing the sinc Function

This example evaluates and graphs the two-dimensional *sinc* function, $\sin(r)/r$, between the x and y directions. `R` is the distance from the origin, which is at the center of the matrix. Adding `eps` (a MATLAB command that returns a small floating-point number) avoids the indeterminate 0/0 at the origin.

```
[X,Y] = meshgrid(-8:.5:8);
R = sqrt(X.^2 + Y.^2) + eps;
Z = sin(R)./R;
mesh(X,Y,Z,'EdgeColor','black')
```

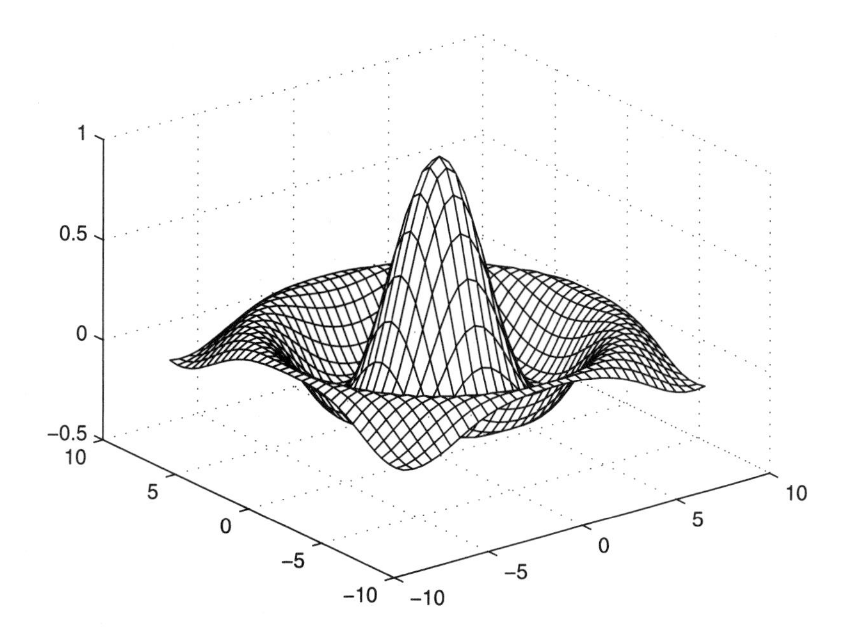

By default, MATLAB colors the mesh using the current colormap. However, this example uses a single-colored mesh by specifying the `EdgeColor` surface property. See the `surface` reference page for a list of all surface properties.

You can create a mesh with see-through faces by disabling hidden line removal.

```
hidden off
```

See the `hidden` reference page for more information on this option.

Example — Colored Surface Plots

A surface plot is similar to a mesh plot except that MATLAB colors the rectangular faces of the surface. The color of each faces is determined by the values of `Z` and the colormap (a colormap is an ordered list of colors). These statements graph the *sinc* function as a surface plot, specify a colormap, and add a color bar to show the mapping of data to color.

```
surf(X,Y,Z)
colormap hsv
colorbar
```

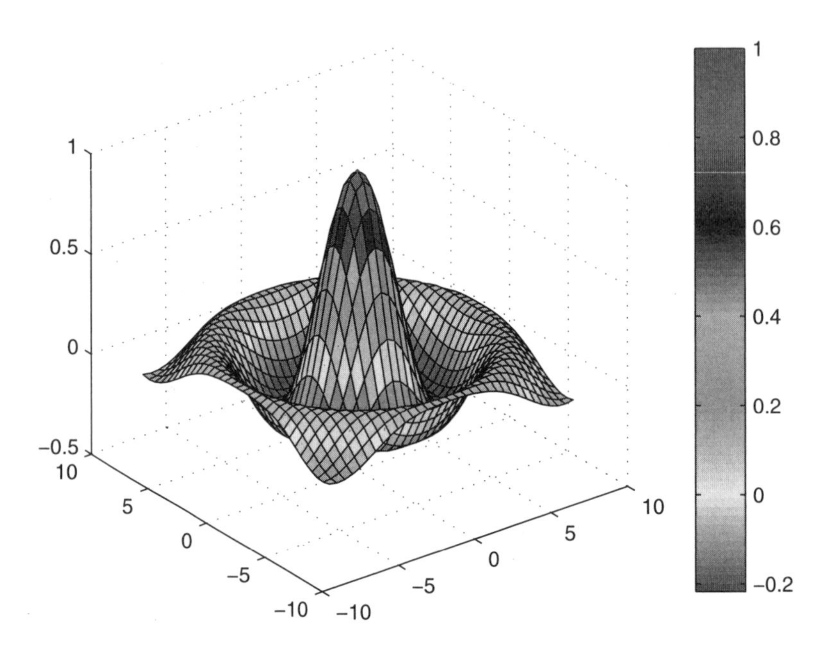

See the `colormap` reference page for information on colormaps.

For More Information See "Creating 3-D Graphs" in the MATLAB documentation for more information on surface plots.

Transparent Surfaces

You can make the faces of a surface transparent to a varying degree. Transparency (referred to as the alpha value) can be specified for the whole object or can be based on an alphamap, which behaves in a way analogous to colormaps. For example,

```
surf(X,Y,Z)
colormap hsv
alpha(.4)
```

produces a surface with a face alpha value of 0.4. Alpha values range from 0 (completely transparent) to 1 (not transparent).

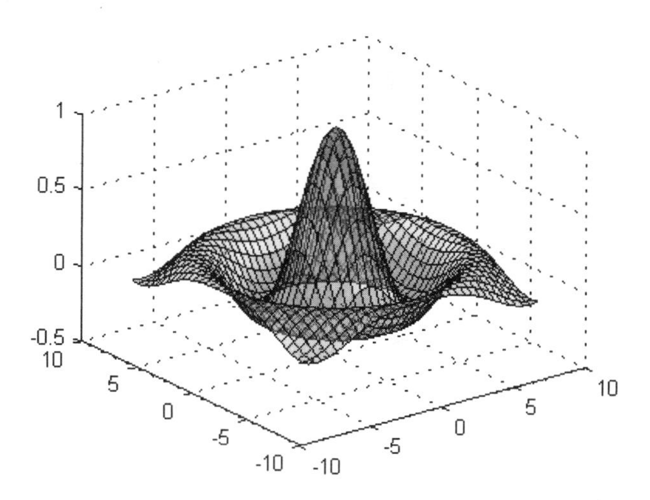

For More Information See "Transparency" in the MATLAB documentation for more information on using transparency.

Surface Plots with Lighting

Lighting is the technique of illuminating an object with a directional light source. In certain cases, this technique can make subtle differences in surface shape easier to see. Lighting can also be used to add realism to three-dimensional graphs.

This example uses the same surface as the previous examples, but colors it red and removes the mesh lines. A light object is then added to the left of the "camera" (the camera is the location in space from where you are viewing the surface).

```
surf(X,Y,Z,'FaceColor','red','EdgeColor','none')
camlight left; lighting phong
```

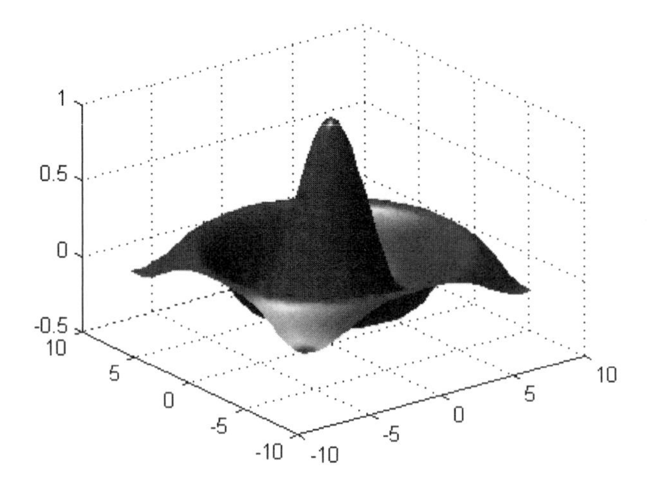

Manipulating the Surface

The figure toolbar and the camera toolbar provide ways to explore 3-D graphics interactively. Display the camera toolbar by selecting **Camera Toolbar** from the figure **View** menu.

The following picture shows both toolbars with the Rotate 3D tool selected.

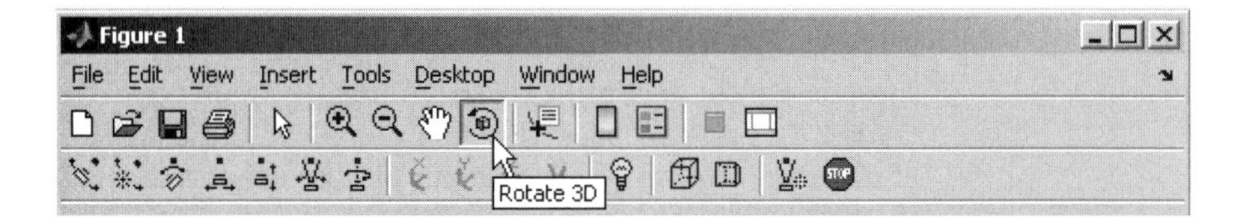

These tools enables you to move the camera around the surface object, zoom, add lighting, and perform other viewing operations without issuing commands.

The following picture shows the surface viewed by orbiting the camera toward the bottom using the Rotate 3D tool. A scene light has been added to illuminate the underside of the surface, which is not lit by the light added in the previous section.

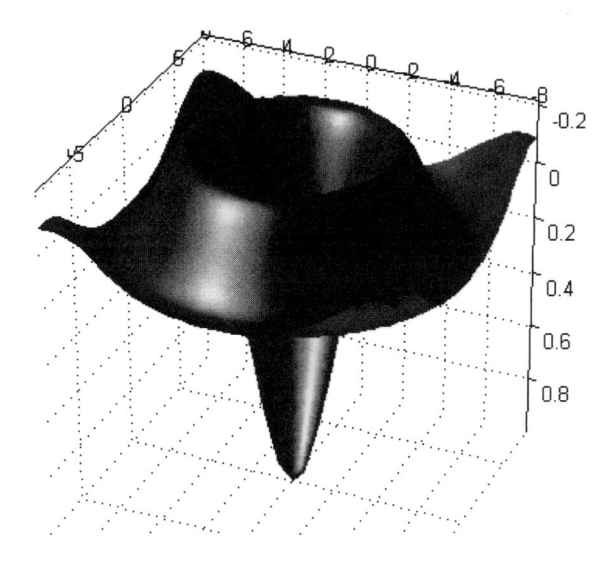

For More Information See "Lighting as a Visualization Tool" and "View Control with the Camera Toolbar" in the MATLAB documentation for information on these techniques.

Images

Two-dimensional arrays can be displayed as *images*, where the array elements determine brightness or color of the images. For example, the statements

```
load durer
whos
Name          Size          Bytes  Class

  X           648x509       2638656  double array
  caption     2x28              112  char array
  map         128x3            3072  double array
```

load the file durer.mat, adding three variables to the workspace. The matrix X is a 648-by-509 matrix and map is a 128-by-3 matrix that is the colormap for this image.

MAT-files, such as durer.mat, are binary files that can be created on one platform and later read by MATLAB on a different platform.

The elements of X are integers between 1 and 128, which serve as indices into the colormap, map. Then

```
image(X)
colormap(map)
axis image
```

reproduces Dürer's etching shown at the beginning of this book. A high-resolution scan of the magic square in the upper right corner is available in another file. Type

```
load detail
```

and then use the up arrow key on your keyboard to reexecute the image, colormap, and axis commands. The statement

```
colormap(hot)
```

adds some twentieth century colorization to the sixteenth century etching. The function hot generates a colormap containing shades of reds, oranges, and yellows. Typically a given image matrix has a specific colormap associated with it. See the colormap reference page for a list of other predefined colormaps.

Reading and Writing Images

You can read standard image files (TIFF, JPEG, BMP, etc.) into MATLAB using the `imread` function. The type of data returned by `imread` depends on the type of image you are reading.

You can write MATLAB data to a variety of standard image formats using the `imwrite` function. See the reference pages for these functions for more information and examples.

For More Information See "Displaying Bit-Mapped Images" in the MATLAB documentation for information on the image processing capabilities of MATLAB.

Printing Graphics

You can print a MATLAB figure directly on a printer connected to your computer or you can export the figure to one of the standard graphics file formats supported by MATLAB. There are two ways to print and export figures:

- Use the **Print** or **Export Setup** options under the **File** menu
- Use the `print` command to print or export the figure

See “Preparing Graphs for Presentation” on page 5-29 for an example.

Printing from the Menu

There are four menu options under the **File** menu that pertain to printing:

- The **Page Setup** option displays a dialog box that enables you to adjust characteristics of the figure on the printed page.
- The **Print Setup** option displays a dialog box that sets printing defaults, but does not actually print the figure.
- The **Print Preview** option enables you to view the figure the way it will look on the printed page.
- The **Print** option displays a dialog box that lets you select standard printing options and print the figure.

Generally, use **Print Preview** to determine whether the printed output is what you want. If not, use the **Page Setup** dialog box to change the output settings. Select the **Page Setup** dialog box **Help** button to display information on how to set up the page.

Exporting Figure to Graphics Files

The **Export Setup** option in the **File** menu enables you to set a variety of figure characteristics, such as size and font type, as well as apply predefined templates to achieve standard-looking graphics files. After setup, you can export the figure to a number of standard graphics file formats.

Using the Print Command

The `print` command provides more flexibility in the type of output sent to the printer and allows you to control printing from M-files. The result can be sent directly to your default printer or stored in a specified file. A wide variety of output formats, including TIFF, JPEG, and PostScript, is available.

For example, this statement saves the contents of the current figure window as color Encapsulated Level 2 PostScript in the file called `magicsquare.eps`. It also includes a TIFF preview, which enables most word processors to display the picture.

```
print -depsc2 -tiff magicsquare.eps
```

To save the same figure as a TIFF file with a resolution of 200 dpi, use the command

```
print -dtiff -r200 magicsquare.tiff
```

If you type `print` on the command line,

```
print
```

MATLAB prints the current figure on your default printer.

For More Information See the `print` reference page and "Printing and Exporting" in the MATLAB documentation for more information on printing.

Handle Graphics

Handle Graphics® refers to a system of graphics objects that MATLAB uses to implement graphing and visualization functions. Each object created has a fixed set of properties. You can use these properties to control the behavior and appearance of your graph.

When you call a plotting function, MATLAB creates the graph using various graphics objects, such as a figure window, axes, lines, text, and so on. MATLAB enables you to query the value of each property and set the values of most properties.

For example, the following statement creates a figure with a white background color and without displaying the figure toolbar.

```
figure('Color','white','Toolbar','none')
```

Using the Handle

Whenever MATLAB creates a graphics object, it assigns an identifier (called a *handle*) to the object. You can use this handle to access the object's properties with the `set` and `get` functions. For example, the following statements create a graph and return a handle to a lineseries object in `h`.

```
x = 1:10;
y = x.^3;
h = plot(x,y);
```

You can use the handle `h` to set the properties of the lineseries object. For example, you can set its `Color` property:

```
set(h,'Color','red')
```

You can also specify properties when you call the plotting function.

```
h = plot(x,y,'Color','red');
```

When you query the lineseries properties,

```
get(h,'LineWidth')
```

MATLAB returns the answer:

```
ans =
    0.5000
```

Use the handle to see what properties a particular object contains.

```
get(h)
```

Graphics Objects

Graphics objects are the basic elements used to display graphs and user interface components. These objects are organized into a hierarchy, as shown by the following diagram.

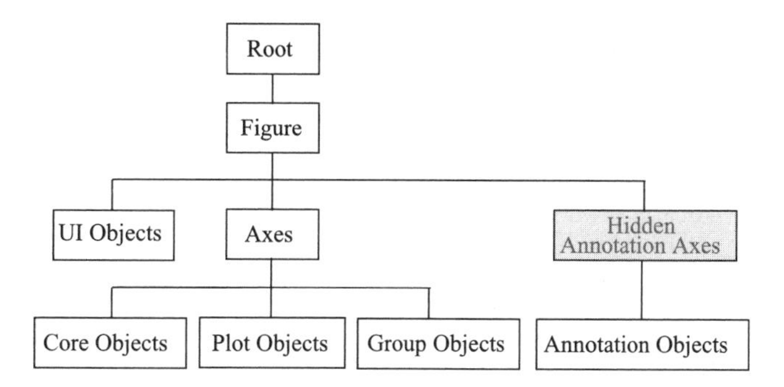

Key Graphics Objects

When you call a function to create a graph, MATLAB creates a hierarchy of graphics objects. For example, calling the `plot` function creates the following graphics objects:

- Lineseries plot objects — Represent the data passed to the `plot` function
- Axes — Provide a frame of reference and scaling for the plotted lineseries
- Text — Label the axes tick marks and are used for titles and annotations
- Figures — Are the windows that contain axes toolbars, menus, etc.

Different types of graphs use different objects to represent data: however, all data objects are contained in axes and all objects (except root) are contained in figures.

The root is an abstract object that primarily stores information about your computer or MATLAB state. You cannot create an instance of the root object.

For More Information See "Handle Graphics Objects" in the MATLAB documentation for information on graphics objects.

User interface objects are used to create graphical user interfaces (GUIs). These objects include components like push buttons, editable text boxes, and list boxes.

For More Information See "Creating Graphical User Interfaces" in the MATLAB documentation for more information on user interface objects.

Creating Objects

Plotting functions (like `plot` and `surf`) call the appropriate low-level function to draw their respective graph. For information about an object's properties, see the Handle Graphics Property Browser in the MATLAB online documentation.

Commands for Working with Objects

This table lists commands commonly used when working with objects.

Function	Purpose
`allchild`	Find all children of specified objects
`ancestor`	Find ancestor of graphics object
`copyobj`	Copy graphics object
`delete`	Delete an object
`findall`	Find all graphics objects (including hidden handles)
`findobj`	Find the handles of objects having specified property values
`gca`	Return the handle of the current axes

Function	Purpose
`gcf`	Return the handle of the current figure
`gco`	Return the handle of the current object
`get`	Query the values of an object's properties
`ishandle`	True if value is valid object handle
`set`	Set the values of an object's properties

Setting Object Properties

All object properties have default values. However, you might find it useful to change the settings of some properties to customize your graph. There are two ways to set object properties:

- Specify values for properties when you create the object.
- Set the property value on an object that already exists.

Setting Properties from Plotting Commands

You can specify object property value pairs as arguments to many plotting functions, such as `plot`, `mesh`, and `surf`.

For example, plotting commands that create lineseries or surfaceplot objects enable you to specify property name/property value pairs as arguments. The command

```
surf(x,y,z,'FaceColor','interp',...
          'FaceLighting','gouraud')
```

plots the data in the variables `x`, `y`, and `z` using a surfaceplot object with interpolated face color and employing the Gouraud face light technique. You can set any of the object's properties this way.

Setting Properties of Existing Objects

To modify the property values of existing objects, you can use the `set` command or the Property Editor. This section describes how to use the `set` command. See "Using the Property Editor" on page 5-17 for more information.

Most plotting functions return the handles of the objects that they create so you can modify the objects using the set command. For example, these statements plot a five-by-five matrix (creating five lineseries, one per column) and then set the Marker property to a square and the MarkerFaceColor property to green.

```
h = plot(magic(5));
set(h,'Marker','s','MarkerFaceColor','g')
```

In this case, h is a vector containing five handles, one for each of the five lineseries in the graph. The set statement sets the Marker and MarkerFaceColor properties of all lineseries to the same values.

Setting Multiple Property Values

If you want to set the properties of each lineseries to a different value, you can use cell arrays to store all the data and pass it to the set command. For example, create a plot and save the lineseries handles.

```
h = plot(magic(5));
```

Suppose you want to add different markers to each lineseries and color the marker's face color the same color as the lineseries. You need to define two cell arrays — one containing the property names and the other containing the desired values of the properties.

The prop_name cell array contains two elements.

```
prop_name(1) = {'Marker'};
prop_name(2) = {'MarkerFaceColor'};
```

The prop_values cell array contains 10 values: five values for the Marker property and five values for the MarkerFaceColor property. Notice that prop_values is a two-dimensional cell array. The first dimension indicates which handle in h the values apply to and the second dimension indicates which property the value is assigned to.

```
prop_values(1,1) = {'s'};
prop_values(1,2) = {get(h(1),'Color')};
prop_values(2,1) = {'d'};
prop_values(2,2) = {get(h(2),'Color')};
prop_values(3,1) = {'o'};
prop_values(3,2) = {get(h(3),'Color')};
prop_values(4,1) = {'p'};
prop_values(4,2) = {get(h(4),'Color')};
```

```
prop_values(5,1) = {'h'};
prop_values(5,2) = {get(h(5),'Color')};
```

The `MarkerFaceColor` is always assigned the value of the corresponding line's color (obtained by getting the lineseries `Color` property with the `get` command).

After defining the cell arrays, call `set` to specify the new property values.

```
set(h,prop_name,prop_values)
```

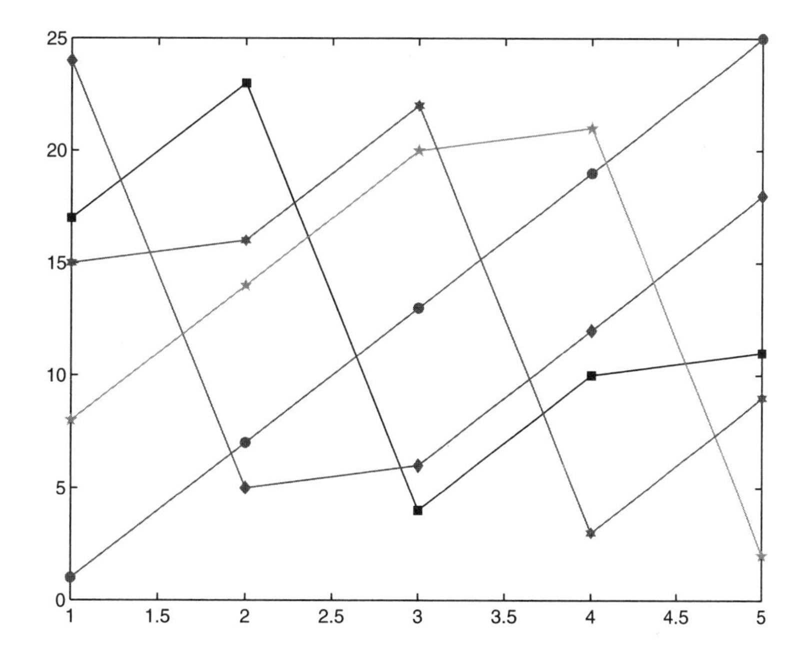

Specifying the Axes or Figure

MATLAB always creates an axes or figure if one does not exist when you issue a plotting command. However, when you are creating a graphics M-file, it is good practice to explicitly create and specify the parent axes and figure, particularly if others will use your program. Specifying the parent prevents the following problems:

- Your M-file overwrites the graph in the current figure. Note that a figure becomes the current figure whenever a user clicks on it.
- The current figure might be in an unexpected state and not behave as your program expects.

The following examples shows a simple M-file that plots a function and the mean of the function over the specified range.

```
function myfunc(x)
% x = -10:.005:40; Here's a value you can use for x
y = [1.5*cos(x) + 6*exp(-.1*x) + exp(.07*x).*sin(3*x)];
ym = mean(y);
hfig = figure('Name','Function and Mean',...
       'Pointer','fullcrosshair');
hax = axes('Parent',hfig);
plot(hax,x,y)
hold on
plot(hax,[min(x) max(x)],[ym ym],'Color','red')
hold off
ylab = get(hax,'YTick');
set(hax,'YTick',sort([ylab ym]))
title ('y = 1.5cos(x) + 6e^{-0.1x} + e^{0.07x}sin(3x)')
xlabel('X Axis'); ylabel('Y Axis')
```

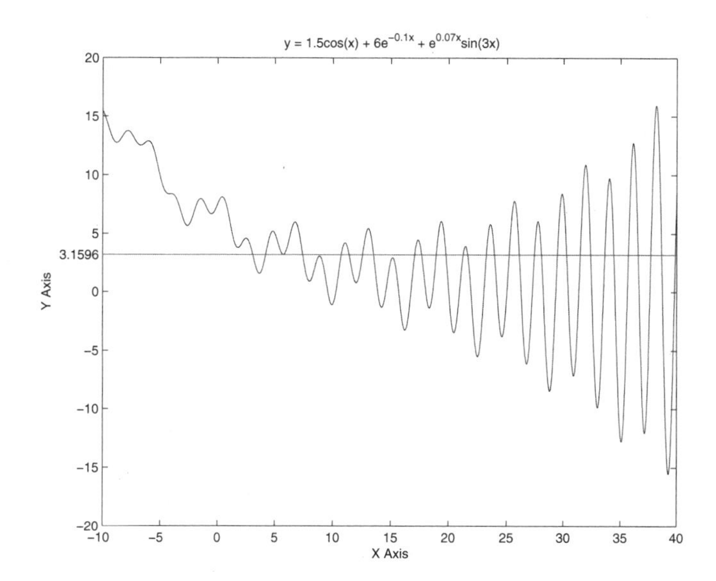

Finding the Handles of Existing Objects

The `findobj` function enables you to obtain the handles of graphics objects by searching for objects with particular property values. With `findobj` you can specify the values of any combination of properties, which makes it easy to pick one object out of many. `findobj` also recognizes regular expressions (`regexp`).

For example, you might want to find the blue line with square marker having blue face color.You can also specify which figures or axes to search, if there are more than one. The following sections provide examples illustrating how to use `findobj`.

Finding All Objects of a Certain Type

Because all objects have a `Type` property that identifies the type of object, you can find the handles of all occurrences of a particular type of object. For example,

```
h = findobj('Type','patch');
```

finds the handles of all patch objects.

Finding Objects with a Particular Property

You can specify multiple properties to narrow the search. For example,

```
h = findobj('Type','line','Color','r','LineStyle',':');
```

finds the handles of all red dotted lines.

Limiting the Scope of the Search

You can specify the starting point in the object hierarchy by passing the handle of the starting figure or axes as the first argument. For example,

```
h = findobj(gca,'Type','text','String','\pi/2');
```

finds the string $\pi/2$ only within the current axes.

Using findobj as an Argument

Because `findobj` returns the handles it finds, you can use it in place of the handle argument. For example,

```
set(findobj('Type','line','Color','red'),'LineStyle',':')
```

finds all red lines and sets their line style to dotted.

Animations

MATLAB provides three ways of generating moving, animated graphics:

- “Erase Mode Method” on page 5-71 — Continually erase and then redraw the objects on the screen, making incremental changes with each redraw.
- “Creating Movies” on page 5-73 — Save a number of different pictures and then play them back as a movie.
- Using AVI files. See `avifile` for more information and examples.

Erase Mode Method

Using the `EraseMode` property is appropriate for long sequences of simple plots where the change from frame to frame is minimal. Here is an example showing simulated Brownian motion. Specify a number of points, such as

```
n = 20
```

and a temperature or velocity, such as

```
s = .02
```

The best values for these two parameters depend upon the speed of your particular computer. Generate `n` random points with (x,y) coordinates between $-1/2$ and $+1/2$.

```
x = rand(n,1)-0.5;
y = rand(n,1)-0.5;
```

Plot the points in a square with sides at -1 and +1. Save the handle for the vector of points and set its `EraseMode` to `xor`. This tells the MATLAB graphics system not to redraw the entire plot when the coordinates of one point are changed, but to restore the background color in the vicinity of the point using an exclusive or operation.

```
h = plot(x,y,'.');
axis([-1 1 -1 1])
axis square
grid off
set(h,'EraseMode','xor','MarkerSize',18)
```

Now begin the animation. Here is an infinite `while` loop, which you can eventually exit by typing **Ctrl+C**. Each time through the loop, add a small amount of normally distributed random noise to the coordinates of the points. Then, instead of creating an entirely new plot, simply change the `XData` and `YData` properties of the original plot.

```
while 1
   drawnow
   x = x + s*randn(n,1);
   y = y + s*randn(n,1);
   set(h,'XData',x,'YData',y)
end
```

See how long it takes for one of the points to get outside the square and how long before all the points are outside the square.

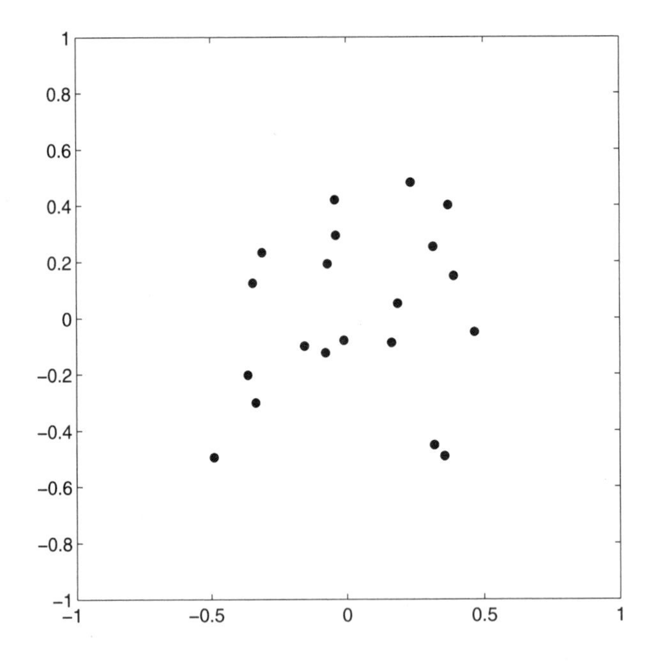

Creating Movies

If you increase the number of points in the Brownian motion example to `n = 300` and `s = .02`, the motion is no longer very fluid; it takes too much time to draw each time step. It becomes more effective to save a predetermined number of frames as bitmaps and to play them back as a *movie*.

First, decide on the number of frames,

```
nframes = 50;
```

Next, set up the first plot as before, except using the default `EraseMode` (`normal`).

```
x = rand(n,1)-0.5;
y = rand(n,1)-0.5;
h = plot(x,y,'.');
set(h,'MarkerSize',18);
axis([-1 1 -1 1])
axis square
grid off
```

Generate the movie and use `getframe` to capture each frame.

```
for k = 1:nframes
   x = x + s*randn(n,1);
   y = y + s*randn(n,1);
   set(h,'XData',x,'YData',y)
   M(k) = getframe;
end
```

Finally, play the movie 30 times.

```
movie(M,30)
```

6

Programming

This chapter introduces programming constructs, multidimensional arrays and other data structures, and MATLAB functions.

Flow Control

MATLAB has several flow control constructs:

- "if" on page 6-2
- "switch and case" on page 6-4
- "for" on page 6-5
- "while" on page 6-6
- "continue" on page 6-6
- "break" on page 6-7
- "try - catch" on page 6-8
- "return" on page 6-8

if

The `if` statement evaluates a logical expression and executes a group of statements when the expression is *true*. The optional `elseif` and `else` keywords provide for the execution of alternate groups of statements. An `end` keyword, which matches the `if`, terminates the last group of statements. The groups of statements are delineated by the four keywords — no braces or brackets are involved.

The MATLAB algorithm for generating a magic square of order n involves three different cases: when n is odd, when n is even but not divisible by 4, or when n is divisible by 4. This is described by

```
if rem(n,2) ~= 0
   M = odd_magic(n)
elseif rem(n,4) ~= 0
   M = single_even_magic(n)
else
   M = double_even_magic(n)
end
```

In this example, the three cases are mutually exclusive, but if they weren't, the first *true* condition would be executed.

It is important to understand how relational operators and `if` statements work with matrices. When you want to check for equality between two variables, you might use

```
if A == B, ...
```

This is valid MATLAB code, and does what you expect when `A` and `B` are scalars. But when `A` and `B` are matrices, `A == B` does not test *if* they are equal, it tests *where* they are equal; the result is another matrix of 0's and 1's showing element-by-element equality. (In fact, if `A` and `B` are not the same size, then `A == B` is an error.)

```
A = magic(4);     B = A;     B(1,1) = 0;

A == B
ans =
     0     1     1     1
     1     1     1     1
     1     1     1     1
     1     1     1     1
```

The proper way to check for equality between two variables is to use the `isequal` function,

```
if isequal(A,B), ...
```

`isequal` returns a *scalar* logical value of `1` (representing `true`) or `0` (`false`), instead of a matrix, as the expression to be evaluated by the `if` function. Using the `A` and `B` matrices from above, you get

```
isequal(A, B)
ans =
    0
```

Here is another example to emphasize this point. If `A` and `B` are scalars, the following program will never reach the "unexpected situation". But for most pairs of matrices, including our magic squares with interchanged columns, none of the matrix conditions `A > B`, `A < B`, or `A == B` is true for *all* elements and so the `else` clause is executed.

```
if A > B
   'greater'
elseif A < B
   'less'
elseif A == B
   'equal'
else
   error('Unexpected situation')
end
```

Several functions are helpful for reducing the results of matrix comparisons to scalar conditions for use with `if`, including

```
isequal
isempty
all
any
```

switch and case

The `switch` statement executes groups of statements based on the value of a variable or expression. The keywords `case` and `otherwise` delineate the groups. Only the first matching case is executed. There must always be an `end` to match the `switch`.

The logic of the magic squares algorithm can also be described by

```
switch (rem(n,4)==0) + (rem(n,2)==0)
   case 0
      M = odd_magic(n)
   case 1
      M = single_even_magic(n)
   case 2
      M = double_even_magic(n)
   otherwise
      error('This is impossible')
end
```

Note Unlike the C language `switch` statement, MATLAB `switch` does not fall through. If the first `case` statement is `true`, the other `case` statements do not execute. So, `break` statements are not required.

---

for

The `for` loop repeats a group of statements a fixed, predetermined number of times. A matching `end` delineates the statements.

```
for n = 3:32
   r(n) = rank(magic(n));
end
r
```

The semicolon terminating the inner statement suppresses repeated printing, and the `r` after the loop displays the final result.

It is a good idea to indent the loops for readability, especially when they are nested.

```
for i = 1:m
   for j = 1:n
      H(i,j) = 1/(i+j);
   end
end
```

while

The `while` loop repeats a group of statements an indefinite number of times under control of a logical condition. A matching `end` delineates the statements.

Here is a complete program, illustrating `while`, `if`, `else`, and `end`, that uses interval bisection to find a zero of a polynomial.

```
a = 0; fa = -Inf;
b = 3; fb = Inf;
while b-a > eps*b
   x = (a+b)/2;
   fx = x^3-2*x-5;
   if sign(fx) == sign(fa)
      a = x; fa = fx;
   else
      b = x; fb = fx;
   end
end
x
```

The result is a root of the polynomial $x^3 - 2x - 5$, namely

```
x =
   2.09455148154233
```

The cautions involving matrix comparisons that are discussed in the section on the `if` statement also apply to the `while` statement.

continue

The `continue` statement passes control to the next iteration of the `for` loop or `while` loop in which it appears, skipping any remaining statements in the body of the loop. In nested loops, `continue` passes control to the next iteration of the `for` loop or `while` loop enclosing it.

The example below shows a `continue` loop that counts the lines of code in the file `magic.m`, skipping all blank lines and comments. A `continue` statement is used to advance to the next line in `magic.m` without incrementing the count whenever a blank line or comment line is encountered.

```
fid = fopen('magic.m','r');
count = 0;
while ~feof(fid)
    line = fgetl(fid);
    if isempty(line) | strncmp(line,'%',1)
        continue
    end
    count = count + 1;
end
disp(sprintf('%d lines',count));
```

break

The `break` statement lets you exit early from a `for` loop or `while` loop. In nested loops, `break` exits from the innermost loop only.

Here is an improvement on the example from the previous section. Why is this use of `break` a good idea?

```
a = 0; fa = -Inf;
b = 3; fb = Inf;
while b-a > eps*b
   x = (a+b)/2;
   fx = x^3-2*x-5;
   if fx == 0
      break
   elseif sign(fx) == sign(fa)
      a = x; fa = fx;
   else
      b = x; fb = fx;
   end
end
x
```

try - catch

The general form of a try-catch statement sequence is

```
try
   statement
   ...
   statement
catch
   statement
   ...
   statement
end
```

In this sequence the statements between try and catch are executed until an error occurs. The statements between catch and end are then executed. Use lasterr to see the cause of the error. If an error occurs between catch and end, MATLAB terminates execution unless another try-catch sequence has been established.

return

return terminates the current sequence of commands and returns control to the invoking function or to the keyboard. return is also used to terminate keyboard mode. A called function normally transfers control to the function that invoked it when it reaches the end of the function. You can insert a return statement within the called function to force an early termination and to transfer control to the invoking function.

Other Data Structures

This section introduces you to some other data structures in MATLAB, including

- "Multidimensional Arrays" on page 6-9
- "Cell Arrays" on page 6-11
- "Characters and Text" on page 6-13
- "Structures" on page 6-16

Multidimensional Arrays

Multidimensional arrays in MATLAB are arrays with more than two subscripts. One way of creating a multidimensional array is by calling `zeros`, `ones`, `rand`, or `randn` with more than two arguments. For example,

```
R = randn(3,4,5);
```

creates a 3-by-4-by-5 array with a total of 3x4x5 = 60 normally distributed random elements.

A three-dimensional array might represent three-dimensional physical data, say the temperature in a room, sampled on a rectangular grid. Or it might represent a sequence of matrices, $A^{(k)}$, or samples of a time-dependent matrix, $A(t)$. In these latter cases, the (i, j)th element of the kth matrix, or the t_kth matrix, is denoted by `A(i,j,k)`.

MATLAB and Dürer's versions of the magic square of order 4 differ by an interchange of two columns. Many different magic squares can be generated by interchanging columns. The statement

```
p = perms(1:4);
```

generates the 4! = 24 permutations of `1:4`. The `k`th permutation is the row vector `p(k,:)`. Then

```
A = magic(4);
M = zeros(4,4,24);
for k = 1:24
   M(:,:,k) = A(:,p(k,:));
end
```

stores the sequence of 24 magic squares in a three-dimensional array, `M`. The size of `M` is

```
size(M)

ans =
     4     4    24
```

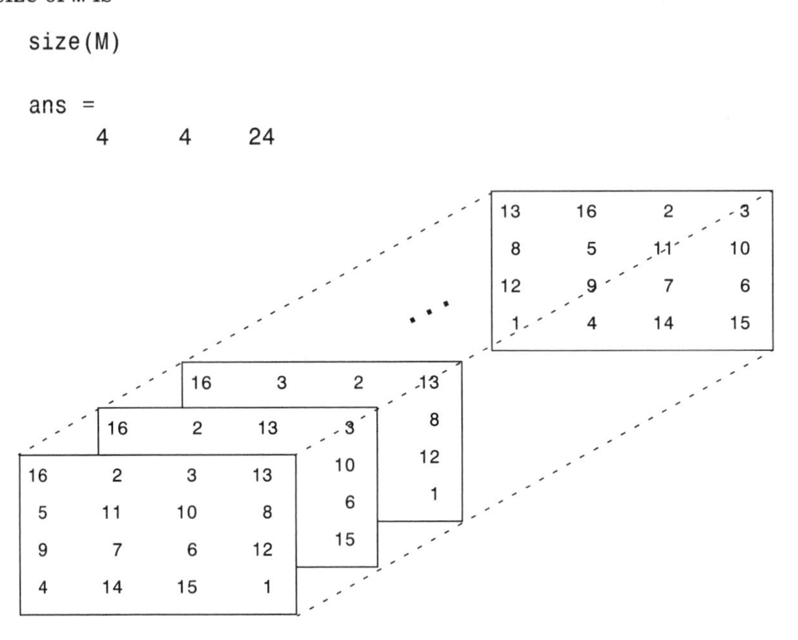

Note The order of the matrices shown in this illustration might differ from your results. The `perms` function always returns all permutations of the input vector, but the order of the permutations might be different for different MATLAB versions.

The statement

```
sum(M,d)
```

computes sums by varying the `d`th subscript. So

```
sum(M,1)
```

is a 1-by-4-by-24 array containing 24 copies of the row vector

```
34    34    34    34
```

and

```
sum(M,2)
```

is a 4-by-1-by-24 array containing 24 copies of the column vector

```
34
34
34
34
```

Finally,

```
S = sum(M,3)
```

adds the 24 matrices in the sequence. The result has size 4-by-4-by-1, so it looks like a 4-by-4 array.

```
S =
   204   204   204   204
   204   204   204   204
   204   204   204   204
   204   204   204   204
```

Cell Arrays

Cell arrays in MATLAB are multidimensional arrays whose elements are copies of other arrays. A cell array of empty matrices can be created with the `cell` function. But, more often, cell arrays are created by enclosing a miscellaneous collection of things in curly braces, `{}`. The curly braces are also used with subscripts to access the contents of various cells. For example,

```
C = {A sum(A) prod(prod(A))}
```

produces a 1-by-3 cell array. The three cells contain the magic square, the row vector of column sums, and the product of all its elements. When `C` is displayed, you see

```
C =
    [4x4 double]    [1x4 double]    [20922789888000]
```

This is because the first two cells are too large to print in this limited space, but the third cell contains only a single number, 16!, so there is room to print it.

Here are two important points to remember. First, to retrieve the contents of one of the cells, use subscripts in curly braces. For example, `C{1}` retrieves the magic square and `C{3}` is 16. Second, cell arrays contain *copies* of other arrays, not *pointers* to those arrays. If you subsequently change `A`, nothing happens to `C`.

You can use three-dimensional arrays to store a sequence of matrices of the *same* size. Cell arrays can be used to store a sequence of matrices of *different* sizes. For example,

```
M = cell(8,1);
for n = 1:8
   M{n} = magic(n);
end
M
```

produces a sequence of magic squares of different order.

```
M =
    [           1]
    [ 2x2  double]
    [ 3x3  double]
    [ 4x4  double]
    [ 5x5  double]
    [ 6x6  double]
    [ 7x7  double]
    [ 8x8  double]
```

64	2	3	61	60	6	7	57
9	55	54	12	13	51	50	16
17	47	46	20	21	43	42	24
40	26	27	37	36	30	31	33
32	34	35	29	28	38	39	25
41	23	22	44	45	19	18	48
49	15	14	52	53	11	10	56
8	58	59	5	4	62	63	1

16	2	3	13
5	11	10	8
9	7	6	12
4	14	15	1

8	1	6
3	5	7
4	9	2

1	3
4	2

1

You can retrieve the 4-by-4 magic square matrix with

```
M{4}
```

Characters and Text

Enter text into MATLAB using single quotes. For example,

```
s = 'Hello'
```

The result is not the same kind of numeric matrix or array you have been dealing with up to now. It is a 1-by-5 character array.

Internally, the characters are stored as numbers, but not in floating-point format. The statement

```
a = double(s)
```

converts the character array to a numeric matrix containing floating-point representations of the ASCII codes for each character. The result is

```
a =
    72    101    108    108    111
```

The statement

```
s = char(a)
```

reverses the conversion.

Converting numbers to characters makes it possible to investigate the various fonts available on your computer. The printable characters in the basic ASCII character set are represented by the integers `32:127`. (The integers less than 32 represent nonprintable control characters.) These integers are arranged in an appropriate 6-by-16 array with

```
F = reshape(32:127,16,6)';
```

The printable characters in the extended ASCII character set are represented by `F+128`. When these integers are interpreted as characters, the result depends on the font currently being used. Type the statements

```
char(F)
char(F+128)
```

and then vary the font being used for the Command Window. Select **Preferences** from the **File** menu to change the font. If you include tabs in lines of code, use a fixed-width font, such as Monospaced, to align the tab positions on different lines.

Concatenation with square brackets joins text variables together into larger strings. The statement

```
h = [s, ' world']
```

joins the strings horizontally and produces

```
h =
   Hello world
```

The statement

```
v = [s; 'world']
```

joins the strings vertically and produces

```
v =
   Hello
   world
```

Note that a blank has to be inserted before the `'w'` in `h` and that both words in `v` have to have the same length. The resulting arrays are both character arrays; `h` is 1-by-11 and `v` is 2-by-5.

To manipulate a body of text containing lines of different lengths, you have two choices — a padded character array or a cell array of strings. When creating a character array, you must make each row of the array the same length. (Pad the ends of the shorter rows with spaces.) The `char` function does this padding for you. For example,

```
S = char('A','rolling','stone','gathers','momentum.')
```

produces a 5-by-9 character array.

```
S =
A
rolling
stone
gathers
momentum.
```

Alternatively, you can store the text in a cell array. For example,

```
C = {'A';'rolling';'stone';'gathers';'momentum.'}
```

creates a 5-by-1 cell array that requires no padding because each row of the array can have a different length.

```
C =
    'A'
    'rolling'
    'stone'
    'gathers'
    'momentum.'
```

You can convert a padded character array to a cell array of strings with

```
C = cellstr(S)
```

and reverse the process with

```
S = char(C)
```

Structures

Structures are multidimensional MATLAB arrays with elements accessed by textual *field designators*. For example,

```
S.name = 'Ed Plum';
S.score = 83;
S.grade = 'B+'
```

creates a scalar structure with three fields.

```
S =
     name: 'Ed Plum'
    score: 83
    grade: 'B+'
```

Like everything else in MATLAB, structures are arrays, so you can insert additional elements. In this case, each element of the array is a structure with several fields. The fields can be added one at a time,

```
S(2).name = 'Toni Miller';
S(2).score = 91;
S(2).grade = 'A-';
```

or an entire element can be added with a single statement.

```
S(3) = struct('name','Jerry Garcia',...
               'score',70,'grade','C')
```

Now the structure is large enough that only a summary is printed.

```
S =
1x3 struct array with fields:
    name
    score
    grade
```

There are several ways to reassemble the various fields into other MATLAB arrays. They are all based on the notation of a *comma-separated list*. If you type

```
S.score
```

it is the same as typing

```
S(1).score, S(2).score, S(3).score
```

This is a comma-separated list. Without any other punctuation, it is not very useful. It assigns the three scores, one at a time, to the default variable `ans` and dutifully prints out the result of each assignment. But when you enclose the expression in square brackets,

```
[S.score]
```

it is the same as

```
[S(1).score, S(2).score, S(3).score]
```

which produces a numeric row vector containing all the scores.

```
ans =
    83    91    70
```

Similarly, typing

```
S.name
```

just assigns the names, one at a time, to `ans`. But enclosing the expression in curly braces,

```
{S.name}
```

creates a 1-by-3 cell array containing the three names.

```
ans =
    'Ed Plum'    'Toni Miller'    'Jerry Garcia'
```

And

```
char(S.name)
```

calls the char function with three arguments to create a character array from the name fields,

```
ans =
Ed Plum
Toni Miller
Jerry Garcia
```

Dynamic Field Names

The most common way to access the data in a structure is by specifying the name of the field that you want to reference. Another means of accessing structure data is to use dynamic field names. These names express the field as a variable expression that MATLAB evaluates at run-time. The dot-parentheses syntax shown here makes `expression` a dynamic field name.

```
structName.(expression)
```

Index into this field using the standard MATLAB indexing syntax. For example, to evaluate `expression` into a field name and obtain the values of that field at columns 1 through 25 of row 7, use

```
structName.(expression)(7,1:25)
```

Dynamic Field Names Example. The `avgscore` function shown below computes an average test score, retrieving information from the `testscores` structure using dynamic field names:

```
function avg = avgscore(testscores, student, first, last)
for k = first:last
   scores(k) = testscores.(student).week(k);
end
avg = sum(scores)/(last - first + 1);
```

You can run this function using different values for the dynamic field `student`.

```
avgscore(testscores, 'Ann Lane', 1, 20)
ans =
   83.5000

avgscore(testscores, 'William King', 1, 20)
ans =
   92.1000
```

Scripts and Functions

Topics covered in this section are

MATLAB is a powerful programming language as well as an interactive computational environment. Files that contain code in the MATLAB language are called M-files. You create M-files using a text editor, then use them as you would any other MATLAB function or command.

There are two kinds of M-files:

- Scripts, which do not accept input arguments or return output arguments. They operate on data in the workspace.
- Functions, which can accept input arguments and return output arguments. Internal variables are local to the function.

If you're a new MATLAB programmer, just create the M-files that you want to try out in the current directory. As you develop more of your own M-files, you will want to organize them into other directories and personal toolboxes that you can add to your MATLAB search path.

If you duplicate function names, MATLAB executes the one that occurs first in the search path.

To view the contents of an M-file, for example, `myfunction.m`, use

```
type myfunction
```

Scripts

When you invoke a *script*, MATLAB simply executes the commands found in the file. Scripts can operate on existing data in the workspace, or they can create new data on which to operate. Although scripts do not return output arguments, any variables that they create remain in the workspace, to be used in subsequent computations. In addition, scripts can produce graphical output using functions like `plot`.

For example, create a file called `magicrank.m` that contains these MATLAB commands.

```
% Investigate the rank of magic squares
r = zeros(1,32);
for n = 3:32
   r(n) = rank(magic(n));
end
r
bar(r)
```

Typing the statement

```
magicrank
```

causes MATLAB to execute the commands, compute the rank of the first 30 magic squares, and plot a bar graph of the result. After execution of the file is complete, the variables `n` and `r` remain in the workspace.

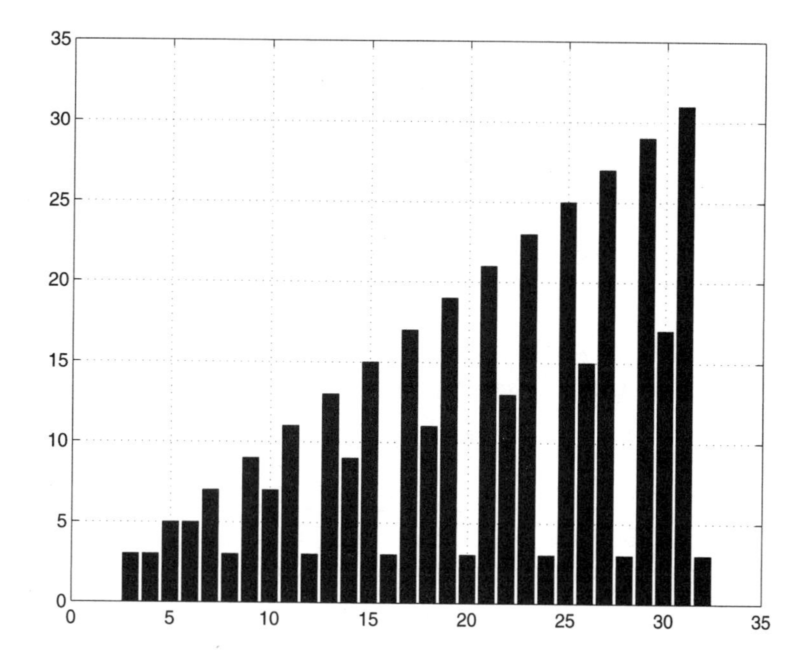

Functions

Functions are M-files that can accept input arguments and return output arguments. The names of the M-file and of the function should be the same. Functions operate on variables within their own workspace, separate from the workspace you access at the MATLAB command prompt.

A good example is provided by `rank`. The M-file `rank.m` is available in the directory

```
toolbox/matlab/matfun
```

You can see the file with

```
type rank
```

Here is the file.

```
function r = rank(A,tol)
%   RANK Matrix rank.
%   RANK(A) provides an estimate of the number of linearly
%   independent rows or columns of a matrix A.
%   RANK(A,tol) is the number of singular values of A
%   that are larger than tol.
%   RANK(A) uses the default tol = max(size(A)) * norm(A) * eps.

s = svd(A);
if nargin==1
   tol = max(size(A)') * max(s) * eps;
end
r = sum(s > tol);
```

The first line of a function M-file starts with the keyword `function`. It gives the function name and order of arguments. In this case, there are up to two input arguments and one output argument.

The next several lines, up to the first blank or executable line, are comment lines that provide the help text. These lines are printed when you type

```
help rank
```

The first line of the help text is the H1 line, which MATLAB displays when you use the `lookfor` command or request `help` on a directory.

The rest of the file is the executable MATLAB code defining the function. The variable `s` introduced in the body of the function, as well as the variables on the first line, `r`, `A` and `tol`, are all *local* to the function; they are separate from any variables in the MATLAB workspace.

This example illustrates one aspect of MATLAB functions that is not ordinarily found in other programming languages — a variable number of arguments. The `rank` function can be used in several different ways.

```
rank(A)
r = rank(A)
r = rank(A,1.e-6)
```

Many M-files work this way. If no output argument is supplied, the result is stored in `ans`. If the second input argument is not supplied, the function computes a default value. Within the body of the function, two quantities named `nargin` and `nargout` are available which tell you the number of input and output arguments involved in each particular use of the function. The `rank` function uses `nargin`, but does not need to use `nargout`.

Types of Functions

MATLAB offers several different types of functions to use in your programming.

Anonymous Functions

An *anonymous function* is a simple form of MATLAB function that does not require an M-file. It consists of a single MATLAB expression and any number of input and output arguments. You can define an anonymous function right at the MATLAB command line, or within an M-file function or script. This gives you a quick means of creating simple functions without having to create M-files each time.

The syntax for creating an anonymous function from an expression is

```
f = @(arglist)expression
```

The statement below creates an anonymous function that finds the square of a number. When you call this function, MATLAB assigns the value you pass in to variable `x`, and then uses `x` in the equation `x.^2`.

```
sqr = @(x) x.^2;
```

To execute the `sqr` function defined above, type

```
a = sqr(5)
a =
   25
```

Primary and Subfunctions

All functions that are not anonymous must be defined within an M-file. Each M-file has a required *primary function* that appears first in the file, and any number of *subfunctions* that follow the primary. Primary functions have a wider scope than subfunctions. That is, primary functions can be invoked from outside of their M-file (from the MATLAB command line or from functions in other M-files) while subfunctions cannot. Subfunctions are visible only to the primary function and other subfunctions within their own M-file.

The `rank` function shown in the section on "Functions" on page 6-21 is an example of a primary function.

Private Functions

A *private function* is a type of primary M-file function. Its unique characteristic is that it is visible only to a limited group of other functions. This type of function can be useful if you want to limit access to a function, or when you choose not to expose the implementation of a function.

Private functions reside in subdirectories with the special name `private`. They are visible only to functions in the parent directory. For example, assume the directory `newmath` is on the MATLAB search path. A subdirectory of `newmath` called `private` can contain functions that only the functions in `newmath` can call.

Because private functions are invisible outside the parent directory, they can use the same names as functions in other directories. This is useful if you want to create your own version of a particular function while retaining the original in another directory. Because MATLAB looks for private functions before standard M-file functions, it will find a private function named `test.m` before a nonprivate M-file named `test.m`.

Nested Functions

You can define functions within the body of any MATLAB M-file function. These are said to be *nested* within the outer function. A nested function contains any or all of the components of any other M-file function. In this example, function `B` is nested in function `A`.

```
function x = A(p1, p2)
...
B(p2)
   function y = B(p3)
   ...
   end
...
end
```

Like other functions, a nested function has its own workspace where variables used by the function are stored. But it also has access to the workspaces of all functions in which it is nested. So, for example, a variable that has a value assigned to it by the primary function can be read or overwritten by a function nested at any level within the primary. Similarly, a variable that is assigned in a nested function can be read or overwritten by any of the functions containing that function.

Function Overloading

Overloaded functions act the same way as overloaded functions in most computer languages. Overloaded functions are useful when you need to create a function that responds to different types of inputs accordingly. For instance, you might want one of your functions to accept both double-precision and integer input, but to handle each type somewhat differently. You can make this difference invisible to the user by creating two separate functions having the same name, and designating one to handle `double` types and one to handle integers. When you call the function, MATLAB chooses which M-file to dispatch to based on the type of the input arguments.

Global Variables

If you want more than one function to share a single copy of a variable, simply declare the variable as `global` in all the functions. Do the same thing at the command line if you want the base workspace to access the variable. The global declaration must occur before the variable is actually used in a function. Although it is not required, using capital letters for the names of global variables helps distinguish them from other variables. For example, create an M-file called `falling.m`.

```
function h = falling(t)
global GRAVITY
h = 1/2*GRAVITY*t.^2;
```

Then interactively enter the statements

```
global GRAVITY
GRAVITY = 32;
y = falling((0:.1:5)');
```

The two global statements make the value assigned to GRAVITY at the command prompt available inside the function. You can then modify GRAVITY interactively and obtain new solutions without editing any files.

Passing String Arguments to Functions

You can write MATLAB functions that accept string arguments without the parentheses and quotes. That is, MATLAB interprets

```
foo a b c
```

as

```
foo('a','b','c')
```

However, when you use the unquoted form, MATLAB cannot return output arguments. For example,

```
legend apples oranges
```

creates a legend on a plot using the strings apples and oranges as labels. If you want the legend command to return its output arguments, then you must use the quoted form.

```
[legh,objh] = legend('apples','oranges');
```

In addition, you cannot use the unquoted form if any of the arguments is not a string.

Constructing String Arguments in Code

The quoted form enables you to construct string arguments within the code. The following example processes multiple data files, August1.dat, August2.dat, and so on. It uses the function int2str, which converts an integer to a character, to build the filename.

```
for d = 1:31
   s = ['August' int2str(d) '.dat'];
   load(s)
   % Code to process the contents of the d-th file
end
```

A Cautionary Note

While the unquoted syntax is convenient, it can be used incorrectly without causing MATLAB to generate an error. For example, given a matrix A,

```
A =
       0    -6    -1
       6     2   -16
      -5    20   -10
```

The eig command returns the eigenvalues of A.

```
eig(A)
ans =
  -3.0710
  -2.4645+17.6008i
  -2.4645-17.6008i
```

The following statement is not allowed because A is not a string; however, MATLAB does not generate an error.

```
eig A
ans =
    65
```

MATLAB actually takes the eigenvalue of the ASCII numeric equivalent of the letter A (which is the number 65).

The eval Function

The eval function works with text variables to implement a powerful text macro facility. The expression or statement

```
eval(s)
```

uses the MATLAB interpreter to evaluate the expression or execute the statement contained in the text string s.

The example of the previous section could also be done with the following code, although this would be somewhat less efficient because it involves the full interpreter, not just a function call.

```
for d = 1:31
   s = ['load August' int2str(d) '.dat'];
   eval(s)
   % Process the contents of the d-th file
end
```

Function Handles

You can create a handle to any MATLAB function and then use that handle as a means of referencing the function. A function handle is typically passed in an argument list to other functions, which can then execute, or *evaluate*, the function using the handle.

Construct a function handle in MATLAB using the *at* sign, `@`, before the function name. The following example creates a function handle for the `sin` function and assigns it to the variable `fhandle`.

```
fhandle = @sin;
```

You can call a function by means of its handle in the same way that you would call the function using its name. The syntax is

```
fhandle(arg1, arg2, ...);
```

The function `plot_fhandle`, shown below, receives a function handle and data, generates y-axis data using the function handle, and plots it.

```
function x = plot_fhandle(fhandle, data)
plot(data, fhandle(data))
```

When you call `plot_fhandle` with a handle to the `sin` function and the argument shown below, the resulting evaluation produces a sine wave plot.

```
plot_fhandle(@sin, -pi:0.01:pi)
```

Function Functions

A class of functions called "function functions" works with nonlinear functions of a scalar variable. That is, one function works on another function. The function functions include

- Zero finding
- Optimization

- Quadrature
- Ordinary differential equations

MATLAB represents the nonlinear function by a function M-file. For example, here is a simplified version of the function `humps` from the `matlab/demos` directory.

```
function y = humps(x)
y = 1./((x-.3).^2 + .01) + 1./((x-.9).^2 + .04) - 6;
```

Evaluate this function at a set of points in the interval $0 \le x \le 1$ with

```
x = 0:.002:1;
y = humps(x);
```

Then plot the function with

```
plot(x,y)
```

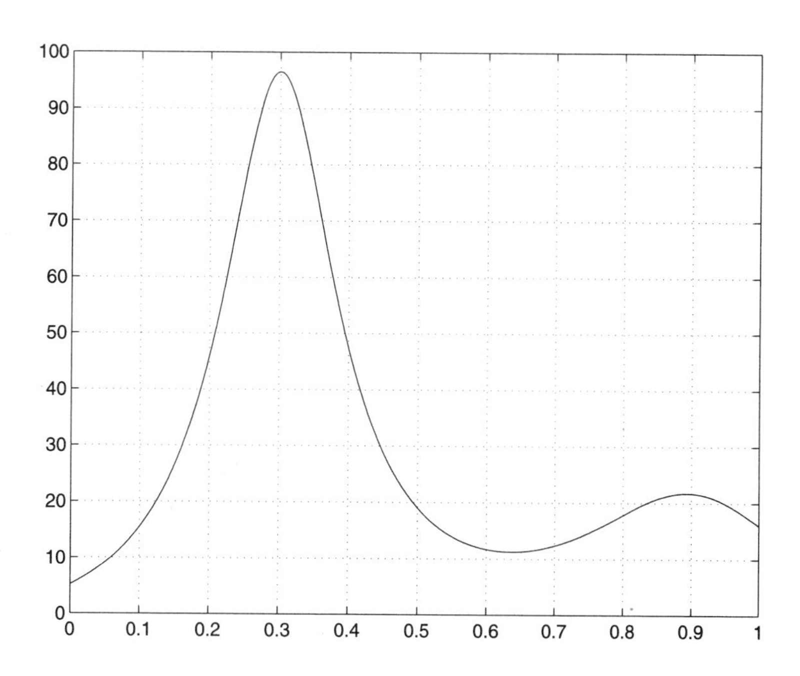

The graph shows that the function has a local minimum near $x = 0.6$. The function `fminsearch` finds the *minimizer*, the value of x where the function takes on this minimum. The first argument to `fminsearch` is a function handle to the function being minimized and the second argument is a rough guess at the location of the minimum.

```
p = fminsearch(@humps,.5)
p =
    0.6370
```

To evaluate the function at the minimizer,

```
humps(p)

ans =
   11.2528
```

Numerical analysts use the terms *quadrature* and *integration* to distinguish between numerical approximation of definite integrals and numerical integration of ordinary differential equations. MATLAB quadrature routines are `quad` and `quadl`. The statement

```
Q = quadl(@humps,0,1)
```

computes the area under the curve in the graph and produces

```
Q =
   29.8583
```

Finally, the graph shows that the function is never zero on this interval. So, if you search for a zero with

```
z = fzero(@humps,.5)
```

you will find one outside the interval

```
z =
   -0.1316
```

Vectorization

One way to make your MATLAB programs run faster is to vectorize the algorithms you use in constructing the programs. Where other programming languages might use `for` loops or `DO` loops, MATLAB can use vector or matrix operations. A simple example involves creating a table of logarithms.

```
x = .01;
for k = 1:1001
   y(k) = log10(x);
   x = x + .01;
end
```

A vectorized version of the same code is

```
x = .01:.01:10;
y = log10(x);
```

For more complicated code, vectorization options are not always so obvious.

For More Information See “Improving Performance and Memory Usage” in the MATLAB Programming documentation for other techniques that you can use.

Preallocation

If you can't vectorize a piece of code, you can make your `for` loops go faster by preallocating any vectors or arrays in which output results are stored. For example, this code uses the function `zeros` to preallocate the vector created in the `for` loop. This makes the `for` loop execute significantly faster.

```
r = zeros(32,1);
for n = 1:32
    r(n) = rank(magic(n));
end
```

Without the preallocation in the previous example, the MATLAB interpreter enlarges the `r` vector by one element each time through the loop. Vector preallocation eliminates this step and results in faster execution.

7

Creating Graphical User Interfaces

This chapter introduces GUIDE, the MATLAB graphical user interface development environment, which is a tool that you can use to create graphical user interfaces.

What Is GUIDE?

GUIDE, the MATLAB graphical user interface development environment, provides a set of tools for creating graphical user interfaces (GUIs). These tools greatly simplify the process of designing and building GUIs. You can use the GUIDE tools to

- Lay out the GUI.

  Using the GUIDE Layout Editor, you can lay out a GUI easily by clicking and dragging GUI components — such as panels, buttons, text fields, sliders, menus, and so on — into the layout area. GUIDE stores the GUI layout in a FIG-file.

- Program the GUI.

  GUIDE automatically generates an M-file that controls how the GUI operates. The M-file initializes the GUI and contains a framework for the most commonly used callbacks for each component — the commands that execute when a user clicks a GUI component. Using the M-file editor, you can add code to the callbacks to perform the functions you want.

Laying Out a GUI

Starting GUIDE

Start GUIDE by typing `guide` at the MATLAB command prompt. This displays the **GUIDE Quick Start** dialog, as shown in the following figure.

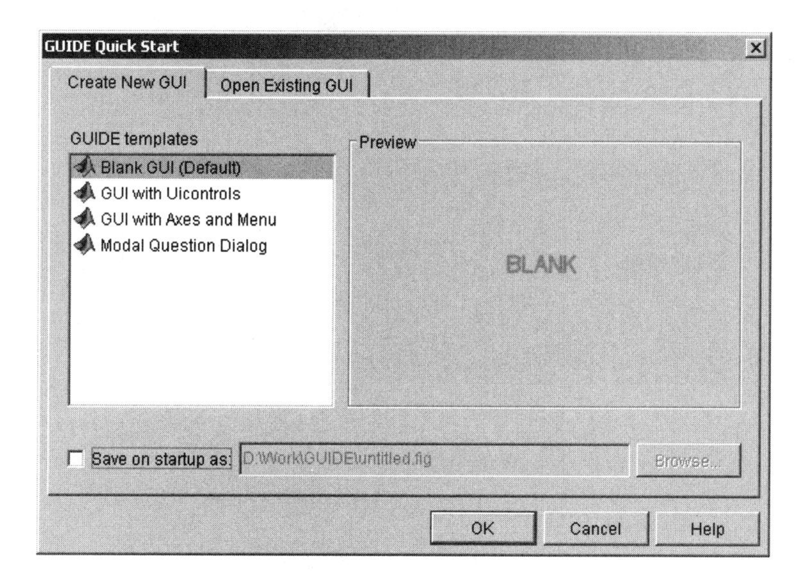

From the **GUIDE Quick Start** dialog, you can

- Create a new GUI from one of the GUIDE templates — prebuilt GUIs that you can modify for your own purposes.
- Open an existing GUI.

The Layout Editor

When you open a GUI in GUIDE, it is displayed in the Layout Editor, which is the control panel for all of the GUIDE tools. The following figure shows the Layout Editor with a blank GUI template.

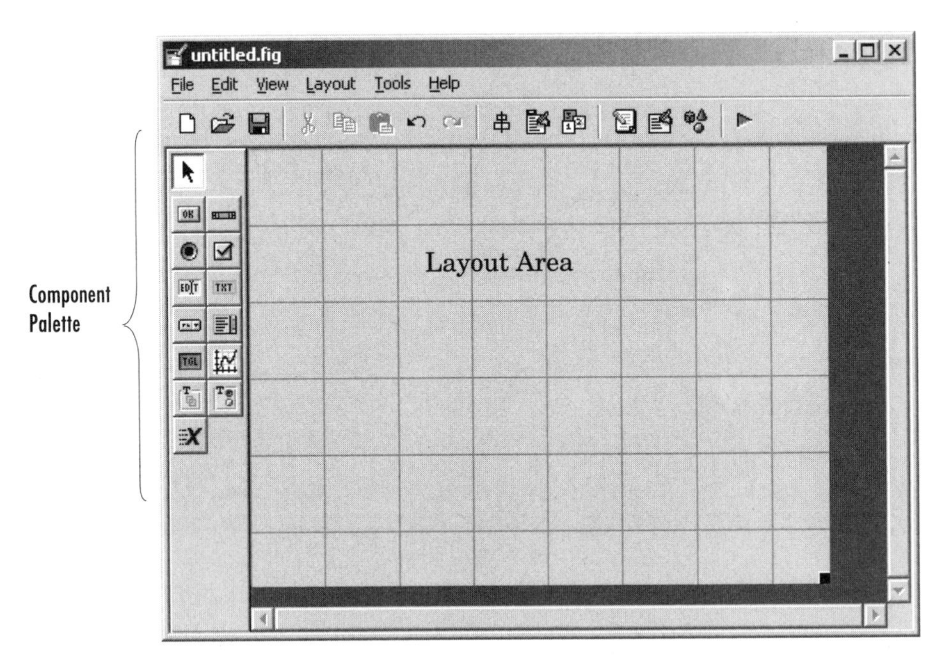

You can lay out your GUI by dragging components, such as panels, push buttons, pop-up menus, or axes, from the component palette, at the left side of the Layout Editor, into the layout area. For example, if you drag a push button into the layout area, it appears as in the following figure.

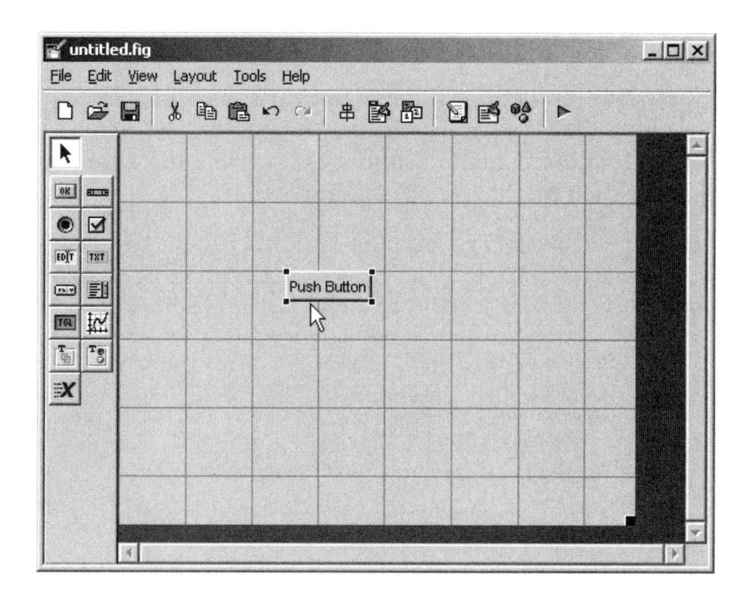

You can also use the Layout Editor to create menus and set basic properties of the GUI components.

To get started using the Layout Editor and setting property values, see "Creating a GUI" in the MATLAB documentation.

Programming a GUI

After laying out the GUI and setting component properties, the next step is to program the GUI. You program the GUI by coding one or more callbacks for each of its components. Callbacks are functions that execute in response to some action by the user. A typical action is clicking a push button.

A GUI's callbacks are found in an M-file that GUIDE generates automatically. GUIDE adds templates for the most commonly used callbacks to this M-file, but you may want to add others. Use the M-file Editor to edit this file.

The following figure shows the Callback template for a push button.

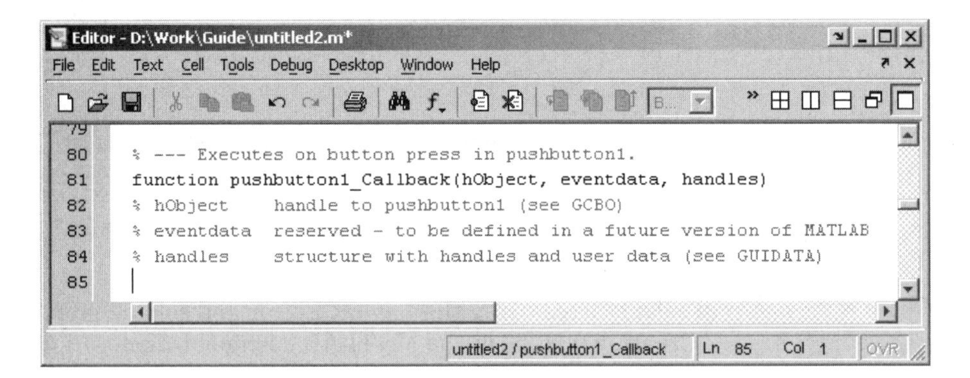

To learn more about programming a GUI, see “Creating a GUI” in the MATLAB documentation.

8

Desktop Tools and Development Environment

This chapter introduces the MATLAB development environment and the tools you can use to manage your work in MATLAB.

Desktop Overview

Use desktop tools to manage your work in MATLAB. You can also use MATLAB functions to perform the equivalent of most of the features found in the desktop tools.

The following illustration shows the default configuration of the MATLAB desktop. You can modify the setup to meet your needs.

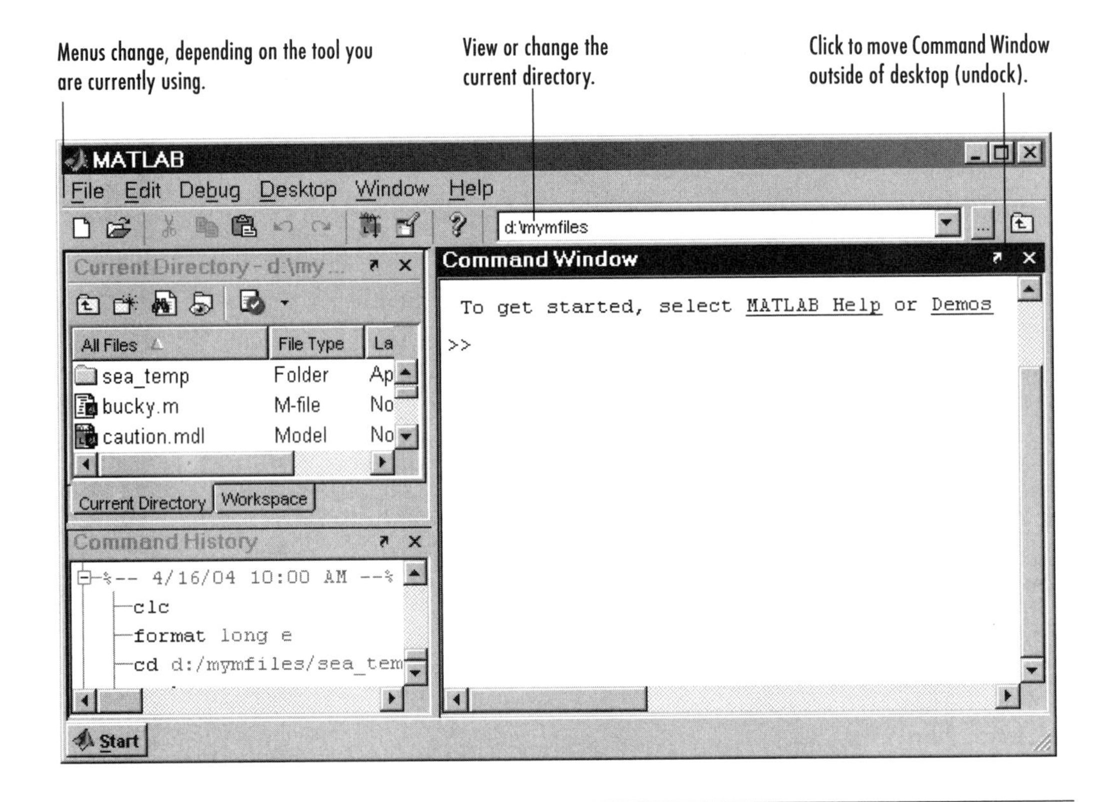

For More Information For an overview of the desktop tools, watch the video tutorials, accessible by typing `demo matlab desktop`. For complete details, see the MATLAB Desktop Tools and Development Environment documentation.

Arranging the Desktop

These are some common ways to customize the desktop:

- Show or hide desktop tools via the **Desktop** menu.
- Resize any tool by dragging one of its edges.
- Move a tool outside of the desktop by clicking the undock button in the tool's title bar.
- Reposition a tool within the desktop by dragging its title bar to the new location. Tools can occupy the same position, as shown for the Current Directory and Workspace browser in the preceding illustration, in which case, you access a tool via its tab.
- Change fonts and other options by using **File -> Preferences**.

Start Button

The MATLAB **Start** button provides easy access to tools, demos, shortcuts, and documentation. Click the **Start** button to see the options.

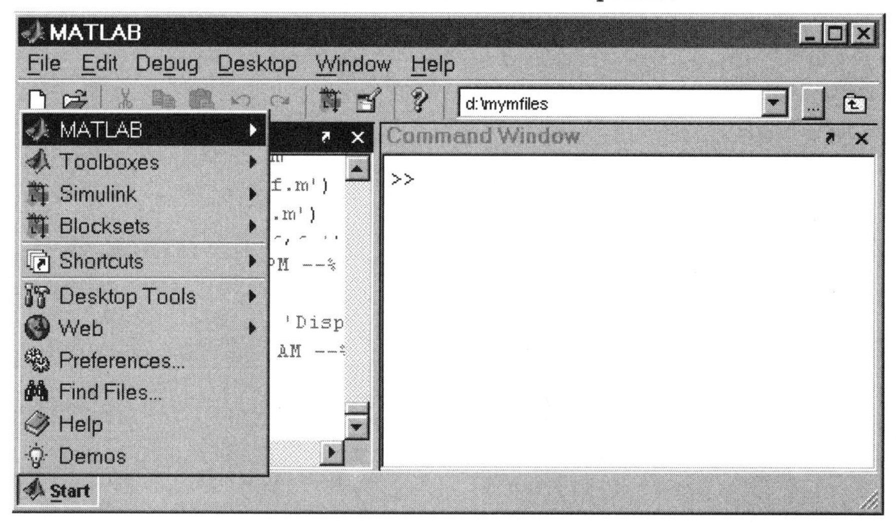

For More Information See "Desktop" in the MATLAB Desktop Tools and Development Environment documentation.

Command Window and Command History

Command Window

Use the Command Window to enter variables and to run functions and M-file scripts.

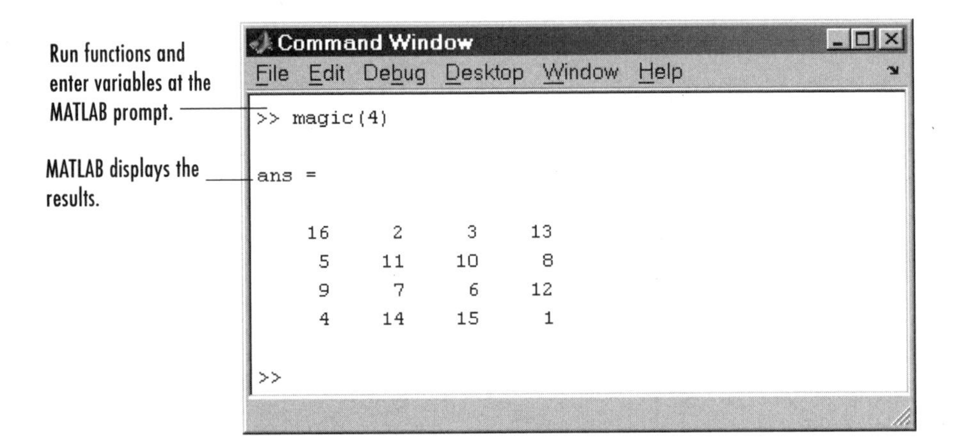

Press the up arrow key ↑ to recall a statement you previously typed. Edit the statement as needed and then press **Enter** to run it. For more information about entering statements in the Command Window, see "Controlling Command Window Input and Output" on page 4-28.

For More Information See "Running Functions" in the MATLAB Desktop Tools and Development Environment documentation for complete details.

Command History

Statements you enter in the Command Window are logged in the Command History. From the Command History, you can view previously run statements, as well as copy and execute selected statements. You can also create an M-file from selected statements.

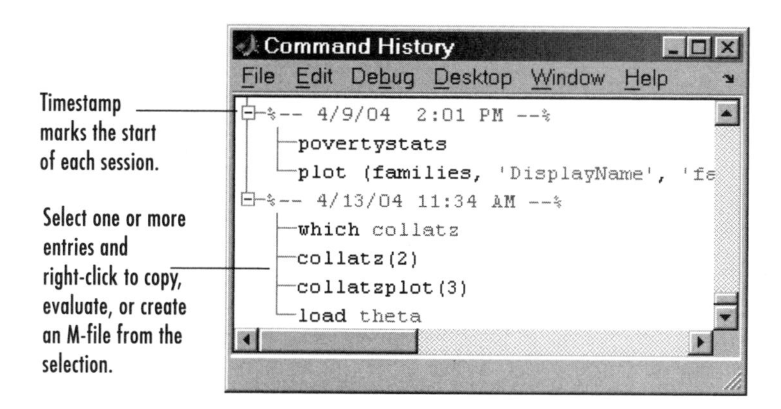

To save the input and output from a MATLAB session to a file, use the `diary` function.

For More Information See "Command History" in the MATLAB Desktop Tools and Development Environment documentation, and the reference page for the `diary` function.

Help Browser

Use the Help browser to search for and view documentation and demos for all your MathWorks products. The Help browser is an HTML viewer integrated into the MATLAB desktop.

To open the Help browser, click the help button ? in the desktop toolbar.

The Help browser consists of two panes, the **Help Navigator**, which you use to find information, and the display pane, where you view the information. These are the key features:

- **Contents** tab — View the titles and tables of contents of the documentation.
- **Index** tab — Find specific index entries (selected keywords) in the documentation.
- **Search** tab — Look for specific words in the documentation.
- **Demos** tab — View and run demonstrations for your MathWorks products.

While viewing the documentation, you can

- Browse to other pages — Use the arrows at the tops and bottoms of the pages to move through the document, or use the back and forward buttons in the toolbar to go to previously viewed pages.
- Bookmark pages — Use the **Favorites** menu.
- Print a page — Click the print button in the toolbar.
- Find a term in the page — Click the find icon (binoculars) in the toolbar.
- Copy or evaluate a selection — Select text, such as code from an example, then right-click and use a context menu item to copy the selection or evaluate (run) it.

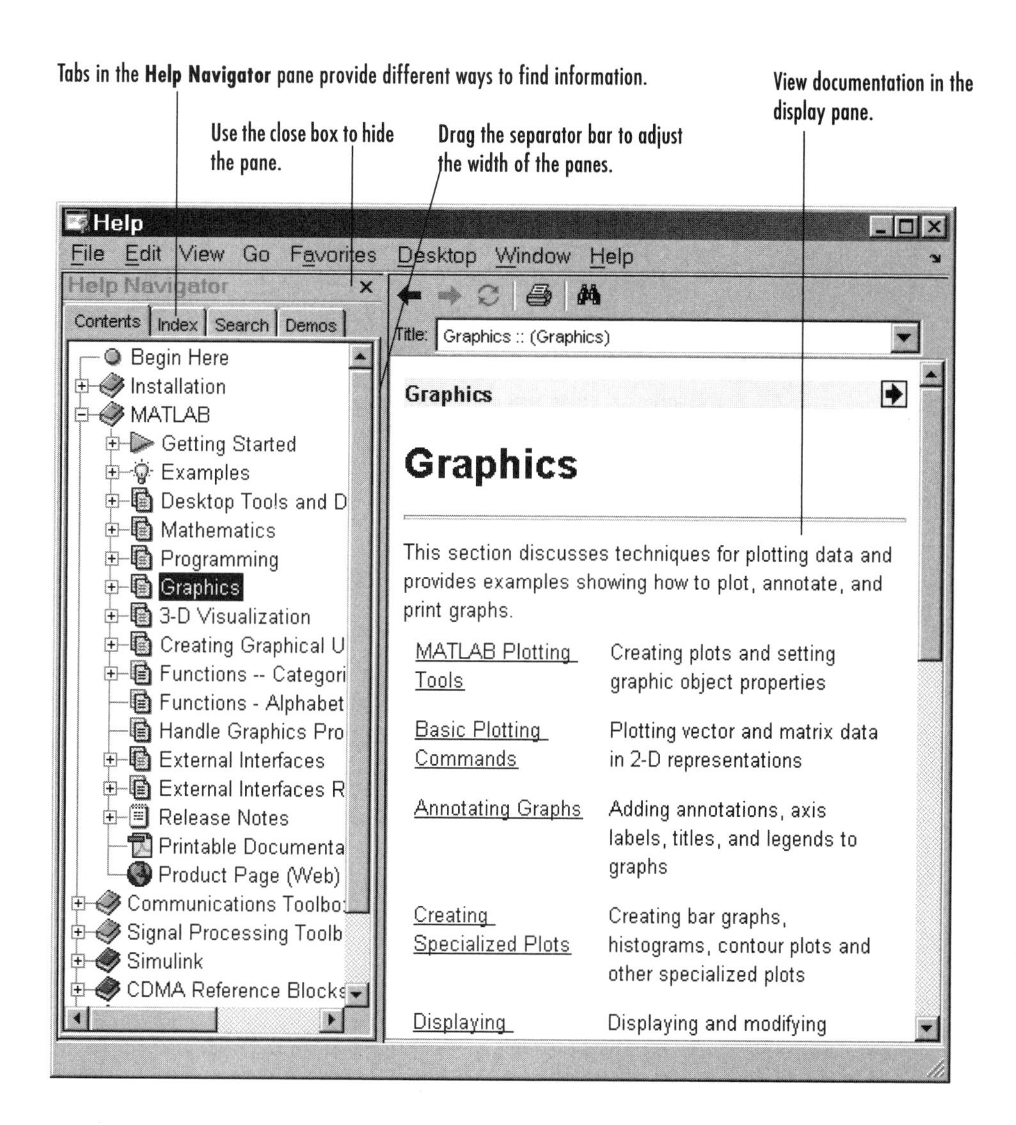
Tabs in the Help Navigator pane provide different ways to find information.
Use the close box to hide the pane.
Drag the separator bar to adjust the width of the panes.
View documentation in the display pane.
Help
File Edit View Go Favorites Desktop Window Help
Help Navigator
Contents Index Search Demos
Begin Here
Installation
MATLAB
Getting Started
Examples
Desktop Tools and D
Mathematics
Programming
Graphics
3-D Visualization
Creating Graphical U
Functions -- Categori
Functions - Alphabet
Handle Graphics Pro
External Interfaces
External Interfaces R
Release Notes
Printable Documenta
Product Page (Web)
Communications Toolbo
Signal Processing Toolb
Simulink
CDMA Reference Blocks
Title: Graphics :: (Graphics)
Graphics
Graphics
This section discusses techniques for plotting data and provides examples showing how to plot, annotate, and print graphs.
MATLAB Plotting Tools
Creating plots and setting graphic object properties
Basic Plotting Commands
Plotting vector and matrix data in 2-D representations
Annotating Graphs
Adding annotations, axis labels, titles, and legends to graphs
Creating Specialized Plots
Creating bar graphs, histograms, contour plots and other specialized plots
Displaying
Displaying and modifying

Other Forms of Help

In addition to the Help browser, you can use help functions. To get help for a specific function, use the `doc` function. For example, `doc format` displays documentation for the `format` function in the Help browser.

To see a briefer form of the documentation for a function, type `help` followed by the function name. The resulting help text appears in the Command Window. It shows function names in all capital letters to distinguish them from the surrounding text. When you use the function names, type them in lowercase or they will not run. Some functions actually consist of both uppercase and lowercase letters, and the help text clearly indicates that. For those functions, match the case used in the `help` function.

Other means for getting help include contacting Technical Support (`http://www.mathworks.com/support`) and participating in the newsgroup for MATLAB users, `comp.soft-sys.matlab`.

For More Information See "Help for Using MATLAB" in the MATLAB Desktop Tools and Development Environment documentation, and the reference pages for the `doc` and `help` functions.

Current Directory Browser and Search Path

MATLAB file operations use the current directory and the search path as reference points. Any file you want to run must either be in the current directory or on the search path.

Current Directory

A quick way to view or change the current directory is by using the current directory field in the desktop toolbar, shown here.

To search for, view, open, and make changes to MATLAB related directories and files, use the MATLAB Current Directory browser. Alternatively, you can use the functions `dir`, `cd`, and `delete`. Use the Visual Directory and Directory Reports to help you manage M-files.

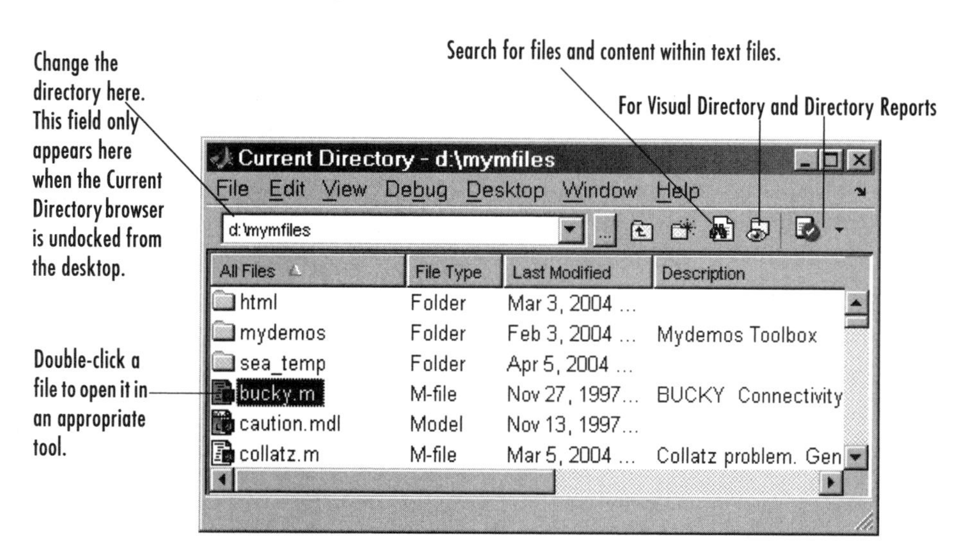

For More Information See “File Management Operations” in the MATLAB Desktop Tools and Development Environment documentation, and the reference pages for the `dir`, `cd`, and `delete` functions.

Search Path

MATLAB uses a *search path* to find M-files and other MATLAB related files, which are organized in directories on your file system. Any file you want to run in MATLAB must reside in the current directory or in a directory that is on the search path. When you create M-files and related files for MATLAB, add the directories in which they are located to the MATLAB search path. By default, the files supplied with MATLAB and other MathWorks products are included in the search path.

To see which directories are on the search path or to change the search path, select **File -> Set Path** and use the resulting **Set Path** dialog box. Alternatively, you can use the `path` function to view the search path, `addpath` to add directories to the path, and `rmpath` to remove directories from the path.

For More Information See “Search Path” in the MATLAB Desktop Tools and Development Environment documentation, and the reference pages for the `path`, `addpath`, and `rmpath` functions.

Workspace Browser and Array Editor

The MATLAB workspace consists of the set of variables (named arrays) built up during a MATLAB session and stored in memory. You add variables to the workspace by using functions, running M-files, and loading saved workspaces.

Workspace Browser

To view the workspace and information about each variable, use the Workspace browser, or use the functions `who` and `whos`.

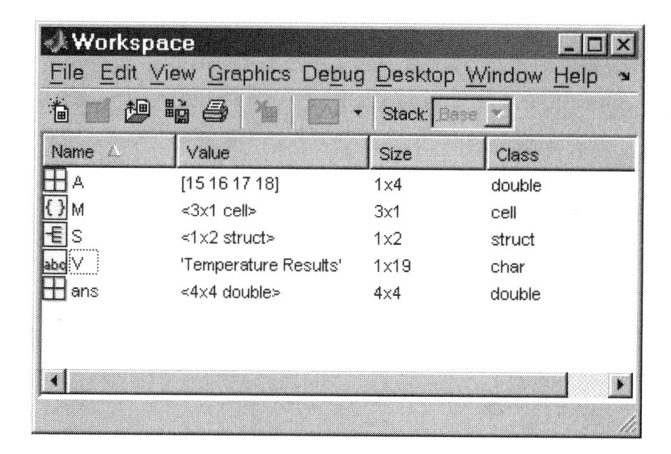

To delete variables from the workspace, select the variables and select **Edit -> Delete**. Alternatively, use the `clear` function.

The workspace is not maintained after you end the MATLAB session. To save the workspace to a file that can be read during a later MATLAB session, select **File -> Save**, or use the `save` function. This saves the workspace to a binary file called a MAT-file, which has a `.mat` extension. You can use options to save to different formats. To read in a MAT-file, select **File -> Import Data**, or use the `load` function.

For More Information See "MATLAB Workspace" in the MATLAB Desktop Tools and Development Environment documentation, and the reference pages for the `who`, `clear`, `save`, and `load` functions.

Array Editor

Double-click a variable in the Workspace browser, or use `openvar variablename`, to see it in the Array Editor. Use the Array Editor to view and edit a visual representation of variables in the workspace.

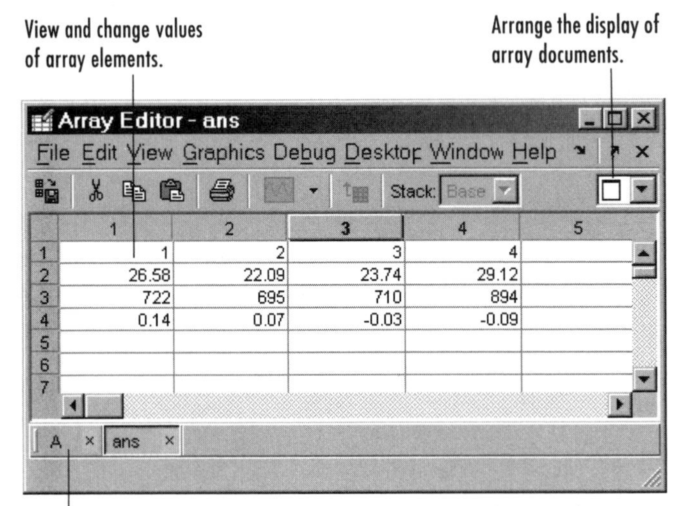

For More Information See "Viewing and Editing Workspace Variables with the Array Editor" in the MATLAB Desktop Tools and Development Environment documentation, and the reference page for the `openvar` function.

Editor/Debugger

Use the Editor/Debugger to create and debug M-files, which are programs you write to run MATLAB functions. The Editor/Debugger provides a graphical user interface for text editing, as well as for M-file debugging. To create or edit an M-file use **File -> New** or **File -> Open**, or use the `edit` function.

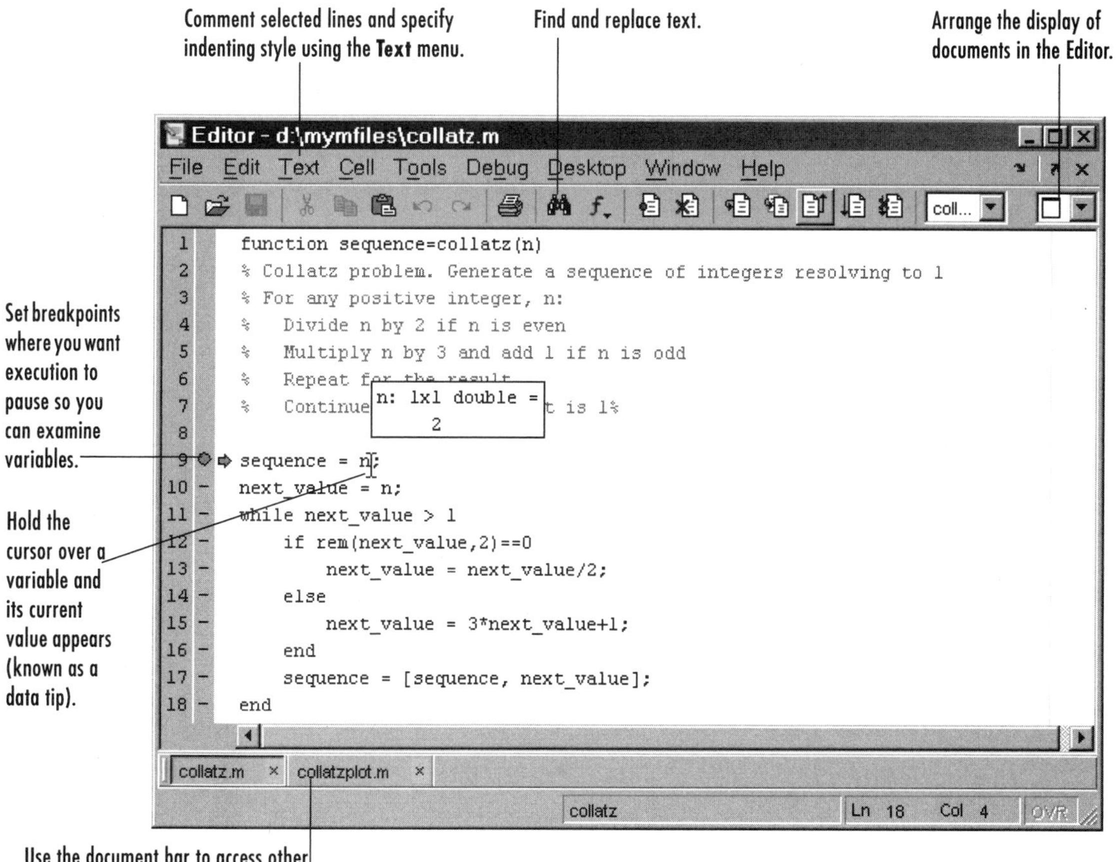

You can use any text editor to create M-files, such as Emacs. Use preferences (accessible from the desktop **File** menu) to specify that editor as the default. If you use another editor, you can still use the MATLAB Editor/Debugger for debugging, or you can use debugging functions, such as `dbstop`, which sets a breakpoint.

If you just need to view the contents of an M-file, you can display the contents in the Command Window using the `type` function.

For More Information See "Editing and Debugging M-Files" in the MATLAB Desktop Tools and Development Environment documentation, and the function reference pages for `edit`, `type`, and `debug`.

M-Lint Code Check and Profiler Reports

MATLAB provides tools to help you manage and improve your M-files, including the M-Lint Code Check and Profiler Reports.

M-Lint Code Check Report

The M-Lint Code Check Report displays potential errors and problems, as well as opportunities for improvement in your M-files. The term "lint" is used by similar tools in other programming languages such as C.

Access the M-Lint Code Check Report and other directory reports from the Current Directory browser. You run a report for all files in the current directory. Alternatively, you can use the `mlint` function to get results for a single M-file.

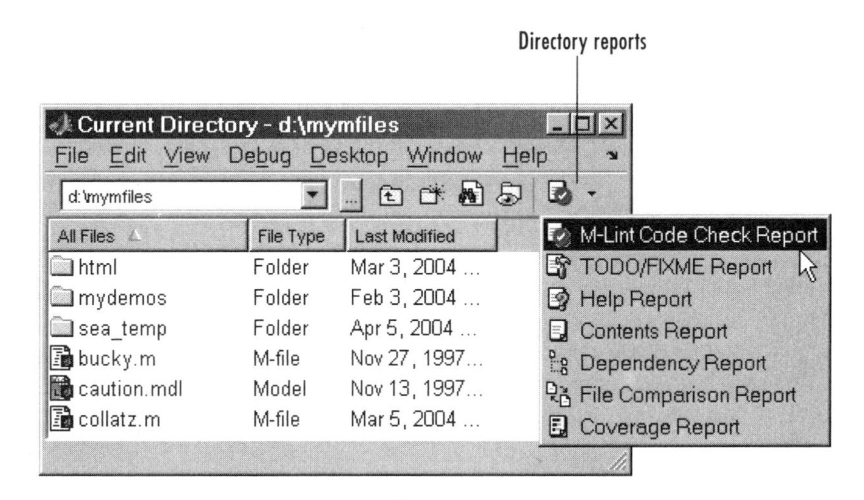

In MATLAB, the M-Lint Code Check Report displays a message for each line of an M-file it determines might be improved. For example, a common M-Lint message is that a variable is defined but never used in the M-file.

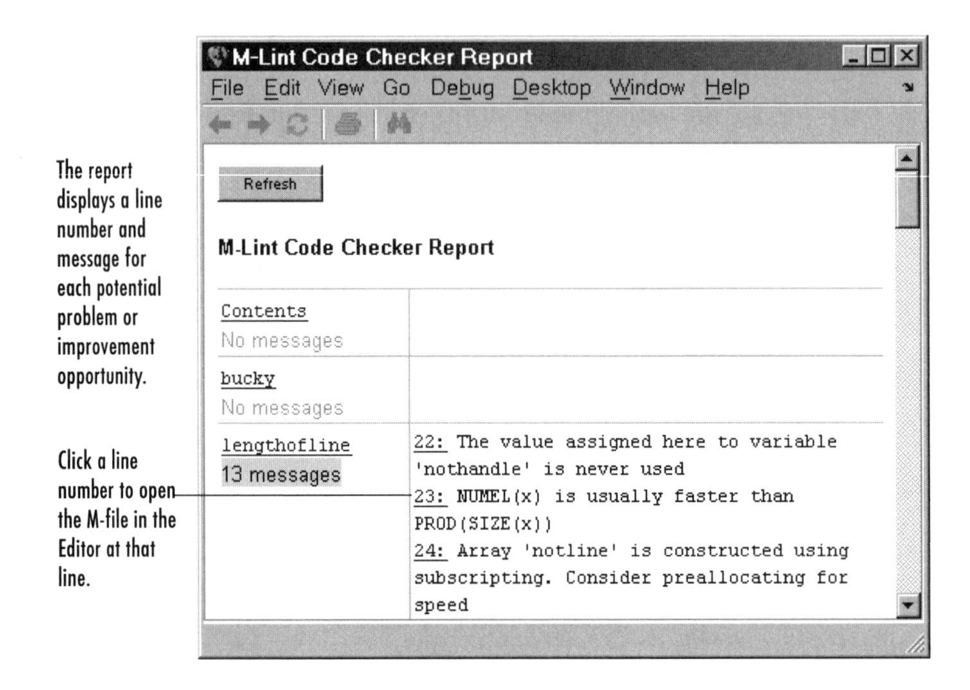

For More Information See "Tuning and Managing M-Files" in the MATLAB Desktop Tools and Development Environment documentation, and the reference page for the `mlint` function.

Profiler

MATLAB includes the Profiler to help you improve the performance of your M-files. Run a MATLAB statement or an M-file in the Profiler and it produces a report of where the time is being spent. Access the Profiler from the **Desktop** menu, or use the `profile` function.

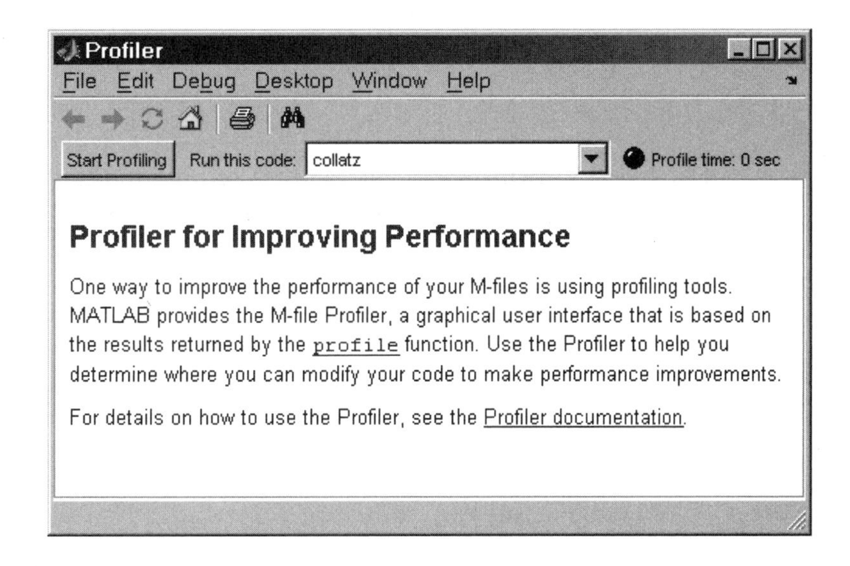

For More Information See "Tuning and Managing M-Files" in the MATLAB Desktop Tools and Development Environment documentation, and the reference page for the `profile` function.

Other Development Environment Features

Additional development environment features include

- Source Control — Access your source control system from within MATLAB.
- Publishing Results — Use the Editor's cell features to publish M-files and results to popular output formats including HTML and Microsoft Word. You can also use MATLAB Notebook to access MATLAB functions from within Microsoft Word.

For More Information See "Source Control" and "Publishing Results" in the MATLAB Desktop Tools and Development Environment documentation.

9

Introducing the Symbolic Math Toolbox

This chapter introduces you to the Symbolic Math Toolbox, and describes how to create and use symbolic objects. It covers the following topics:

What Is the Symbolic Math Toolbox?

The Symbolic Math Toolbox incorporates symbolic computation into the numeric environment of MATLAB. The toolbox is a collection of more than 100 MATLAB functions that provide access to the Maple kernel using a syntax and style that is a natural extension of the MATLAB language. The Symbolic Math Toolbox supplements MATLAB numeric and graphical facilities with several other types of mathematical computation, which are summarized in following table.

Facility	Covers
Calculus	Differentiation, integration, limits, summation, and Taylor series
Linear Algebra	Inverses, determinants, eigenvalues, singular value decomposition, and canonical forms of symbolic matrices
Simplification	Methods of simplifying algebraic expressions
Solution of Equations	Symbolic and numerical solutions to algebraic and differential equations
Variable-Precision Arithmetic	Numerical evaluation of mathematical expressions to any specified accuracy
Transforms	Fourier, Laplace, z-transform, and corresponding inverse transforms

The computational engine underlying the toolboxes is the kernel of Maple, a system developed primarily at the University of Waterloo, Canada and, more recently, at the Eidgenössiche Technische Hochschule, Zürich, Switzerland. Maple is marketed and supported by Waterloo Maple, Inc.

Symbolic Objects

The Symbolic Math Toolbox defines a new MATLAB data type called a *symbolic object*. (See "Programming and Data Types" in the MATLAB documentation for an introduction to MATLAB classes and objects.) Internally, a symbolic object is a data structure that stores a string representation of the symbol. The Symbolic Math Toolbox uses symbolic objects to represent symbolic variables, expressions, and matrices. The actual computations involving symbolic objects are performed primarily by Maple, mathematical software developed by Waterloo Maple, Inc.

The following example illustrates the difference between a standard MATLAB data type, such as `double`, and the corresponding symbolic object. The MATLAB command

```
sqrt(2)
```

returns a floating-point decimal number:

```
ans =
    1.4142
```

On the other hand, if you convert 2 to a symbolic object using the `sym` command, and then take its square root by entering

```
a = sqrt(sym(2))
```

the result is

```
a =
2^(1/2)
```

MATLAB gives the result `2^(1/2)`, which means $2^{1/2}$, using symbolic notation for the square root operation, without actually calculating a numerical value. MATLAB records this symbolic expression in the string that represents `2^(1/2)`. You can always obtain the numerical value of a symbolic object with the `double` command:

```
double(a)
ans =
    1.4142
```

Notice that the result is indented, which tells you it has data type `double`. Symbolic results are not indented.

When you create a fraction involving symbolic objects, MATLAB records the numerator and denominator. For example:

```
sym(2)/sym(5)
ans =
2/5
```

MATLAB performs arithmetic on symbolic objects differently than it does on standard data types. If you add two fractions that are of data type `double`, MATLAB gives the answer as a decimal fraction. For example:

```
2/5 + 1/3
ans =
0.7333
```

If you add the same fractions as symbolic objects, MATLAB finds their common denominator and combines them by the usual procedure for adding rational numbers:

```
sym(2)/sym(5) + sym(1)/sym(3)
ans =
11/15
```

The Symbolic Math Toolbox enables you to perform a variety of symbolic calculations that arise in mathematics and science. These are described in detail in Chapter 10, "Using the Symbolic Math Toolbox."

Creating Symbolic Variables and Expressions

The sym command lets you construct symbolic variables and expressions. For example, the commands

```
x = sym('x')
a = sym('alpha')
```

create a symbolic variable x that prints as x and a symbolic variable a that prints as alpha.

Suppose you want to use a symbolic variable to represent the golden ratio

$$\rho = \frac{1+\sqrt{5}}{2}$$

The command

```
rho = sym('(1 + sqrt(5))/2')
```

achieves this goal. Now you can perform various mathematical operations on rho. For example,

```
f = rho^2 - rho - 1
```

returns

```
f =

(1/2+1/2*5^(1/2))^2-3/2-1/2*5^(1/2)
```

You can simplify this answer by entering

```
simplify(f)
```

which returns

```
ans =
0
```

Now suppose you want to study the quadratic function $f = ax^2 + bx + c$. One approach is to enter the command

```
f = sym('a*x^2 + b*x + c')
```

which assigns the symbolic expression $ax^2 + bx + c$ to the variable f. However, in this case, the Symbolic Math Toolbox does not create variables corresponding to the terms of the expression, a, b, c, and x. To perform symbolic math operations (e.g., integration, differentiation, substitution, etc.) on f, you need to create the variables explicitly. A better alternative is to enter the commands

```
a = sym('a')
b = sym('b')
c = sym('c')
x = sym('x')
```

or simply

```
syms a b c x
```

Then enter

```
f = sym('a*x^2 + b*x + c')
```

In general, you can use sym or syms to create symbolic variables. We recommend you use syms because it requires less typing.

Note To create a symbolic expression that is a constant, you must use the sym command. For example, to create the expression whose value is 5, enter f = sym('5'). Note that the command f = 5 does *not* define f as a symbolic expression.

If you set a variable equal to a symbolic expression, and then apply the syms command to the variable, MATLAB removes the previously defined expression from the variable. For example,

```
syms a b
f = a + b
```

returns

```
f =
a+b
```

If you then enter

```
syms f
f
```

MATLAB returns

```
f =
f
```

You can use the syms command to clear variables of definitions that you assigned to them previously in your MATLAB session. However, syms does not clear the properties of the variables in the Maple workspace. See "Clearing Variables in the Maple Workspace" on page 9-12 for more information.

The findsym Command

To determine what symbolic variables are present in an expression, use the findsym command. For example, given the symbolic expressions f and g defined by

```
syms a b n t x z
f = x^n; g = sin(a*t + b);
```

you can find the symbolic variables in f by entering

```
findsym(f)
ans =
n, x
```

Similarly, you can find the symbolic variables in g by entering

```
findsym(g)
ans =
a, b, t
```

The subs Command

You can substitute a numerical value for a symbolic variable using the `subs` command. For example, to substitute the value $x = 2$ in the symbolic expression,

```
f = 2*x^2 - 3*x + 1
```

enter the command

```
subs(f,2)
```

This returns $f(2)$:

```
ans =
      3
```

Note To substitute a matrix `A` into the symbolic expression `f`, use the command `polyvalm(sym2poly(f), A)`, which replaces all occurrences of `x` by `A`, and replaces the constant term of `f` with the constant times an identity matrix.

When your expression contains more than one variable, you can specify the variable for which you want to make the substitution. For example, to substitute the value $x = 3$ in the symbolic expression,

```
syms x y
f = x^2*y + 5*x*sqrt(y)
```

enter the command

```
subs(f, x, 3)
```

This returns

```
ans =
9*y+15*y^(1/2)
```

On the other hand, to substitute $y = 3$, enter

```
subs(f, y, 3)
ans =
3*x^2+5*x*3^(1/2)
```

The Default Symbolic Variable

If you do not specify a variable to substitute for, MATLAB chooses a default variable according to the following rule. For one-letter variables, MATLAB chooses the letter closest to x in the alphabet. If there are two letters equally close to x, MATLAB chooses the one that comes later in the alphabet. In the preceding function, `subs(f, 3)` returns the same answer as `subs(f, x, 3)`.

You can use the `findsym` command to determine the default variable. For example,

```
syms s t
g = s + t;
findsym(g,1)
```

returns the default variable:

```
ans =
t
```

See "Substitutions" on page 10-50 to learn more about substituting for variables.

Symbolic and Numeric Conversions

Consider the ordinary MATLAB quantity

```
t = 0.1
```

The `sym` function has four options for returning a symbolic representation of the numeric value stored in `t`. The `'f'` option

```
sym(t,'f')
```

returns a symbolic floating-point representation

```
'1.999999999999a'*2^(-4)
```

The `'r'` option

```
sym(t,'r')
```

returns the rational form

```
1/10
```

This is the default setting for `sym`. That is, calling `sym` without a second argument is the same as using `sym` with the `'r'` option:

```
sym(t)

ans =
1/10
```

The third option `'e'` returns the rational form of `t` plus the difference between the theoretical rational expression for `t` and its actual (machine) floating-point value in terms of `eps` (the floating-point relative accuracy):

```
sym(t,'e')

ans =
1/10+eps/40
```

The fourth option `'d'` returns the decimal expansion of `t` up to the number of significant digits specified by `digits`:

```
sym(t,'d')
```

```
ans =
.10000000000000000555111512312578
```

The default value of `digits` is 32 (hence, `sym(t,'d')` returns a number with 32 significant digits), but if you prefer a shorter representation, use the `digits` command as follows:

```
digits(7)
sym(t,'d')

ans =
.1000000
```

A particularly effective use of `sym` is to convert a matrix from numeric to symbolic form. The command

```
A = hilb(3)
```

generates the 3-by-3 Hilbert matrix:

```
A =

    1.0000    0.5000    0.3333
    0.5000    0.3333    0.2500
    0.3333    0.2500    0.2000
```

By applying `sym` to `A`

```
A = sym(A)
```

you can obtain the symbolic (infinitely precise) form of the 3-by-3 Hilbert matrix:

```
A =

[   1, 1/2, 1/3]
[ 1/2, 1/3, 1/4]
[ 1/3, 1/4, 1/5]
```

Constructing Real and Complex Variables

The sym command allows you to specify the mathematical properties of symbolic variables by using the 'real' option. That is, the statements

```
x = sym('x','real'); y = sym('y','real');
```

or more efficiently

```
syms x y real
z = x + i*y
```

create symbolic variables x and y that have the added mathematical property of being real variables. Specifically this means that the expression

```
f = x^2 + y^2
```

is strictly nonnegative. Hence, z is a complex variable and can be manipulated as such. Thus, the commands

```
conj(x), conj(z), expand(z*conj(z))
```

return

```
x, x-i*y, x^2+y^2
```

respectively. The conj command is the complex conjugate operator for the toolbox. If conj(x) == x returns 1, then x is a real variable.

Clearing Variables in the Maple Workspace

When you declare x to be real with the command

```
syms x real
```

a becomes a symbolic object in the MATLAB workspace and a positive real variable in the Maple kernel workspace. If you later want to remove the real property from x, enter

```
syms a unreal
```

Note that entering

```
clear x
```

only clears x in the MATLAB workspace. If you then enter syms x, MATLAB still treats x as a positive real number.

Creating Abstract Functions

If you want to create an abstract (i.e., indeterminant) function $f(x)$, type

```
f = sym('f(x)')
```

Then `f` acts like $f(x)$ and can be manipulated by the toolbox commands. For example, to construct the first difference ratio, type

```
df = (subs(f,'x','x+h') - f)/'h'
```

or

```
syms x h
df = (subs(f,x,x+h)-f)/h
```

which returns

```
df =
(f(x+h)-f(x))/h
```

This application of `sym` is useful when computing Fourier, Laplace, and z-transforms.

Using sym to Access Maple Functions

Similarly, you can access Maple's factorial function `k!` using `sym`:

```
kfac = sym('k!')
```

To compute 6! or n!, type

```
syms k n
subs(kfac,k,6), subs(kfac,k,n)

ans =
720

ans =
n!
```

Example: Creating a Symbolic Matrix

A circulant matrix has the property that each row is obtained from the previous one by cyclically permuting the entries one step forward. You can create the circulant matrix `A` whose elements are `a`, `b`, and `c`, using the commands

```
syms a b c
A = [a b c; b c a; c a b]
```

which return

```
A =
[ a, b, c ]
[ b, c, a ]
[ c, a, b ]
```

Since A is circulant, the sum over each row and column is the same. To check this for the first row and second column, enter the command

```
sum(A(1,:))
```

which returns

```
ans =
a+b+c
```

The command

```
sum(A(1,:)) == sum(A(:,2)) % This is a logical test.
```

returns

```
ans =
     1
```

Now replace the (2,3) entry of A with beta and the variable b with alpha. The commands

```
syms alpha beta;
A(2,3) = beta;
A = subs(A,b,alpha)
```

return

```
A =
[     a, alpha,     c]
[ alpha,     c,  beta]
[     c,     a, alpha]
```

From this example, you can see that using symbolic objects is very similar to using regular MATLAB numeric objects.

Creating Symbolic Math Functions

There are two ways to create functions:

- Use symbolic expressions
- Create an M-file

Using Symbolic Expressions

The sequence of commands

```
syms x y z
r = sqrt(x^2 + y^2 + z^2)
t = atan(y/x)
f = sin(x*y)/(x*y)
```

generates the symbolic expressions `r`, `t`, and `f`. You can use `diff`, `int`, `subs`, and other Symbolic Math Toolbox functions to manipulate such expressions.

Creating an M-File

M-files permit a more general use of functions. Suppose, for example, you want to create the `sinc` function `sin(x)/x`. To do this, create an M-file in the `@sym` directory:

```
function z = sinc(x)
%SINC The symbolic sinc function
%     sin(x)/x. This function
%     accepts a sym as the input argument.
if isequal(x,sym(0))
   z = 1;
else
   z = sin(x)/x;
end
```

You can extend such examples to functions of several variables. See "Programming and Data Types" in the MATLAB documentation for a more detailed discussion on object-oriented programming.

10

Using the Symbolic Math Toolbox

This chapter explains how to use the Symbolic Math Toolbox to perform many common mathematical operations. It covers the following topics:

Calculus

The Symbolic Math Toolbox provides functions to do the basic operations of calculus. The following sections describe these functions:

Differentiation

To illustrate how to take derivatives using the Symbolic Math Toolbox, first create a symbolic expression:

```
syms x
f = sin(5*x)
```

The command

```
diff(f)
```

differentiates `f` with respect to `x`:

```
ans =
5*cos(5*x)
```

As another example, let

```
g = exp(x)*cos(x)
```

where `exp(x)` denotes e^x, and differentiate `g`:

```
diff(g)
ans =
exp(x)*cos(x)-exp(x)*sin(x)
```

To take the second derivative of g, enter

```
diff(g,2)
ans =
-2*exp(x)*sin(x)
```

You can get the same result by taking the derivative twice:

```
diff(diff(g))
ans =
-2*exp(x)*sin(x)
```

In this example, MATLAB automatically simplifies the answer. However, in some cases, MATLAB might not simply an answer, in which case you can use the `simplify` command. For an example of this, see "More Examples" on page 10-5.

Note that to take the derivative of a constant, you must first define the constant as a symbolic expression. For example, entering

```
c = sym('5');
diff(c)
```

returns

```
ans =
0
```

If you just enter

```
diff(5)
```

MATLAB returns

```
ans =
     []
```

because 5 is not a symbolic expression.

Derivatives of Expressions with Several Variables

To differentiate an expression that contains more than one symbolic variable, you must specify the variable that you want to differentiate with respect to. The `diff` command then calculates the partial derivative of the expression with respect to that variable. For example, given the symbolic expression

```
syms s t
f = sin(s*t)
```

the command

```
diff(f,t)
```

calculates the partial derivative $\partial f / \partial t$. The result is

```
ans =
cos(s*t)*s
```

To differentiate `f` with respect to the variable `s`, enter

```
diff(f,s)
```

which returns:

```
ans =
cos(s*t)*t
```

If you do not specify a variable to differentiate with respect to, MATLAB chooses a default variable by the same rule described in "The subs Command" on page 9-8. For one-letter variables, the default variable is the letter closest to x in the alphabet. In the preceding example, `diff(f)` takes the derivative of `f` with respect to `t` because t is closer to x in the alphabet than s is. To determine the default variable that MATLAB differentiates with respect to, use the `findsym` command:

```
findsym(f,1)
ans =
t
```

To calculate the second derivative of `f` with respect to `t`, enter

```
diff(f,t,2)
```

which returns

```
ans =
-sin(s*t)*s^2
```

Note that `diff(f,2)` returns the same answer because `t` is the default variable.

More Examples

To further illustrate the `diff` command, define `a`, `b`, `x`, `n`, `t`, and `theta` in the MATLAB workspace by entering

```
syms a b x n t theta
```

The table below illustrates the results of entering `diff(f)`.

f	diff(f)
`x^n`	`x^n*n/x`
`sin(a*t+b)`	`cos(a*t+b)*a`
`exp(i*theta)`	`i*exp(i*theta)`

In the first example, MATLAB does not automatically simplify the answer. To simplify the answer, enter

```
simplify(diff(x^n))
ans =
x^(n-1)*n
```

To differentiate the Bessel function of the first kind, `besselj(nu,z)`, with respect to `z`, type

```
syms nu z
b = besselj(nu,z);
db = diff(b)
```

which returns

```
db =
-besselj(nu+1,z)+nu/z*besselj(nu,z)
```

The `diff` function can also take a symbolic matrix as its input. In this case, the differentiation is done element-by-element. Consider the example

```
syms a x
A = [cos(a*x),sin(a*x);-sin(a*x),cos(a*x)]
```

which returns

```
A =
[  cos(a*x),  sin(a*x)]
[ -sin(a*x),  cos(a*x)]
```

The command

```
diff(A)
```

returns

```
ans =
[ -sin(a*x)*a,  cos(a*x)*a]
[ -cos(a*x)*a, -sin(a*x)*a]
```

You can also perform differentiation of a column vector with respect to a row vector. Consider the transformation from Euclidean (x, y, z) to spherical (r, λ, φ) coordinates as given by $x = r\cos\lambda\cos\varphi$, $y = r\cos\lambda\sin\varphi$, and $z = r\sin\lambda$. Note that λ corresponds to elevation or latitude while φ denotes azimuth or longitude.

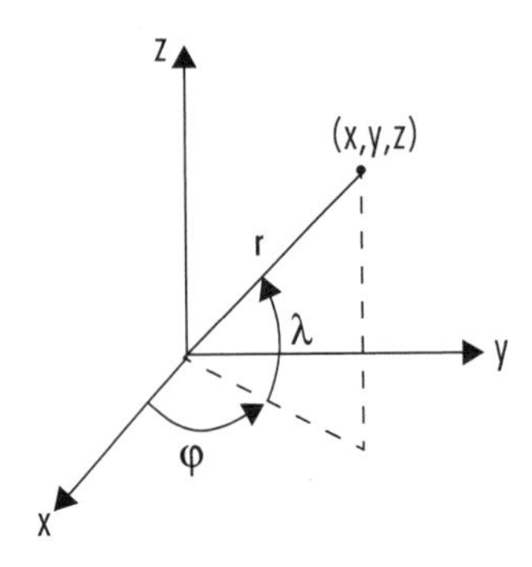

To calculate the Jacobian matrix, J, of this transformation, use the `jacobian` function. The mathematical notation for J is

$$J = \frac{\partial(x, y, x)}{\partial(r, \lambda, \varphi)}$$

For the purposes of toolbox syntax, use `l` for λ and `f` for φ. The commands

```
syms r l f
x = r*cos(l)*cos(f); y = r*cos(l)*sin(f); z = r*sin(l);
J = jacobian([x; y; z], [r l f])
```

return the Jacobian

```
J =
[    cos(l)*cos(f), -r*sin(l)*cos(f), -r*cos(l)*sin(f)]
[    cos(l)*sin(f), -r*sin(l)*sin(f),  r*cos(l)*cos(f)]
[           sin(l),         r*cos(l),                0]
```

and the command

```
detJ = simple(det(J))
```

returns

```
detJ =
-cos(l)*r^2
```

Notice that the first argument of the `jacobian` function must be a column vector and the second argument a row vector. Moreover, since the determinant of the Jacobian is a rather complicated trigonometric expression, you can use the `simple` command to make trigonometric substitutions and reductions (simplifications). See "Simplifications and Substitutions" on page 10-41 for more details on simplification.

A table summarizing `diff` and `jacobian` follows.

Mathematical Operator	**MATLAB Command**
$\frac{df}{dx}$	`diff(f)` or `diff(f,x)`
$\frac{df}{da}$	`diff(f,a)`

Mathematical Operator	MATLAB Command
$\frac{d^2 f}{db^2}$	`diff(f,b,2)`
$J = \frac{\partial(r, t)}{\partial(u, v)}$	`J = jacobian([r;t],[u,v])`

Limits

The fundamental idea in calculus is to make calculations on functions as a variable "gets close to" or approaches a certain value. Recall that the definition of the derivative is given by a limit

$$f'(x) = \lim_{h \to 0} \frac{f(x+h) - f(x)}{h}$$

provided this limit exists. The Symbolic Math Toolbox enables you to calculate the limits of functions directly. The commands

```
syms h n x
limit( (cos(x+h) - cos(x))/h,h,0 )
```

which return

```
ans =
-sin(x)
```

and

```
limit( (1 + x/n)^n,n,inf )
```

which returns

```
ans =
exp(x)
```

illustrate two of the most important limits in mathematics: the derivative (in this case of $\cos x$) and the exponential function.

One-Sided Limits

You can also calculate one-sided limits with the Symbolic Math Toolbox. For example, you can calculate the limit of $x/|x|$, whose graph is shown in the following figure, as x approaches 0 from the left or from the right.

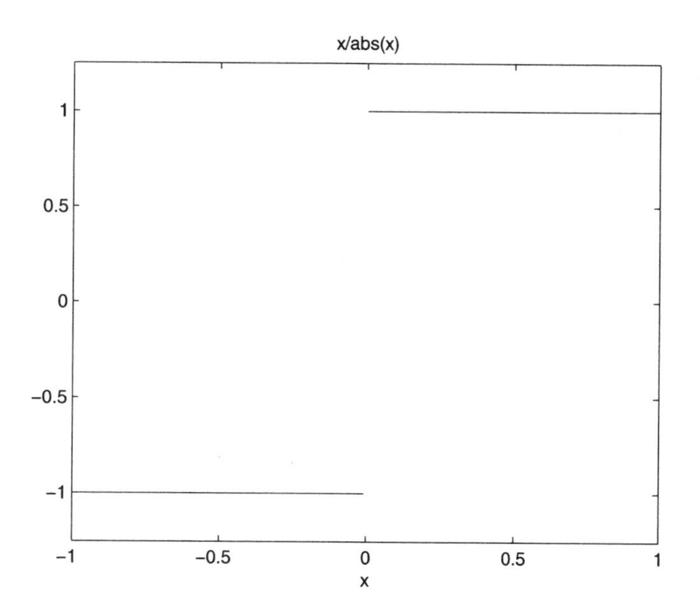

To calculate the limit as x approaches 0 from the left,

$$\lim_{x \to 0^-} \frac{x}{|x|}$$

enter

```
limit(x/abs(x),x,0,'left')
```

This returns

```
ans =
 -1
```

To calculate the limit as x approaches 0 from the right,

$$\lim_{x \to 0^+} \frac{x}{|x|} = 1$$

enter

```
limit(x/abs(x),x,0,'right')
```

This returns

```
ans =
1
```

Since the limit from the left does not equal the limit from the right, the two-sided limit does not exist. In the case of undefined limits, MATLAB returns `NaN` (not a number). For example,

```
limit(x/abs(x),x,0)
```

returns

```
ans =
NaN
```

Observe that the default case, `limit(f)` is the same as `limit(f,x,0)`. Explore the options for the `limit` command in this table, where `f` is a function of the symbolic object `x`.

Mathematical Operation	**MATLAB Command**
$\lim_{x \to 0} f(x)$	`limit(f)`
$\lim_{x \to a} f(x)$	`limit(f,x,a)` or `limit(f,a)`
$\lim_{x \to a-} f(x)$	`limit(f,x,a,'left')`
$\lim_{x \to a+} f(x)$	`limit(f,x,a,'right')`

Integration

If `f` is a symbolic expression, then

```
int(f)
```

attempts to find another symbolic expression, `F`, so that `diff(F) = f`. That is, `int(f)` returns the indefinite integral or antiderivative of `f` (provided one exists in closed form). Similar to differentiation,

```
int(f,v)
```

uses the symbolic object `v` as the variable of integration, rather than the variable determined by `findsym`. See how `int` works by looking at this table.

Mathematical Operation	MATLAB Command
$\int x^n dx = \frac{x^{n+1}}{n+1}$	`int(x^n)` or `int(x^n,x)`
$\int_0^{\pi/2} \sin(2x)dx = 1$	`int(sin(2*x),0,pi/2)` or `int(sin(2*x),x,0,pi/2)`

$g = \cos(at+b)$
$\int g(t)dt = \sin(at+b)/a$
	`g = cos(a*t + b)`
	`int(g)` or
	`int(g,t)`

$\int J_1(z)dz = -J_0(z)$	`int(besselj(1,z))` or `int(besselj(1,z),z)`

In contrast to differentiation, symbolic integration is a more complicated task. A number of difficulties can arise in computing the integral:

- The antiderivative, `F`, may not exist in closed form.
- The antiderivative may define an unfamiliar function.
- The antiderivative may exist, but the software can't find the it.
- The software could find the antiderivative on a larger computer, but runs out of time or memory on the available machine.

Nevertheless, in many cases, MATLAB can perform symbolic integration successfully. For example, create the symbolic variables

```
syms a b theta x y n u z
```

The following table illustrates integration of expressions containing those variables.

f	int(f)
`x^n`	`x^(n+1)/(n+1)`
`y^(-1)`	`log(y)`
`n^x`	`1/log(n)*n^x`
`sin(a*theta+b)`	`-1/a*cos(a*theta+b)`
`1/(1+u^2)`	`atan(u)`
`exp(-x^2)`	`1/2*pi^(1/2)*erf(x)`

In the last example, `exp(-x^2)`, there is no formula for the integral involving standard calculus expressions, such as trigonometric and exponential functions. In this case, MATLAB returns an answer in terms of the error function `erf`.

If MATLAB is unable to find an answer to the integral of a function `f`, it just returns `int(f)`.

Definite integration is also possible. The commands

```
int(f,a,b)
```

and

```
int(f,v,a,b)
```

are used to find a symbolic expression for

$$\int_a^b f(x)dx \text{ and } \int_a^b f(v)dv$$

respectively.

Here are some additional examples.

f	a, b	int(f,a,b)
`x^7`	`0, 1`	`1/8`
`1/x`	`1, 2`	`log(2)`
`log(x)*sqrt(x)`	`0, 1`	`-4/9`
`exp(-x^2)`	`0, inf`	`1/2*pi^(1/2)`
`besselj(1,z)^2`	`0, 1`	`1/12*hypergeom([3/2, 3/2], [2, 5/2, 3],-1)`

For the Bessel function (`besselj`) example, it is possible to compute a numerical approximation to the value of the integral, using the `double` function. The commands

```
syms z
a = int(besselj(1,z)^2,0,1)
```

return

```
a =
1/12*hypergeom([3/2, 3/2],[2, 5/2, 3],-1)
```

and the command

```
a = double(a)
```

returns

```
a =
  0.0717
```

Integration with Real Parameters

One of the subtleties involved in symbolic integration is the "value" of various parameters. For example, if a is any positive real number, the expression

$$e^{-ax^2}$$

is the positive, bell shaped curve that tends to 0 as x tends to $\pm\infty$. You can create an example of this curve, for $a = 1/2$, using the following commands:

```
syms x
a = sym(1/2);
f = exp(-a*x^2);
ezplot(f)
```

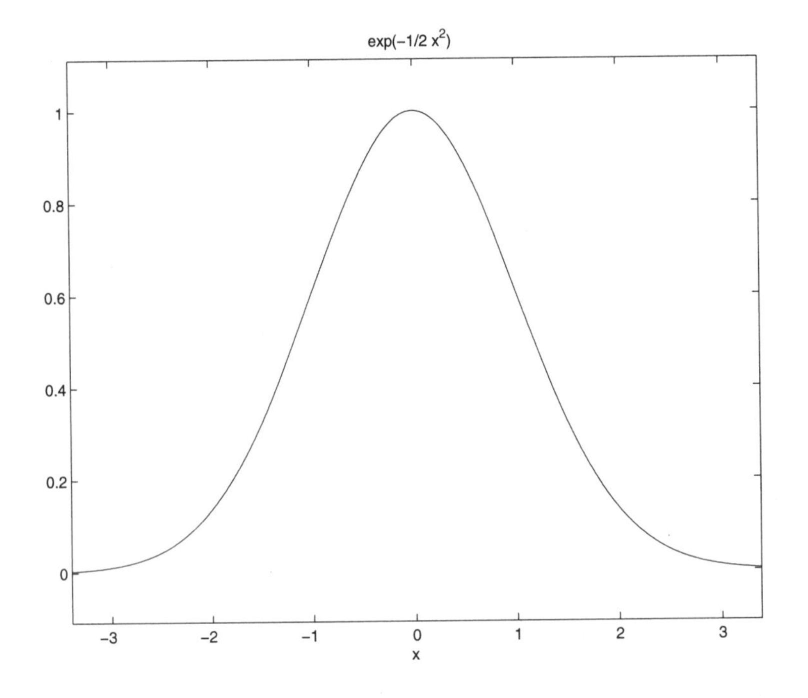

However, if you try to calculate the integral

$$\int_{-\infty}^{\infty} e^{-ax^2}\,dx$$

without assigning a value to a, MATLAB assumes that a represents a complex number, and therefore returns a complex answer. If you are only interested in the case when a is a positive real number, you can calculate the integral as follows:

```
syms a positive;
```

The argument `positive` in the `syms` command restricts a to have positive values. Now you can calculate the preceding integral using the commands

```
syms x;
f = exp(-a*x^2);
int(f,x,-inf,inf)
```

This returns

```
ans =
1/(a)^(1/2)*pi^(1/2)
```

If you want to calculate the integral

$$\int_{-\infty}^{\infty} e^{-ax^2} dx$$

for any real number a, not necessarily positive, you can declare a to be real with the following commands:

```
syms a real
f=exp(-a*x^2);
F = int(f, x, -inf, inf)
```

MATLAB returns

```
F =
PIECEWISE([1/a^(1/2)*pi^(1/2), signum(a) = 1],[Inf, otherwise])
```

You can put this in a more readable form by entering

```
pretty(F)
                            {    1/2
                            { pi
                            { -----            signum(a~) = 1
                            {    1/2
                            { a~
                            {
                            {   Inf               otherwise
```

The ~ after a is simply a reminder that a is real, and `signum(a~)` is the sign of a. So the integral is

$$\frac{\sqrt{\pi}}{\sqrt{a}}$$

when a is positive, just as in the preceding example, and ∞ when a is negative.

You can also declare a sequence of symbolic variables `w`, `y`, `x`, `z` to be real by entering

```
syms w x y z real
```

Integration with Complex Parameters

To calculate the integral

$$\int_{-\infty}^{\infty} e^{-ax^2} dx$$

for complex values of `a`, enter

```
syms a x unreal %
f = exp(-a*x^2);
F = int(f, x, -inf, inf)
```

Note that `syms` is used with the `unreal` option to clear the `real` property that was assigned to a in the preceding example — see "Clearing Variables in the Maple Workspace" on page 9-12.

The preceding commands produce the complex output

```
F =
PIECEWISE([1/a^(1/2)*pi^(1/2), csgn(a) = 1],[Inf, otherwise])
```

You can make this output more readable by entering

```
pretty(F)
                                {   1/2
                                { pi
                                { -----          csgn(a) = 1
                                {  1/2
                                { a
                                {
                                {  Inf            otherwise
```

The expression `csgn(a)` (complex sign of `a`) is defined by

$$\operatorname{csgn}(a) = \begin{cases} 1 & \text{if } \operatorname{Re}(a) > 0, \text{ or } \operatorname{Re}(a) = 0 \text{ and } \operatorname{Im}(a) > 0 \\ -1 & \text{if } \operatorname{Re}(a) < 0, \text{ or } \operatorname{Re}(a) = 0 \text{ and } \operatorname{Im}(a) < 0 \end{cases}$$

The condition csgn(a) = 1 corresponds to the shaded region of the complex plane shown in the following figure.

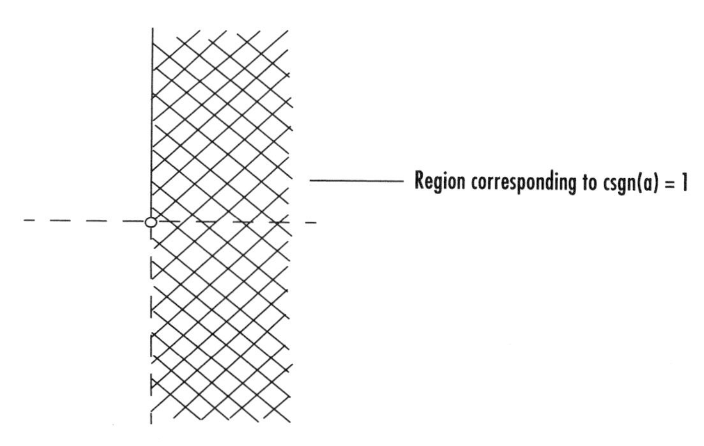

The square root of a in the answer is the unique square root lying in the shaded region.

Symbolic Summation

You can compute symbolic summations, when they exist, by using the `symsum` command. For example, the p-series

$$1 + \frac{1}{2^2} + \frac{1}{3^2} + \ldots$$

sums to $\pi^2/6$, while the geometric series

$$1 + x + x^2 + \ldots$$

sums to $1/(1-x)$, provided $|x| < 1$. Three summations are demonstrated below:

```
syms x k
s1 = symsum(1/k^2,1,inf)
s2 = symsum(x^k,k,0,inf)

s1 =

1/6*pi^2

s2 =

-1/(x-1)
```

Taylor Series

The statements

```
syms x
f = 1/(5+4*cos(x))
T = taylor(f,8)
```

return

```
T =
1/9+2/81*x^2+5/1458*x^4+49/131220*x^6
```

which is all the terms up to, but not including, order eight in the Taylor series for $f(x)$:

$$\sum_{n=0}^{\infty} (x-a)^n \frac{f^{(n)}(a)}{n!}$$

Technically, T is a Maclaurin series, since its basepoint is a = 0.

The command

```
pretty(T)
```

prints T in a format resembling typeset mathematics:

```
                2              4      49    6
1/9 + 2/81 x  + 5/1458 x  + ------ x
                              131220
```

These commands

```
syms x
g = exp(x*sin(x))
t = taylor(g,12,2);
```

generate the first 12 nonzero terms of the Taylor series for g about x = 2.

Next, plot these functions together to see how well this Taylor approximation compares to the actual function g:

```
xd = 1:0.05:3; yd = subs(g,x,xd);
ezplot(t, [1,3]); hold on;
plot(xd, yd, 'r-.')
title('Taylor approximation vs. actual function');
legend('Taylor','Function')
```

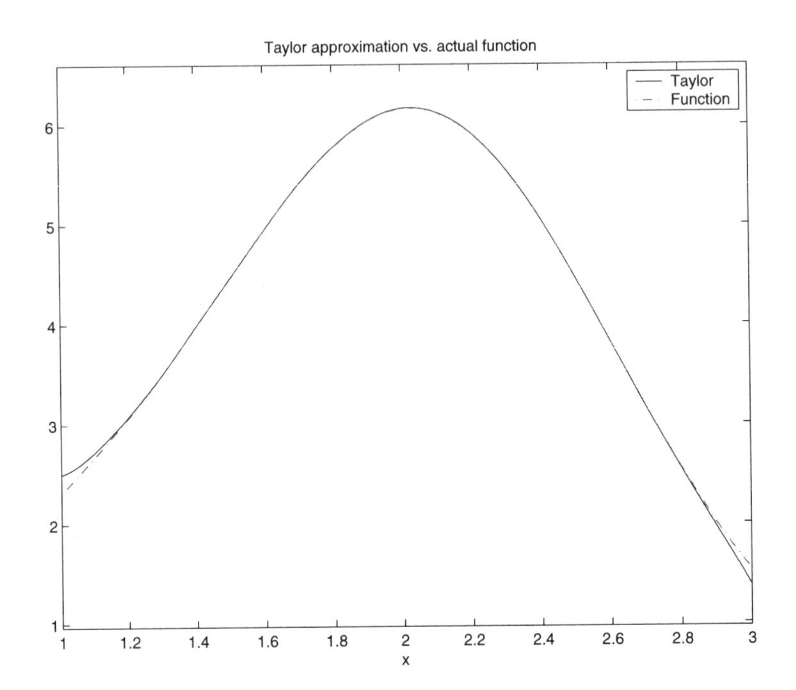

Special thanks to Professor Gunnar Bäckstrøm of UMEA in Sweden for this example.

Calculus Example

This section describes how to analyze a simple function to find its asymptotes, maximum, minimum, and inflection point. The section covers the following topics:

- "Defining the Function" on page 10-21
- "Finding the Asymptotes" on page 10-22
- "Finding the Maximum and Minimum" on page 10-24
- "Finding the Inflection Point" on page 10-26

Defining the Function

The function in this example is

$$f(x) = \frac{3x^2 + 6x - 1}{x^2 + x - 3}$$

To create the function, enter the following commands:

```
syms x
num = 3*x^2 + 6*x -1;
denom = x^2 + x - 3;
f = num/denom
```

This returns

```
f =
(3*x^2+6*x-1)/(x^2+x-3)
```

You can plot the graph of `f` by entering

```
ezplot(f)
```

This displays the following plot.

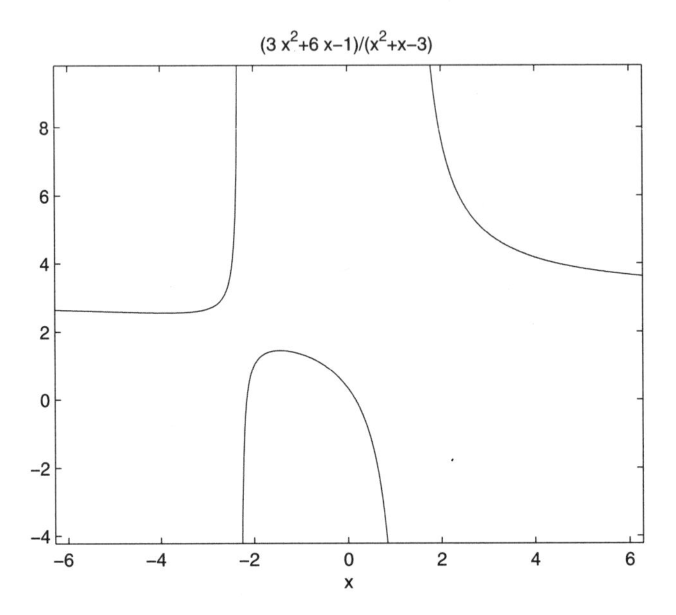

Finding the Asymptotes

To find the horizontal asymptote of the graph of `f`, take the limit of `f` as `x` approaches positive infinity:

```
limit(f, inf)
ans =
3
```

The limit as x approaches negative infinity is also 3. This tells you that the line $y = 3$ is a horizontal asymptote to the graph.

To find the vertical asymptotes of `f`, set the denominator equal to 0 and solve by entering the following command:

```
roots = solve(denom)
```

This returns to solutions to $x^2 + x - 3 = 0$:

```
roots =
[ -1/2+1/2*13^(1/2)]
[ -1/2-1/2*13^(1/2)]
```

This tells you that vertical asymptotes are the lines

$$x = \frac{-1 + \sqrt{13}}{2}$$

and

$$x = \frac{-1 - \sqrt{13}}{2}$$

You can plot the horizontal and vertical asymptotes with the following commands:

```
ezplot(f)
hold on % Keep the graph of f in the figure
% Plot horizontal asymptote
plot([-2*pi 2*pi], [3 3],'g')
% Plot vertical asymptotes
plot(double(roots(1))*[1 1], [-5 10],'r')
plot(double(roots(2))*[1 1], [-5 10],'r')
title('Horizontal and Vertical Asymptotes')
hold off
```

Note that `roots` must be converted to `double` to use the `plot` command.

The preceding commands display the following figure.

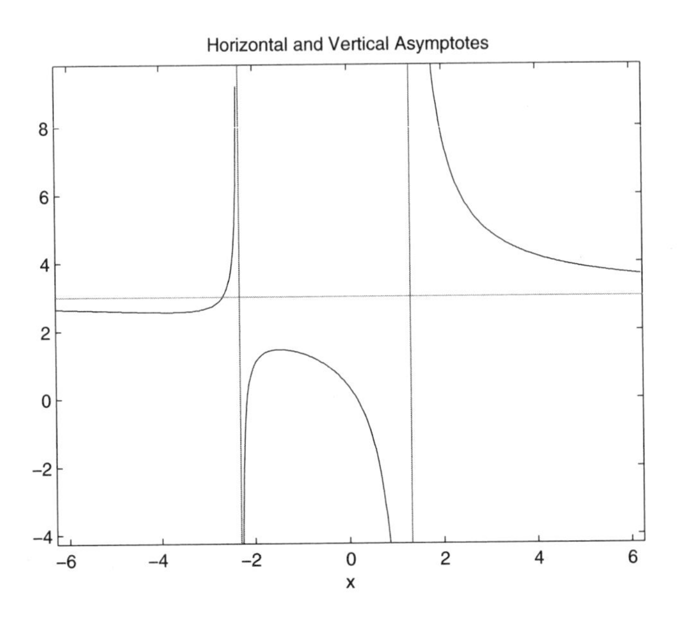

To recover the graph of `f` without the asymptotes, enter

```
ezplot(f)
```

Finding the Maximum and Minimum

You can see from the graph that `f` has a local maximum somewhere between the points $x = 2$ and $x = 3$, and might have a local minimum between $x = -4$ and $x = -2$. To find the x-coordinates of the maximum and minimum, first take the derivative of `f`:

```
f1 = diff(f)
```

This returns

```
f1 = (6*x+6)/(x^2+x-3)-(3*x^2+6*x-1)/(x^2+x-3)^2*(2*x+1)
```

To simplify this expression, enter

```
f1 = simplify(f1)
```

which returns

```
f1 = -(3*x^2+16*x+17)/(x^2+x-3)^2
```

You can display `f1` in a more readable form by entering

```
pretty(f1)
```

which returns

```
                       2
                    3 x  + 16 x + 17
                  - ----------------
                       2         2
                     (x  + x - 3)
```

Next, set the derivative equal to 0 and solve for the critical points:

```
crit_pts = solve(f1)
```

This returns

```
ans =
[ -8/3-1/3*13^(1/2)]
[ -8/3+1/3*13^(1/2)]
```

It is clear from the graph of `f` that it has a local minimum at

$$x_1 = \frac{-8 - \sqrt{13}}{3}$$

and a local maximum at

$$x_2 = \frac{-8 + \sqrt{13}}{3}$$

Note MATLAB does not always return the roots to an equation in the same order.

You can plot the maximum and minimum of `f` with the following commands:

```
ezplot(f)
hold on
```

```
plot(double(crit_pts), double(subs(f,crit_pts)),'ro')
title('Maximum and Minimum of f')
text(-5.5,3.2,'Local minimum')
text(-2.5,2,'Local maximum')
hold off
```

This displays the following figure.

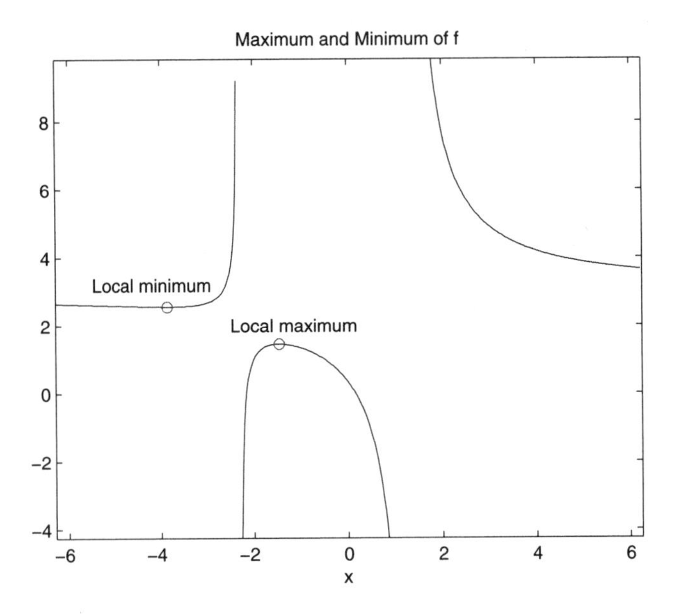

Finding the Inflection Point

To find the inflection point of `f`, set the second derivative equal to 0 and solve.

```
f2 = diff(f1);
inflec_pt = solve(f2);
double(inflec_pt)
```

This returns

```
ans =
  -5.2635
  -1.3682 - 0.8511i
  -1.3682 + 0.8511i
```

In this example, only the first entry is a real number, so this is the only inflection point. (Note that in other examples, the real solutions might not be the first entries of the answer.) Since you are only interested in the real solutions, you can discard the last two entries, which are complex numbers.

```
inflec_pt = inflec_pt(1)
```

To see the symbolic expression for the inflection point, enter

```
pretty(simplify(inflec_pt))
```

This returns

```
                     1/2 2/3                           1/2 1/3
       (676 + 156 13    )     + 52 + 16 (676 + 156 13    )
- 1/6 ----------------------------------------------------
                                         1/2 1/3
                         (676 + 156 13    )
```

To plot the inflection point, enter

```
ezplot(f, [-9 6])
hold on
plot(double(inflec_pt), double(subs(f,inflec_pt)),'ro')
title('Inflection Point of f')
text(-7,2,'Inflection point')
hold off
```

The extra argument, `[-9 6]`, in `ezplot` extends the range of x values in the plot so that you see the inflection point more clearly, as shown in the following figure.

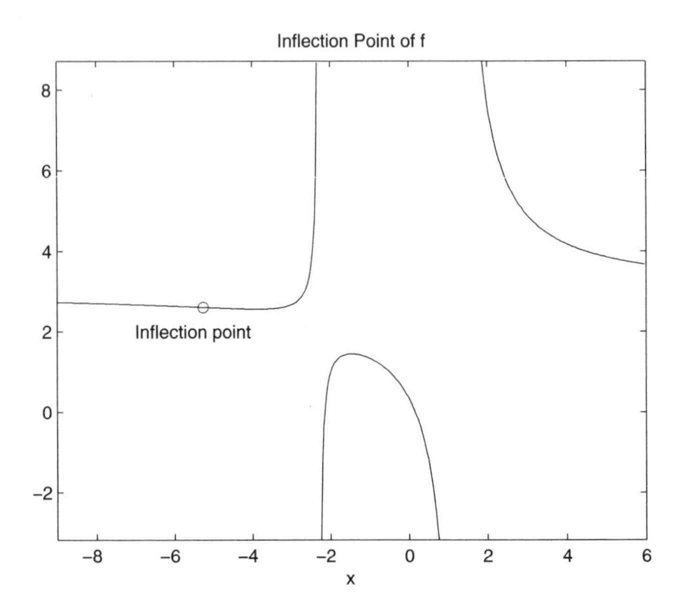

Extended Calculus Example

This section presents an extended example that illustrates how to find the maxima and minima of a function. The section covers the following topics:

- "Defining the Function" on page 10-28
- "Finding the Zeros of f3" on page 10-30
- "Finding the Maxima and Minima of f2" on page 10-33
- "Integrating" on page 10-35

Defining the Function

The starting point for the example is the function

$$f(x) = \frac{1}{5 + 4\cos(x)}$$

You can create the function with the commands

```
syms x
f = 1/(5+4*cos(x))
```

which return

```
f =
1/(5+4*cos(x))
```

The example shows how to find the maximum and minimum of the second derivative of $f(x)$. To compute the second derivative, enter

```
f2 = diff(f,2)
```

which returns

```
f2 =
32/(5+4*cos(x))^3*sin(x)^2+4/(5+4*cos(x))^2*cos(x)
```

Equivalently, you can type `f2 = diff(f,x,2)`. The default scaling in `ezplot` cuts off part of the graph of `f2`. You can set the axes limits manually to see the entire function:

```
ezplot(f2)
axis([-2*pi 2*pi -5 2])
title('Graph of f2')
```

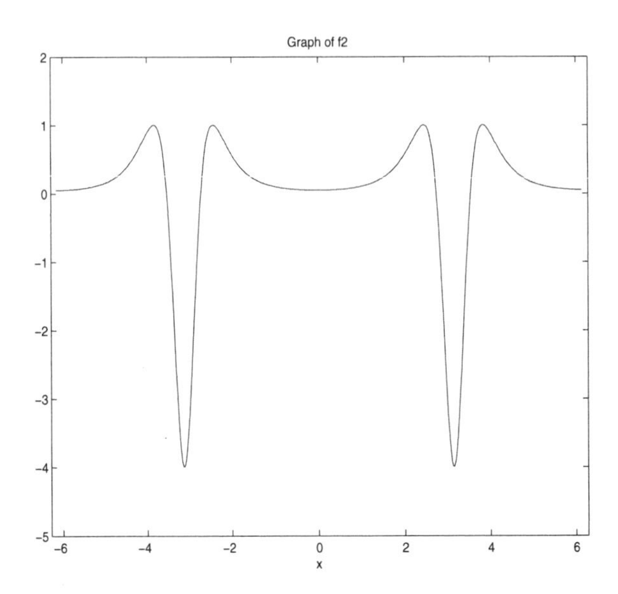

From the graph, it appears that the maximum value of $f''(x)$ is 1 and the minimum value is -4. As you will see, this is not quite true. To find the exact values of the maximum and minimum, you only need to find the maximum and minimum on the interval $(-\pi\ \pi]$. This is true because $f''(x)$ is periodic with period 2π, so that the maxima and minima are simply repeated in each translation of this interval by an integer multiple of 2π. The next two sections explain how to do find the maxima and minima.

Finding the Zeros of f3

The maxima and minima of $f''(x)$ occur at the zeros of $f'''(x)$. The statements

```
f3 = diff(f2);
pretty(f3)
```

compute $f'''(x)$ and display it in a more readable form:

```
                3
          sin(x)               sin(x) cos(x)               sin(x)
384 --------------- + 96 --------------- - 4 ---------------
                   4                     3                     2
    (5 + 4 cos(x))         (5 + 4 cos(x))         (5 + 4 cos(x))
```

You can simplify this expression using the statements

```
f3 = simple(f3);
pretty(f3)

                        2                           2
  sin(x) (96 sin(x)  + 80 cos(x) + 80 cos(x)  - 25)
4 -------------------------------------------------
                                      4
                     (5 + 4 cos(x))
```

Now, to find the zeros of $f'''(x)$, enter

```
zeros = solve(f3)
```

This returns a 5-by-1 symbolic matrix

```
zeros =
[                                                 0]
[        atan((-255-60*19^(1/2))^(1/2),10+3*19^(1/2))]
[       atan(-(-255-60*19^(1/2))^(1/2),10+3*19^(1/2))]
[  atan((-255+60*19^(1/2))^(1/2)/(10-3*19^(1/2)))+pi]
[ -atan((-255+60*19^(1/2))^(1/2)/(10-3*19^(1/2)))-pi]
```

each of whose entries is a zero of $f'''(x)$. The commands

```
format; % Default format of 5 digits
zerosd = double(zeros)
```

convert the zeros to `double` form:

```
zerosd =
        0
        0+ 2.4381i
        0- 2.4381i
   2.4483
  -2.4483
```

So far, you have found three real zeros and two complex zeros. However, as the following graph of `f3` shows, these are not all its zeros:

```
ezplot(f3)
hold on;
plot(zerosd,0*zerosd,'ro') % Plot zeros
plot([-2*pi,2*pi], [0,0],'g-.'); % Plot x-axis
title('Graph of f3')
```

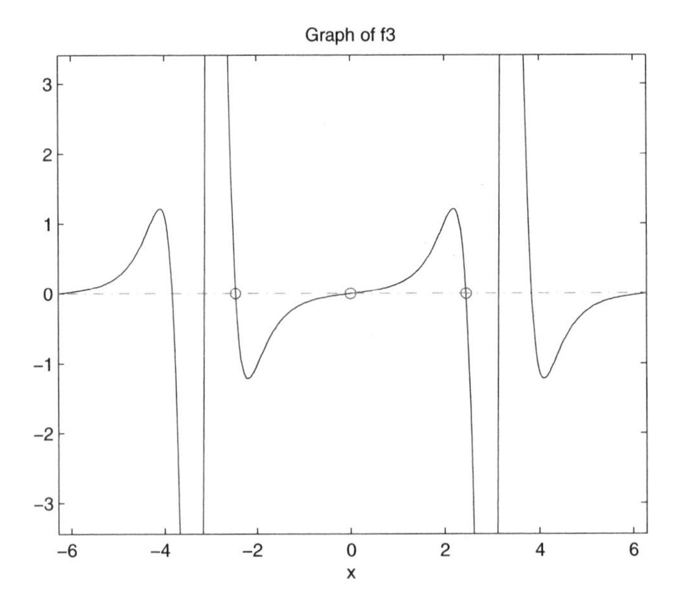

The red circles in the graph correspond to `zerosd(1)`, `zerosd(4)`, and `zerosd(5)`. As you can see in the graph, there are also zeros at $\pm\pi$. The additional zeros occur because $f'''(x)$ contains a factor of $\sin(x)$, which is zero at integer multiples of π. The function, `solve(sin(x))`, however, only finds the zero at $x = 0$.

A complete list of the zeros of $f'''(x)$ in the interval $(-\pi\ \pi]$ is

```
zerosd = [zerosd(1) zerosd(4) zerosd(5) pi];
```

You can display these zeros on the graph of $f'''(x)$ with the following commands:

```
ezplot(f3)
hold on;
plot(zerosd,0*zerosd,'ro')
plot([-2*pi,2*pi], [0,0],'g-.'); % Plot x-axis
title('Zeros of f3')
hold off;
```

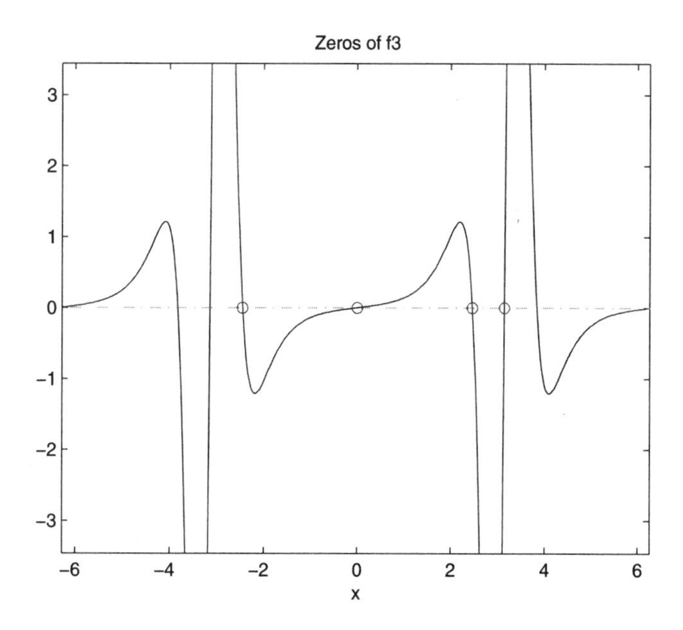

Finding the Maxima and Minima of f2

To find the maxima and minima of $f''(x)$, calculate the value of $f''(x)$ at each of the zeros of $f'''(x)$. To do so, substitute `zeros` into `f2` and display the result below `zeros`:

```
[zerosd; subs(f2,zerosd)]
ans =
        0    2.4483   -2.4483    3.1416
   0.0494    1.0051    1.0051   -4.0000
```

This shows the following:

- $f''(x)$ has an absolute maximum at $x = \pm 2.4483$, whose value is 1.0051.
- $f''(x)$ has an absolute minimum at $x = \pi$, whose value is -4.
- $f''(x)$ has a local minimum at $x = \pi$, whose value is 0.0494.

You can display the maxima and minima with the following commands:

```
clf
ezplot(f2)
axis([-2*pi 2*pi -4.5 1.5])
ylabel('f2');
title('Maxima and Minima of f2')
hold on
plot(zeros, subs(f2,zeros), 'ro')
text(-4, 1.25, 'Absolute maximum')
text(-1,-0.25,'Local minimum')
text(.9, 1.25, 'Absolute maximum')
text(1.6, -4.25, 'Absolute minimum')
hold off;
```

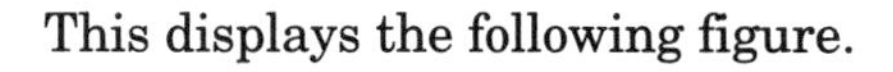

This displays the following figure.

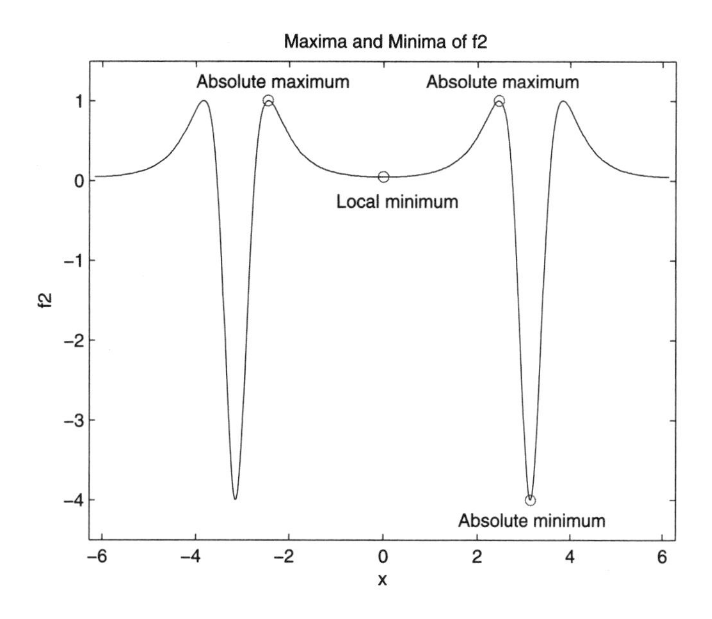

The preceding analysis shows that the actual range of $f''(x)$ is [-4, 1.0051].

Integrating

To see whether integrating $f''(x)$ twice with respect to x recovers the original function $f(x) = 1/(5+4\cos x)$, enter the command

```
g = int(int(f2))
```

which returns

```
g =
-8/(tan(1/2*x)^2+9)
```

This is certainly not the original expression for $f(x)$. Now look at the difference $f(x) - g(x)$.

```
d = f - g
pretty(d)
```

```
      1                   8
----------- + --------------
5 + 4 cos(x)                2
               tan(1/2 x)   + 9
```

You can simplify this using `simple(d)` or `simplify(d)`. Either command produces

```
ans =
1
```

This illustrates the concept that differentiating $f(x)$ twice, then integrating the result twice, produces a function that may differ from $f(x)$ by a linear function of x.

Finally, integrate $f(x)$ once more:

```
F = int(f)
```

The result

```
F =
2/3*atan(1/3*tan(1/2*x))
```

involves the arctangent function.

Note that $F(x)$ is not an antiderivative of $f(x)$ for all real numbers, since it is discontinuous at odd multiples of π, where $\tan x$ is singular. You can see the gaps in $F(x)$ in the following figure.

```
ezplot(F)
```

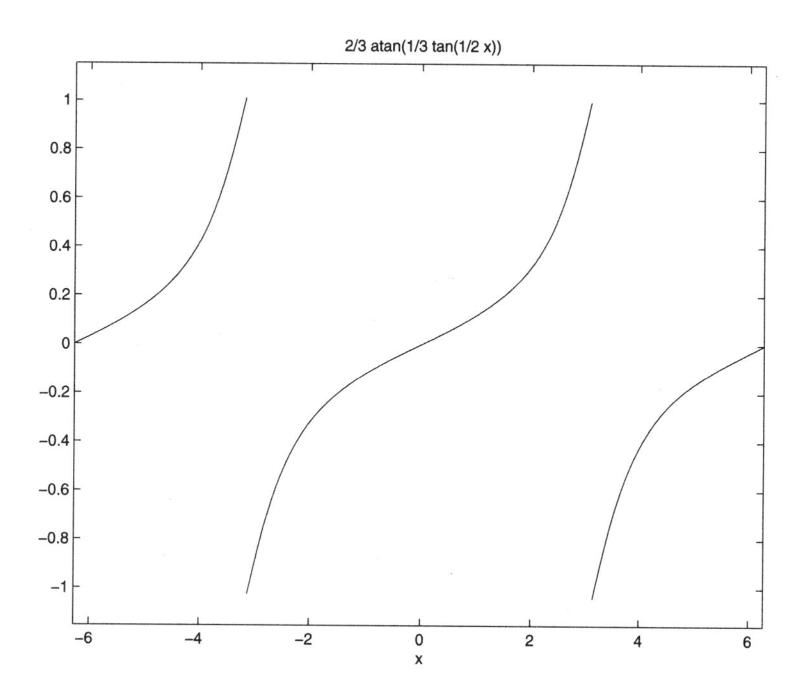

To change $F(x)$ into a true antiderivative of $f(x)$ that is differentiable everywhere, you can add a step function to $F(x)$. The height of the steps is the height of the gaps in the graph of $F(x)$. You can determine the height of the gaps by taking the limits of $F(x)$ as x approaches π from the left and from the right. The limit from the left is

```
limit(F, x, pi, 'left')
ans =
1/3*pi
```

On the other hand, the limit from the right is

```
limit(F, x, pi, 'right')
ans =-1/3*pi
```

The height of the gap is the distance between the left and right hand limits, which is $2\pi/3$, as shown in the following figure.

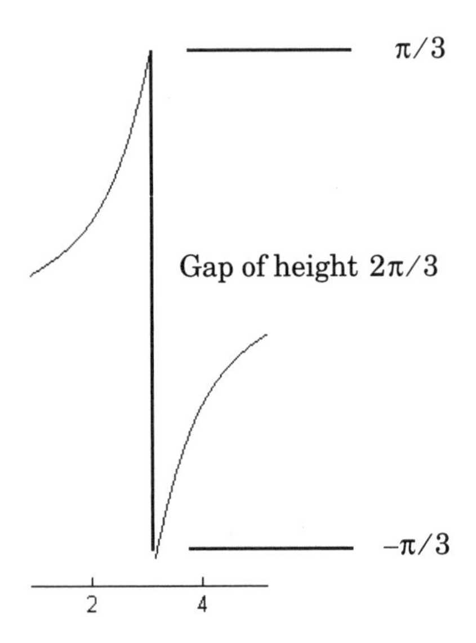

You can create the step function using the `round` function, which rounds numbers to the nearest integer, as follows:

```
J = sym(2*pi/3)*sym('round(x/(2*pi))');
```

Each step has width 2π and the jump from one step to the next is $2\pi/3$, as shown in the following figure.

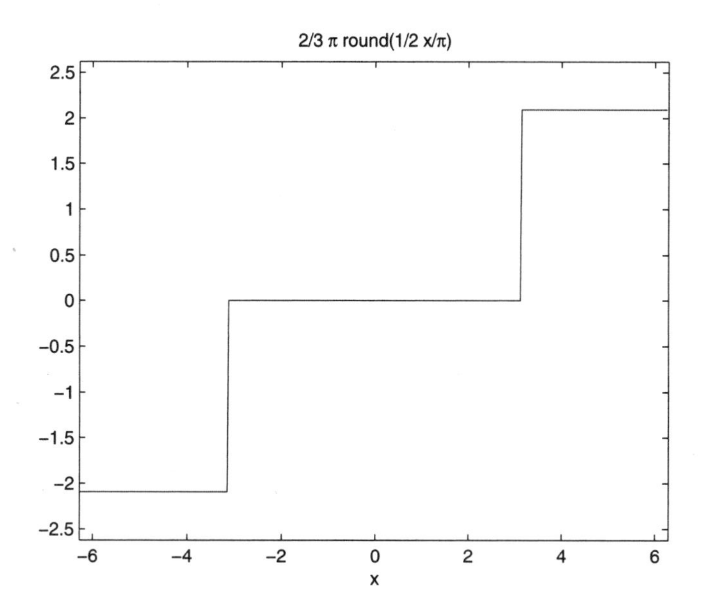

Next, add the step function $J(x)$ to $F(x)$ with the following code:

```
F1 = F+J
F1 =
2/3*atan(1/3*tan(1/2*x))+2/3*pi*round(1/2*x/pi)
```

Adding the step function raises the section of the graph of $F(x)$ on the interval $[\pi \quad 3\pi)$ up by $2\pi/3$, lowers the section on the interval $(-3\pi \quad -\pi]$ down by $2\pi/3$, and so on, as shown in the following figure.

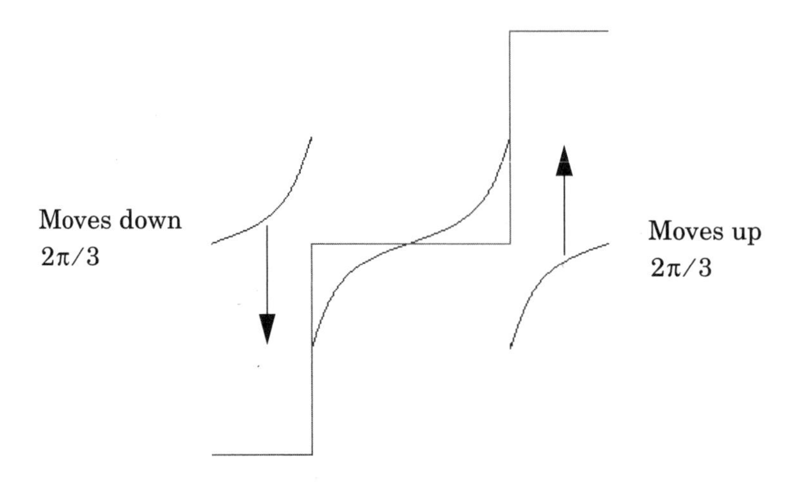

When you plot the result by entering

```
ezplot(F1)
```

you see that this representation does have a continuous graph.

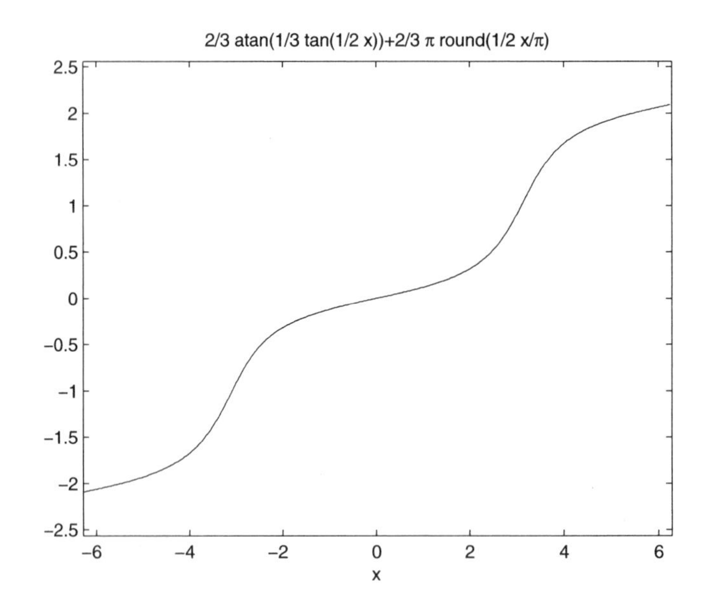

Simplifications and Substitutions

There are several functions that simplify symbolic expressions and are used to perform symbolic substitutions:

Simplifications

Here are three different symbolic expressions.

```
syms x
f = x^3-6*x^2+11*x-6
g = (x-1)*(x-2)*(x-3)
h = -6+(11+(-6+x)*x)*x
```

Here are their prettyprinted forms, generated by

```
pretty(f), pretty(g), pretty(h)

 3      2
x  - 6 x  + 11 x - 6

(x - 1) (x - 2) (x - 3)

-6 + (11 + (-6 + x) x) x
```

These expressions are three different representations of the same mathematical function, a cubic polynomial in x.

Each of the three forms is preferable to the others in different situations. The first form, f, is the most commonly used representation of a polynomial. It is simply a linear combination of the powers of x. The second form, g, is the factored form. It displays the roots of the polynomial and is the most accurate for numerical evaluation near the roots. But, if a polynomial does not have such simple roots, its factored form may not be so convenient. The third form, h, is the Horner, or nested, representation. For numerical evaluation, it involves the fewest arithmetic operations and is the most accurate for some other ranges of x.

The symbolic simplification problem involves the verification that these three expressions represent the same function. It also involves a less clearly defined objective — which of these representations is "the simplest"?

This toolbox provides several functions that apply various algebraic and trigonometric identities to transform one representation of a function into another, possibly simpler, representation. These functions are `collect`, `expand`, `horner`, `factor`, `simplify`, and `simple`.

collect

The statement

```
collect(f)
```

views `f` as a polynomial in its symbolic variable, say `x`, and collects all the coefficients with the same power of `x`. A second argument can specify the variable in which to collect terms if there is more than one candidate. Here are a few examples.

f	collect(f)
`(x-1)*(x-2)*(x-3)`	`x^3-6*x^2+11*x-6`
`x*(x*(x-6)+11)-6`	`x^3-6*x^2+11*x-6`
`(1+x)*t + x*t`	`2*x*t+t`

expand

The statement

```
expand(f)
```

distributes products over sums and applies other identities involving functions of sums as shown in the examples below.

f	expand(f)
a*(x + y)	a*x + a*y
(x-1)*(x-2)*(x-3)	x^3-6*x^2+11*x-6
x*(x*(x-6)+11)-6	x^3-6*x^2+11*x-6
exp(a+b)	exp(a)*exp(b)
cos(x+y)	cos(x)*cos(y)-sin(x)*sin(y)
cos(3*acos(x))	4*x^3-3*x

horner

The statement

```
horner(f)
```

transforms a symbolic polynomial f into its Horner, or nested, representation as shown in the following examples.

f	horner(f)
x^3-6*x^2+11*x-6	-6+(11+(-6+x)*x)*x
1.1+2.2*x+3.3*x^2	11/10+(11/5+33/10*x)*x

factor

If `f` is a polynomial with rational coefficients, the statement

```
factor(f)
```

expresses `f` as a product of polynomials of lower degree with rational coefficients. If `f` cannot be factored over the rational numbers, the result is `f` itself. Here are several examples.

f	factor(f)
`x^3-6*x^2+11*x-6`	`(x-1)*(x-2)*(x-3)`
`x^3-6*x^2+11*x-5`	`x^3-6*x^2+11*x-5`
`x^6+1`	`(x^2+1)*(x^4-x^2+1)`

Here is another example involving `factor`. It factors polynomials of the form `x^n + 1`. This code

```
syms x;
n = (1:9)';
p = x.^n + 1;
f = factor(p);
[p, f]
```

returns a matrix with the polynomials in its first column and their factored forms in its second.

```
[                 x+1,                          x+1 ]
[               x^2+1,                        x^2+1 ]
[               x^3+1,                (x+1)*(x^2-x+1) ]
[               x^4+1,                        x^4+1 ]
[               x^5+1,        (x+1)*(x^4-x^3+x^2-x+1) ]
[               x^6+1,            (x^2+1)*(x^4-x^2+1) ]
[               x^7+1, (x+1)*(1-x+x^2-x^3+x^4-x^5+x^6) ]
[               x^8+1,                        x^8+1 ]
[               x^9+1,      (x+1)*(x^2-x+1)*(x^6-x^3+1) ]
```

As an aside at this point, `factor` can also factor symbolic objects containing integers. This is an alternative to using the `factor` function in the MATLAB `specfun` directory. For example, the following code segment

```
N = sym(1);
for k = 2:11
   N(k) = 10*N(k-1)+1;
end
[N' factor(N')]
```

displays the factors of symbolic integers consisting of 1s:

```
[                    1,                     1]
[                   11,                  (11)]
[                  111,             (3)*(37)]
[                 1111,           (11)*(101)]
[                11111,           (41)*(271)]
[               111111, (3)*(7)*(11)*(13)*(37)]
[              1111111,         (239)*(4649)]
[             11111111,  (11)*(73)*(101)*(137)]
[            111111111,    (3)^2*(37)*(333667)]
[           1111111111, (11)*(41)*(271)*(9091)]
[          11111111111,       (513239)*(21649)]
```

simplify

The `simplify` function is a powerful, general purpose tool that applies a number of algebraic identities involving sums, integral powers, square roots and other fractional powers, as well as a number of functional identities involving trig functions, exponential and log functions, Bessel functions, hypergeometric functions, and the gamma function. Here are some examples.

f	simplify(f)
`x*(x*(x-6)+11)-6`	`x^3-6*x^2+11*x-6`
`(1-x^2)/(1-x)`	`x+1`
`(1/a^3+6/a^2+12/a+8)^(1/3)`	`((2*a+1)^3/a^3)^(1/3)`
`syms x y positive` `log(x*y)`	`log(x)+log(y)`
`exp(x) * exp(y)`	`exp(x+y)`
`besselj(2,x) + besselj(0,x)`	`2/x*besselj(1,x)`
`gamma(x+1)-x*gamma(x)`	`0`
`cos(x)^2 + sin(x)^2`	`1`

simple

The `simple` function has the unorthodox mathematical goal of finding a simplification of an expression that has the fewest number of characters. Of course, there is little mathematical justification for claiming that one expression is "simpler" than another just because its ASCII representation is shorter, but this often proves satisfactory in practice.

The `simple` function achieves its goal by independently applying `simplify`, `collect`, `factor`, and other simplification functions to an expression and keeping track of the lengths of the results. The `simple` function then returns the shortest result.

The `simple` function has several forms, each returning different output. The form

```
simple(f)
```

displays each trial simplification and the simplification function that produced it in the MATLAB Command Window. The `simple` function then returns the shortest result. For example, the command

```
simple(cos(x)^2 + sin(x)^2)
```

displays the following alternative simplifications in the MATLAB Command Window:

```
simplify:
1

radsimp:
cos(x)^2+sin(x)^2

combine(trig):
1

factor:
 cos(x)^2+sin(x)^2

expand:
cos(x)^2+sin(x)^2

combine:
1

convert(exp):
 (1/2*exp(i*x)+1/2/exp(i*x))^2-1/4*(exp(i*x)-1/exp(i*x))^2

convert(sincos):
cos(x)^2+sin(x)^2

convert(tan):
(1-tan(1/2*x)^2)^2/(1+tan(1/2*x)^2)^2+
4*tan(1/2*x)^2/(1+tan(1/2*x)^2)^2

collect(x):
cos(x)^2+sin(x)^2
```

and returns

```
ans =
1
```

This form is useful when you want to check, for example, whether the shortest form is indeed the simplest. If you are not interested in how `simple` achieves its result, use the form

```
f = simple(f)
```

This form simply returns the shortest expression found. For example, the statement

```
f = simple(cos(x)^2+sin(x)^2)
```

returns

```
f =
1
```

If you want to know which simplification returned the shortest result, use the multiple output form:

```
[F, how] = simple(f)
```

This form returns the shortest result in the first variable and the simplification method used to achieve the result in the second variable. For example, the statement

```
[f, how] = simple(cos(x)^2+sin(x)^2)
```

returns

```
f =
1

how =
combine
```

The `simple` function sometimes improves on the result returned by `simplify`, one of the simplifications that it tries. For example, when applied to the examples given for `simplify`, `simple` returns a simpler (or at least shorter) result in two cases.

f	simplify(f)	simple(f)
`(1/a^3+6/a^2+12/a+8)^(1/3)`	`((2*a+1)^3/a^3)^(1/3)`	`(2*a+1)/a`
`syms x y positive` `log(x*y)`	`log(x)+log(y)`	`log(x*y)`

In some cases, it is advantageous to apply `simple` twice to obtain the effect of two different simplification functions. For example, the statements

```
f = (1/a^3+6/a^2+12/a+8)^(1/3);
simple(simple(f))
```

return

```
2+1/a
```

The first application, `simple(f)`, uses `radsimp` to produce `(2*a+1)/a`; the second application uses `combine(trig)` to transform this to `1/a+2`.

The `simple` function is particularly effective on expressions involving trigonometric functions. Here are some examples.

f	simple(f)
`cos(x)^2+sin(x)^2`	`1`
`2*cos(x)^2-sin(x)^2`	`3*cos(x)^2-1`
`cos(x)^2-sin(x)^2`	`cos(2*x)`
`cos(x)+(-sin(x)^2)^(1/2)`	`cos(x)+i*sin(x)`
`cos(x)+i*sin(x)`	`exp(i*x)`
`cos(3*acos(x))`	`4*x^3-3*x`

Substitutions

There are two functions for symbolic substitution: `subexpr` and `subs`.

subexpr

These commands

```
syms a x
s = solve(x^3+a*x+1)
```

solve the equation `x^3+a*x+1 = 0 for x`:

```
s =
[                            1/6*(-108+12*(12*a^3+81)^(1/2))^(1/3)-2*a/
                                      (-108+12*(12*a^3+81)^(1/2))^(1/3)]
[ -1/12*(-108+12*(12*a^3+81)^(1/2))^(1/3)+a/
      (-108+12*(12*a^3+81)^(1/2))^(1/3)+1/2*i*3^(1/2)*(1/
      6*(-108+12*(12*a^3+81)^(1/2))^(1/3)+2*a/
      (-108+12*(12*a^3+81)^(1/2))^(1/3))]
[ -1/12*(-108+12*(12*a^3+81)^(1/2))^(1/3)+a/
      (-108+12*(12*a^3+81)^(1/2))^(1/3)-1/2*i*3^(1/2)*(1/
      6*(-108+12*(12*a^3+81)^(1/2))^(1/3)+2*a/
      (-108+12*(12*a^3+81)^(1/2))^(1/3))]
```

Use the `pretty` function to display s in a more readable form:

```
pretty(s)

s =
        [                          1/3      a                 ]
        [                    1/6 %1    - 2 -----              ]
        [                                   1/3               ]
        [                                 %1                  ]
        [                                                     ]
        [         1/3     a              1/2 /      1/3      a \]
        [- 1/12 %1    + ----- + 1/2 i 3    |1/6 %1    + 2 -----|]
        [                 1/3              |               1/3|]
        [               %1                 \             %1    /]
        [                                                     ]
        [         1/3     a              1/2 /      1/3      a \]
        [- 1/12 %1    + ----- - 1/2 i 3    |1/6 %1    + 2 -----|]
        [                 1/3              |               1/3|]
        [               %1                 \             %1    /]

                                                3      1/2
                          %1 := -108 + 12 (12 a  + 81)
```

The `pretty` command inherits the `%n` (`n`, an integer) notation from Maple to denote subexpressions that occur multiple times in the symbolic object. The `subexpr` function allows you to save these common subexpressions as well as the symbolic object rewritten in terms of the subexpressions. The subexpressions are saved in a column vector called `sigma`.

Continuing with the example

```
r = subexpr(s)
```

returns

```
sigma =
-108+12*(12*a^3+81)^(1/2)
r =
[                               1/6*sigma^(1/3)-2*a/sigma^(1/3)]
[ -1/12*sigma^(1/3)+a/sigma^(1/3)+1/2*i*3^(1/2)*(1/6*sigma^
     (1/3)+2*a/sigma^(1/3))]
```

```
[ -1/12*sigma^(1/3)+a/sigma^(1/3)-1/2*i*3^(1/2)*(1/6*sigma^
     (1/3)+2*a/sigma^(1/3))]
```

Notice that `subexpr` creates the variable `sigma` in the MATLAB workspace. You can verify this by typing `whos`, or the command

```
sigma
```

which returns

```
sigma =
-108+12*(12*a^3+81)^(1/2)
```

subs

The following code finds the eigenvalues and eigenvectors of a circulant matrix A:

```
syms a b c
A = [a b c; b c a; c a b];
[v,E] = eig(A)

v =

[ -(a+(b^2-b*a-c*b-c*a+a^2+c^2)^(1/2)-b)/(a-c),
          -(a-(b^2-b*a-c*b-c*a+a^2+c^2)^(1/2)-b)/(a-c),   1]
[ -(b-c-(b^2-b*a-c*b-c*a+a^2+c^2)^(1/2))/(a-c),
          -(b-c+(b^2-b*a-c*b-c*a+a^2+c^2)^(1/2))/(a-c),   1]
[ 1,
         1,                                               1]


E =

[ (b^2-b*a-c*b-
   c*a+a^2+c^2)^(1/2),                    0,            0]
[                  0,    -(b^2-b*a-c*b-
                         c*a+a^2+c^2)^(1/2),            0]
[                  0,                     0,        b+c+a]
```

Note MATLAB might return the eigenvalues that appear on the diagonal of E in a different order. In this case, the corresponding eigenvectors, which are the columns of v, will also appear in a different order.

Suppose you want to replace the rather lengthy expression

```
(b^2-b*a-c*b-c*a+a^2+c^2)^(1/2)
```

throughout v and E. First, use subexpr

```
v = subexpr(v,'S')
```

which returns

```
S =
(b^2-b*a-c*b-c*a+a^2+c^2)^(1/2)

v =
[ -(a+S-b)/(a-c), -(a-S-b)/(a-c),                1]
[ -(b-c-S)/(a-c), -(b-c+S)/(a-c),                1]
[              1,              1,                1]
```

Next, substitute the symbol S into E with

```
E = subs(E,S,'S')

E =
[     S,      0,      0]
[     0,     -S,      0]
[     0,      0, b+c+a]
```

Now suppose you want to evaluate v at a = 10. You can do this using the subs command:

```
subs(v,a,10)
```

This replaces all occurrences of a in v with 10.

```
[ -(10+S-b)/(10-c), -(10-S-b)/(10-c),                1]
[  -(b-c-S)/(10-c),  -(b-c+S)/(10-c),                1]
[                1,                1,                1]
```

Notice, however, that the symbolic expression that S represents is unaffected by this substitution. That is, the symbol a in S is not replaced by 10. The subs command is also a useful function for substituting in a variety of values for several variables in a particular expression. For example, suppose that in addition to substituting a = 10 in S, you also want to substitute the values for 2 and 10 for b and c, respectively. The way to do this is to set values for a, b, and c in the workspace. Then subs evaluates its input using the existing symbolic and double variables in the current workspace. In the example, you first set

```
a = 10; b = 2; c = 10;
subs(S)

ans =
8
```

To look at the contents of the workspace, type whos, which gives

```
Name      Size          Bytes  Class

A         3x3             878  sym object
E         3x3             888  sym object
S         1x1             186  sym object
a         1x1               8  double array
ans       1x1             140  sym object
b         1x1               8  double array
c         1x1               8  double array
v         3x3             982  sym object
```

a, b, and c are now variables of class double while A, E, S, and v remain symbolic expressions (class sym).

If you want to preserve a, b, and c as symbolic variables, but still alter their value within S, use this procedure.

```
syms a b c
subs(S,{a,b,c},{10,2,10})

ans =
8
```

Typing whos reveals that a, b, and c remain 1-by-1 sym objects.

The `subs` command can be combined with `double` to evaluate a symbolic expression numerically. Suppose you have the following expressions

```
syms t
M = (1-t^2)*exp(-1/2*t^2);
P = (1-t^2)*sech(t);
```

and want to see how `M` and `P` differ graphically.

One approach is to type

```
ezplot(M); hold on; ezplot(P); hold off;
```

but this plot does not readily help us identify the curves.

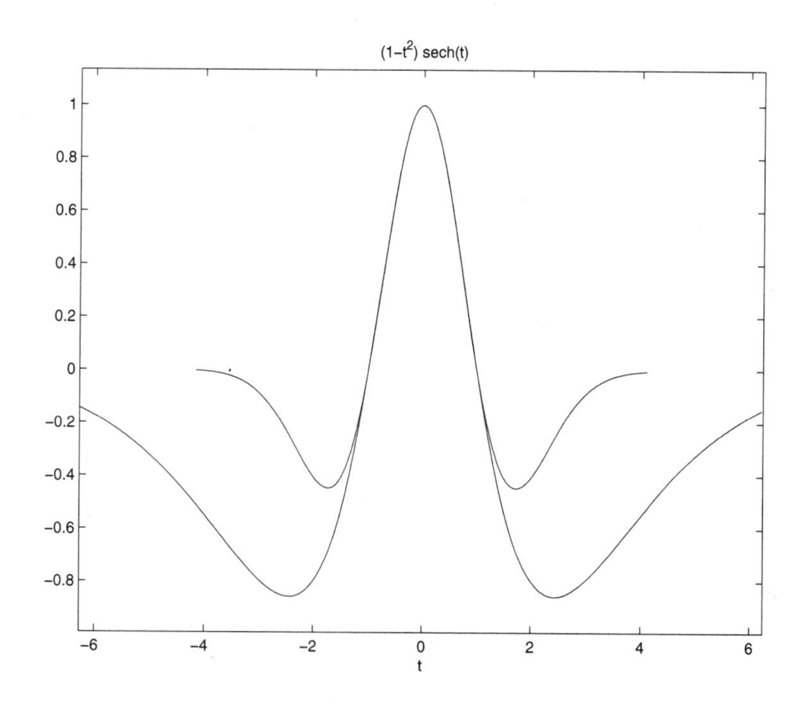

Instead, combine subs, double, and plot

```
T = -6:0.05:6;
MT = double(subs(M,t,T));
PT = double(subs(P,t,T));
plot(T,MT,'b',T,PT,'r-.')
title(' ')
legend('M','P')
xlabel('t'); grid
```

to produce a multicolored graph that indicates the difference between M and P.

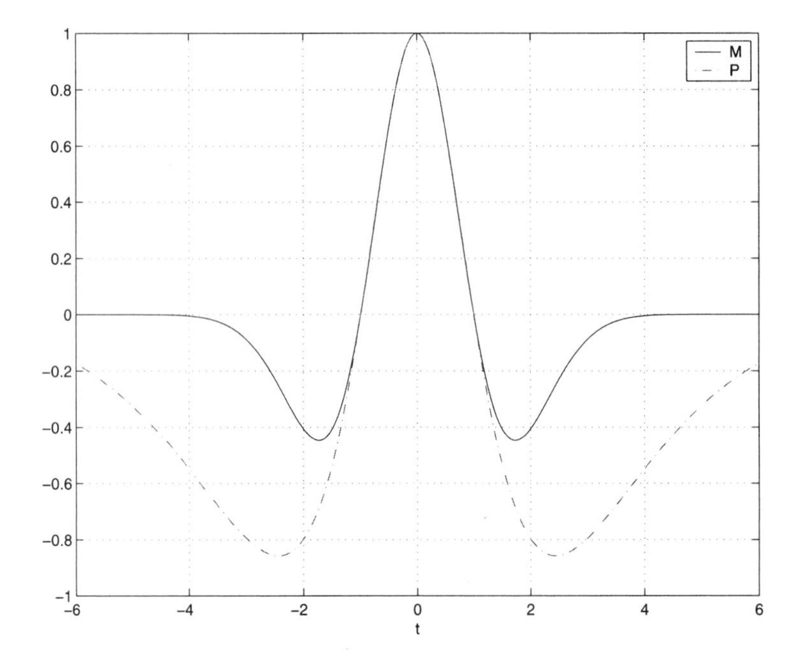

Finally the use of subs with strings greatly facilitates the solution of problems involving the Fourier, Laplace, or z-transforms.

Variable-Precision Arithmetic

Overview

There are three different kinds of arithmetic operations in this toolbox:

Numeric	MATLAB floating-point arithmetic
Rational	Maple's exact symbolic arithmetic
VPA	Maple's variable-precision arithmetic

For example, the MATLAB statements

```
format long
1/2+1/3
```

use numeric computation to produce

```
0.83333333333333
```

With the Symbolic Math Toolbox, the statement

```
sym(1/2)+1/3
```

uses symbolic computation to yield

```
5/6
```

And, also with the toolbox, the statements

```
digits(25)
vpa('1/2+1/3')
```

use variable-precision arithmetic to return

```
.8333333333333333333333333
```

The floating-point operations used by numeric arithmetic are the fastest of the three, and require the least computer memory, but the results are not exact. The number of digits in the printed output of MATLAB double quantities is controlled by the `format` statement, but the internal representation is always the eight-byte floating-point representation provided by the particular computer hardware.

In the computation of the numeric result above, there are actually three roundoff errors, one in the division of 1 by 3, one in the addition of 1/2 to the result of the division, and one in the binary to decimal conversion for the printed output. On computers that use IEEE floating-point standard arithmetic, the resulting internal value is the binary expansion of 5/6, truncated to 53 bits. This is approximately 16 decimal digits. But, in this particular case, the printed output shows only 15 digits.

The symbolic operations used by rational arithmetic are potentially the most expensive of the three, in terms of both computer time and memory. The results are exact, as long as enough time and memory are available to complete the computations.

Variable-precision arithmetic falls in between the other two in terms of both cost and accuracy. A global parameter, set by the function `digits`, controls the number of significant decimal digits. Increasing the number of digits increases the accuracy, but also increases both the time and memory requirements. The default value of `digits` is 32, corresponding roughly to floating-point accuracy.

The Maple documentation uses the term "hardware floating-point" for what you are calling "numeric" or "floating-point" and uses the term "floating-point arithmetic" for what you are calling "variable-precision arithmetic."

Example: Using the Different Kinds of Arithmetic

Rational Arithmetic

By default, the Symbolic Math Toolbox uses rational arithmetic operations, i.e., Maple's exact symbolic arithmetic. Rational arithmetic is invoked when you create symbolic variables using the `sym` function.

The `sym` function converts a double matrix to its symbolic form. For example, if the double matrix is

```
A =
1.1000     1.2000     1.3000
2.1000     2.2000     2.3000
3.1000     3.2000     3.3000
```

its symbolic form, `S = sym(A)`, is

```
S =
[11/10,  6/5, 13/10]
[21/10, 11/5, 23/10]
[31/10, 16/5, 33/10]
```

For this matrix `A`, it is possible to discover that the elements are the ratios of small integers, so the symbolic representation is formed from those integers. On the other hand, the statement

```
E = [exp(1) (1+sqrt(5))/2; log(3) rand]
```

returns a matrix

```
E =
    2.71828182845905    1.61803398874989
    1.09861228866811    0.76209683302739
```

whose elements are not the ratios of small integers, so `sym(E)` reproduces the floating-point representation in a symbolic form:

```
ans =
[ 6121026514868074*2^(-51), 7286977268806824*2^(-52)]
[ 4947709893870346*2^(-52), 6864358026484820*2^(-53)]
```

Variable-Precision Numbers

Variable-precision numbers are distinguished from the exact rational representation by the presence of a decimal point. A power of 10 scale factor, denoted by `'e'`, is allowed. To use variable-precision instead of rational arithmetic, create your variables using the `vpa` function.

For matrices with purely double entries, the `vpa` function generates the representation that is used with variable-precision arithmetic. For example, if you apply `vpa` to the matrix `S` defined in the preceding section, with `digits(4)`, by entering

```
vpa(S)
```

MATLAB returns the output

```
S =
[1.100, 1.200, 1.300]
[2.100, 2.200, 2.300]
[3.100, 3.200, 3.300]
```

Applying `vpa` to the matrix `E` defined in the preceding section, with `digits(25)`, by entering

```
digits(25)
F = vpa(E)
```

returns

```
F =
[2.718281828459045534884808, 1.414213562373094923430017]
[1.098612288668110004152823, .2189591863280899719512718]
```

Converting to Floating-Point

To convert a rational or variable-precision number to its MATLAB floating-point representation, use the `double` function.

In the example, both `double(sym(E))` and `double(vpa(E))` return `E`.

Another Example

The next example is perhaps more interesting. Start with the symbolic expression

```
f = sym('exp(pi*sqrt(163))')
```

The statement

```
double(f)
```

produces the printed floating-point value

```
ans =
     2.625374126407687e+017
```

Using the second argument of vpa to specify the number of digits,

```
vpa(f,18)
```

returns

```
262537412640768744.
```

whereas

```
vpa(f,25)
```

returns

```
262537412640768744.0000000
```

you suspect that f might actually have an integer value. This suspicion is reinforced by the 30 digit value, vpa(f,30)

```
262537412640768743.999999999999
```

Finally, the 40 digit value, vpa(f,40)

```
262537412640768743.9999999999992500725944
```

shows that f is very close to, but not exactly equal to, an integer.

Linear Algebra

Basic Algebraic Operations

Basic algebraic operations on symbolic objects are the same as operations on MATLAB objects of class double. This is illustrated in the following example.

The Givens transformation produces a plane rotation through the angle t. The statements

```
syms t;
G = [cos(t) sin(t); -sin(t) cos(t)]
```

create this transformation matrix.

```
G =
[  cos(t),  sin(t) ]
[ -sin(t),  cos(t) ]
```

Applying the Givens transformation twice should simply be a rotation through twice the angle. The corresponding matrix can be computed by multiplying G by itself or by raising G to the second power. Both

```
A = G*G
```

and

```
A = G^2
```

produce

```
A =
[cos(t)^2-sin(t)^2,    2*cos(t)*sin(t)]
[ -2*cos(t)*sin(t), cos(t)^2-sin(t)^2]
```

The simple function

```
A = simple(A)
```

uses a trigonometric identity to return the expected form by trying several different identities and picking the one that produces the shortest representation.

```
A =
[ cos(2*t), sin(2*t)]
[-sin(2*t), cos(2*t)]
```

The Givens rotation is an orthogonal matrix, so its transpose is its inverse. Confirming this by

```
I = G.' *G
```

which produces

```
I =
[cos(t)^2+sin(t)^2,                 0]
[                0, cos(t)^2+sin(t)^2]
```

and then

```
I = simple(I)
I =
[1, 0]
[0, 1]
```

Linear Algebraic Operations

The following examples show to do several basic linear algebraic operations using the Symbolic Math Toolbox.

The command

```
H = hilb(3)
```

generates the 3-by-3 Hilbert matrix. With `format short`, MATLAB prints

```
H =
1.0000    0.5000    0.3333
0.5000    0.3333    0.2500
0.3333    0.2500    0.2000
```

The computed elements of `H` are floating-point numbers that are the ratios of small integers. Indeed, `H` is a MATLAB array of class `double`. Converting `H` to a symbolic matrix

```
H = sym(H)
```

gives

```
[   1, 1/2, 1/3]
[1/2, 1/3, 1/4]
[1/3, 1/4, 1/5]
```

This allows subsequent symbolic operations on `H` to produce results that correspond to the infinitely precise Hilbert matrix, `sym(hilb(3))`, not its floating-point approximation, `hilb(3)`. Therefore,

```
inv(H)
```

produces

```
[  9,  -36,   30]
[-36,  192, -180]
[ 30, -180,  180]
```

and

```
det(H)
```

yields

```
1/2160
```

You can use the backslash operator to solve a system of simultaneous linear equations. For example, the commands

```
b = [1 1 1]'
x = H\b    % Solve Hx = b
```

produce the solution

```
[  3]
[-24]
[ 30]
```

All three of these results, the inverse, the determinant, and the solution to the linear system, are the exact results corresponding to the infinitely precise, rational, Hilbert matrix. On the other hand, using `digits(16)`, the command

```
V = vpa(hilb(3))
```

returns

```
[                1., .5000000000000000, .3333333333333333]
[.5000000000000000, .3333333333333333, .2500000000000000]
[.3333333333333333, .2500000000000000, .2000000000000000]
```

The decimal points in the representation of the individual elements are the signal to use variable-precision arithmetic. The result of each arithmetic operation is rounded to 16 significant decimal digits. When inverting the matrix, these errors are magnified by the matrix condition number, which for `hilb(3)` is about 500. Consequently,

```
inv(V)
```

which returns

```
ans =
[  9.000000000000179, -36.00000000000080,  30.00000000000067]
[ -36.00000000000080,  192.0000000000042, -180.0000000000040]
[  30.00000000000067, -180.0000000000040,  180.0000000000038]
```

shows the loss of two digits. So does

```
det(V)
```

which gives

```
.462962962962953e-3
```

and

```
V\b
```

which is

```
[ 3.000000000000041]
[-24.00000000000021]
[ 30.00000000000019]
```

Since `H` is nonsingular, calculating the null space of `H` with the command

```
null(H)
```

returns an empty matrix, and calculating the column space of `H` with

```
colspace(H)
```

returns a permutation of the identity matrix. A more interesting example, which the following code shows, is to find a value `s` for `H(1,1)` that makes `H` singular. The commands

```
syms s
H(1,1) = s
Z = det(H)
sol = solve(Z)
```

produce

```
H =
[   s, 1/2, 1/3]
[1/2, 1/3, 1/4]
[1/3, 1/4, 1/5]

Z =
1/240*s-1/270

sol =
8/9
```

Then

```
H = subs(H,s,sol)
```

substitutes the computed value of `sol` for `s` in `H` to give

```
H =
[8/9, 1/2, 1/3]
[1/2, 1/3, 1/4]
[1/3, 1/4, 1/5]
```

Now, the command

```
det(H)
```

returns

```
ans =
0
```

and

```
inv(H)
```

produces an error message

```
??? error using ==> inv
Error, (in inverse) singular matrix
```

because `H` is singular. For this matrix, `Z = null(H)` and `C = colspace(H)` are nontrivial:

```
Z =
[    1]
[   -4]
[10/3]

C =
[      1,      0]
[      0,      1]
[ -3/10,    6/5]
```

It should be pointed out that even though `H` is singular, `vpa(H)` is not. For any integer value `d`, setting

```
digits(d)
```

and then computing

```
det(vpa(H))
inv(vpa(H))
```

results in a determinant of size `10^(-d)` and an inverse with elements on the order of `10^d`.

Eigenvalues

The symbolic eigenvalues of a square matrix `A` or the symbolic eigenvalues and eigenvectors of `A` are computed, respectively, using the commands

```
E = eig(A)
[V,E] = eig(A)
```

The variable-precision counterparts are

```
E = eig(vpa(A))
[V,E] = eig(vpa(A))
```

The eigenvalues of A are the zeros of the characteristic polynomial of A, det(A-x*I), which is computed by

```
poly(A)
```

The matrix H from the last section provides the first example:

```
H =
[8/9, 1/2, 1/3]
[1/2, 1/3, 1/4]
[1/3, 1/4, 1/5]
```

The matrix is singular, so one of its eigenvalues must be zero. The statement

```
[T,E] = eig(H)
```

produces the matrices T and E. The columns of T are the eigenvectors of H:

```
T =

[    1, 28/153+2/153*12589^(1/2),  28/153-2/153*12589^(12)]
[   -4,                        1,                        1]
[ 10/3, 92/255-1/255*12589^(1/2), 292/255+1/255*12589^(12)]
```

Similarly, the diagonal elements of E are the eigenvalues of H:

```
E =

[0,                        0,                        0]
[0, 32/45+1/180*12589^(1/2),                         0]
[0,                        0, 32/45-1/180*12589^(1/2)]
```

It may be easier to understand the structure of the matrices of eigenvectors, T, and eigenvalues, E, if you convert T and E to decimal notation. To do so, proceed as follows. The commands

```
Td = double(T)
Ed = double(E)
```

return

```
Td =
     1.0000    1.6497   -1.2837
    -4.0000    1.0000    1.0000
     3.3333    0.7051    1.5851
```

```
Ed =
     0          0          0
     0     1.3344          0
     0          0     0.0878
```

The first eigenvalue is zero. The corresponding eigenvector (the first column of `Td`) is the same as the basis for the null space found in the last section. The other two eigenvalues are the result of applying the quadratic formula to

```
x^2-64/45*x+253/2160
```

which is the quadratic factor in `factor(poly(H))`.

```
syms x
g = simple(factor(poly(H))/x);
solve(g)

ans =
[ 32/45+1/180*12589^(1/2)]
[ 32/45-1/180*12589^(1/2)]
```

Closed form symbolic expressions for the eigenvalues are possible only when the characteristic polynomial can be expressed as a product of rational polynomials of degree four or less. The Rosser matrix is a classic numerical analysis test matrix that illustrates this requirement. The statement

```
R = sym(gallery('rosser'))
```

generates

```
 R =
[ 611   196  -192   407    -8   -52   -49    29]
[ 196   899   113  -192   -71   -43    -8   -44]
[-192   113   899   196    61    49     8    52]
[ 407  -192   196   611     8    44    59   -23]
[  -8   -71    61     8   411  -599   208   208]
[ -52   -43    49    44  -599   411   208   208]
[ -49    -8     8    59   208   208    99  -911]
[  29   -44    52   -23   208   208  -911    99]
```

The commands

```
p = poly(R);
pretty(factor(p))
```

produce

```
                   2                     2                      2
x (x - 1020) (x  - 1020 x + 100)(x  - 1040500) (x - 1000)
```

The characteristic polynomial (of degree 8) factors nicely into the product of two linear terms and three quadratic terms. You can see immediately that four of the eigenvalues are 0, 1020, and a double root at 1000. The other four roots are obtained from the remaining quadratics. Use

```
eig(R)
```

to find all these values

```
ans =
[                  0]
[               1020]
[    10*10405^(1/2)]
[   -10*10405^(1/2)]
[ 510+100*26^(1/2)]
[ 510-100*26^(1/2)]
[               1000]
[               1000]
```

The Rosser matrix is not a typical example; it is rare for a full 8-by-8 matrix to have a characteristic polynomial that factors into such simple form. If you change the two “corner” elements of R from 29 to 30 with the commands

```
S = R;  S(1,8) = 30;  S(8,1) = 30;
```

and then try

```
p = poly(S)
```

you find

```
p =
 x^8-4040*x^7+5079941*x^6+82706090*x^5-5327831918568*x^4+
4287832912719760*x^3-1082699388411166000*x^2+51264008540948000*x
+40250968213600000
```

You also find that `factor(p)` is `p` itself. That is, the characteristic polynomial cannot be factored over the rationals.

For this modified Rosser matrix

```
F = eig(S)
```

returns

```
F =
[   .21803980548301606860857564424981]
[  999.94691786044276755320289228602]
[  1000.1206982933841335712817075454]
[  1019.5243552632016358324933278291]
[  1019.9935501291629257348091808173]
[  1020.4201882015047278185457498840]
[ -.17053529728768998575200874607757]
[ -1020.0532142558915165931894252600]
```

Notice that these values are close to the eigenvalues of the original Rosser matrix. Further, the numerical values of F are a result of Maple's floating-point arithmetic. Consequently, different settings of digits do not alter the number of digits to the right of the decimal place.

It is also possible to try to compute eigenvalues of symbolic matrices, but closed form solutions are rare. The Givens transformation is generated as the matrix exponential of the elementary matrix

$$A = \begin{bmatrix} 0 & 1 \\ -1 & 0 \end{bmatrix}$$

The Symbolic Math Toolbox commands

```
syms t
A = sym([0 1; -1 0]);
G = expm(t*A)
```

return

```
[  cos(t),  sin(t)]
[ -sin(t),  cos(t)]
```

Next, the command

```
g = eig(G)
```

produces

```
g =
[ cos(t)+(cos(t)^2-1)^(1/2)]
[ cos(t)-(cos(t)^2-1)^(1/2)]
```

you can use `simple` to simplify this form of `g`. Indeed, a repeated application of `simple`

```
for  j = 1:4
   [g,how] = simple(g)
end
```

produces the best result:

```
g =
[ cos(t)+(-sin(t)^2)^(1/2)]
[ cos(t)-(-sin(t)^2)^(1/2)]

how =
mwcos2sin

g =
[ cos(t)+i*sin(t)]
[ cos(t)-i*sin(t)]

how =
radsimp

g =
[   exp(i*t)]
[ 1/exp(i*t)]

how =
convert(exp)

g =
[  exp(i*t)]
[ exp(-i*t)]

how =
simplify
```

Notice the first application of `simple` uses `mwcos2sin` to produce a sum of sines and cosines. Next, `simple` invokes `radsimp` to produce `cos(t) + i*sin(t)` for the first eigenvector. The third application of `simple` uses `convert(exp)` to change the sines and cosines to complex exponentials. The last application of `simple` uses `simplify` to obtain the final form.

Jordan Canonical Form

The Jordan canonical form results from attempts to diagonalize a matrix by a similarity transformation. For a given matrix `A`, find a nonsingular matrix `V`, so that `inv(V)*A*V`, or, more succinctly, `J = V\A*V`, is "as close to diagonal as possible." For almost all matrices, the Jordan canonical form is the diagonal matrix of eigenvalues and the columns of the transformation matrix are the eigenvectors. This always happens if the matrix is symmetric or if it has distinct eigenvalues. Some nonsymmetric matrices with multiple eigenvalues cannot be diagonalized. The Jordan form has the eigenvalues on its diagonal, but some of the superdiagonal elements are one, instead of zero. The statement

```
J = jordan(A)
```

computes the Jordan canonical form of `A`. The statement

```
[V,J] = jordan(A)
```

also computes the similarity transformation. The columns of `V` are the generalized eigenvectors of `A`.

The Jordan form is extremely sensitive to perturbations. Almost any change in `A` causes its Jordan form to be diagonal. This makes it very difficult to compute the Jordan form reliably with floating-point arithmetic. It also implies that `A` must be known exactly (i.e., without round-off error, etc.). Its elements must be integers, or ratios of small integers. In particular, the variable-precision calculation, `jordan(vpa(A))`, is not allowed.

For example, let

```
A = sym([12,32,66,116;-25,-76,-164,-294;
          21,66,143,256;-6,-19,-41,-73])
A =
[   12,   32,   66,  116]
[  -25,  -76, -164, -294]
[   21,   66,  143,  256]
[   -6,  -19,  -41,  -73]
```

Then

```
[V,J] = jordan(A)
```

produces

```
V =
[   4,   -2,    4,    3]
[  -6,    8,  -11,   -8]
[   4,   -7,   10,    7]
[  -1,    2,   -3,   -2]

J =
[ 1, 1, 0, 0]
[ 0, 1, 0, 0]
[ 0, 0, 2, 1]
[ 0, 0, 0, 2]
```

Therefore A has a double eigenvalue at 1, with a single Jordan block, and a double eigenvalue at 2, also with a single Jordan block. The matrix has only two eigenvectors, V(:,1) and V(:,3). They satisfy

```
A*V(:,1) = 1*V(:,1)
A*V(:,3) = 2*V(:,3)
```

The other two columns of V are generalized eigenvectors of grade 2. They satisfy

```
A*V(:,2) = 1*V(:,2) + V(:,1)
A*V(:,4) = 2*V(:,4) + V(:,3)
```

In mathematical notation, with $\mathbf{v}_j$ = v(:,j), the columns of V and eigenvalues satisfy the relationships

$$(A - \lambda_1 I)v_2 = v_1$$

$$(A - \lambda_2 I)v_4 = v_3$$

Singular Value Decomposition

Only the variable-precision numeric computation of the complete singular vector decomposition is available in the toolbox. One reason for this is that the formulas that result from symbolic computation are usually too long and complicated to be of much use. If A is a symbolic matrix of floating-point or variable-precision numbers, then

```
S = svd(A)
```

computes the singular values of A to an accuracy determined by the current setting of digits. And

```
[U,S,V] = svd(A);
```

produces two orthogonal matrices, U and V, and a diagonal matrix, S, so that

```
A = U*S*V';
```

Consider the n-by-n matrix A with elements defined by

```
A(i,j) = 1/(i-j+1/2)
```

For n = 5, the matrix is

```
[  2    -2   -2/3   -2/5   -2/7]
[2/3     2     -2   -2/3   -2/5]
[2/5   2/3      2     -2   -2/3]
[2/7   2/5    2/3      2     -2]
[2/9   2/7    2/5    2/3      2]
```

It turns out many of the singular values of these matrices are close to π.

The most obvious way of generating this matrix is

```
for i=1:n
    for j=1:n
      A(i,j) = sym(1/(i-j+1/2));
   end
end
```

The most efficient way to generate the matrix is

```
[J,I] = meshgrid(1:n);
A = sym(1./(I - J+1/2));
```

Since the elements of A are the ratios of small integers, vpa(A) produces a variable-precision representation, which is accurate to digits precision. Hence

```
S = svd(vpa(A))
```

computes the desired singular values to full accuracy. With `n = 16` and `digits(30)`, the result is

```
S =
[ 1.20968137605668985332455685357 ]
[ 2.69162158686066606774782763594 ]
[ 3.07790297231119748658424727354 ]
[ 3.13504054399744654843898901261 ]
[ 3.14106044663470063805218371924 ]
[ 3.14155754359918083691050658260 ]
[ 3.14159075458605848728982577119 ]
[ 3.14159256925492306470284863102 ]
[ 3.14159265052654880815569479613 ]
[ 3.14159265349961053143856838564 ]
[ 3.14159265358767361712392612384 ]
[ 3.14159265358975439206849907220 ]
[ 3.14159265358979270342635559051 ]
[ 3.14159265358979323325290142781 ]
[ 3.14159265358979323843066846712 ]
[ 3.14159265358979323846255035974 ]
```

There are two ways to compare `S` with `pi`, the floating-point representation of π. In the vector below, the first element is computed by subtraction with variable-precision arithmetic and then converted to a `double`. The second element is computed with floating-point arithmetic:

```
format short e
[double(pi*ones(16,1)-S)  pi-double(S)]
```

The results are

```
1.9319e+00   1.9319e+00
4.4997e-01   4.4997e-01
6.3690e-02   6.3690e-02
6.5521e-03   6.5521e-03
5.3221e-04   5.3221e-04
3.5110e-05   3.5110e-05
1.8990e-06   1.8990e-06
8.4335e-08   8.4335e-08
3.0632e-09   3.0632e-09
9.0183e-11   9.0183e-11
2.1196e-12   2.1196e-12
3.8846e-14   3.8636e-14
5.3504e-16   4.4409e-16
5.2097e-18            0
3.1975e-20            0
9.3024e-23            0
```

Since the relative accuracy of `pi` is `pi*eps`, which is `6.9757e-16`, either column confirms the suspicion that four of the singular values of the `16`-by-`16` example equal π to floating-point accuracy.

Eigenvalue Trajectories

This example applies several numeric, symbolic, and graphic techniques to study the behavior of matrix eigenvalues as a parameter in the matrix is varied. This particular setting involves numerical analysis and perturbation theory, but the techniques illustrated are more widely applicable.

In this example, you consider a 3-by-3 matrix A whose eigenvalues are 1, 2, 3. First, you perturb A by another matrix E and parameter t: $A \to A + tE$. As t increases from 0 to 10^{-6}, the eigenvalues $\lambda_1 = 1$, $\lambda_2 = 2$, $\lambda_3 = 3$ change to $\lambda_1' \approx 1.5596 + 0.2726i$, $\lambda_2' \approx 1.5596 - 0.2726i$, $\lambda_3' \approx 2.8808$.

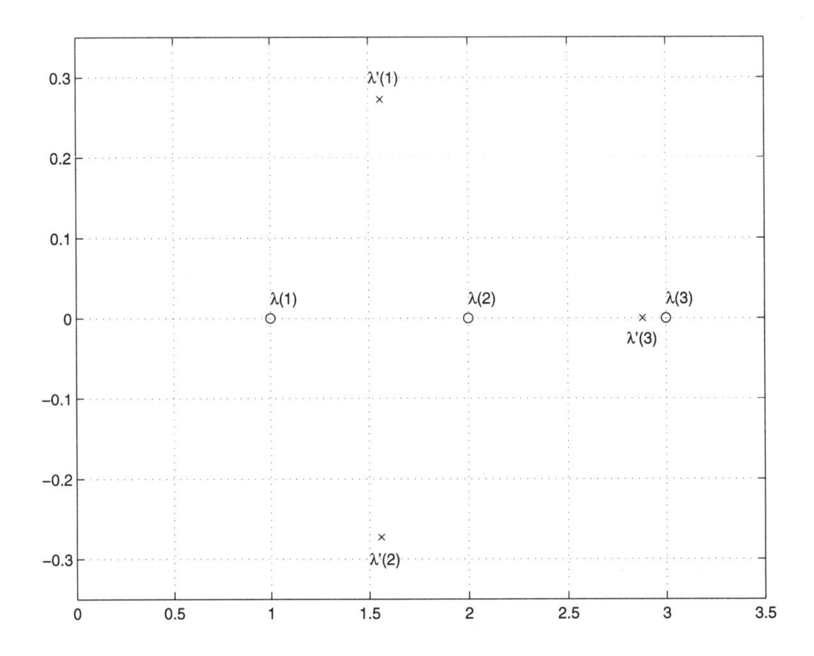

This, in turn, means that for some value of $t = \tau, 0 < \tau < 10^{-6}$, the perturbed matrix $A(t) = A + tE$ has a double eigenvalue $\lambda_1 = \lambda_2$. The example shows how to find the value of t, called τ, where this happens.

The starting point is a MATLAB test example, known as `gallery(3)`.

```
A = gallery(3)
A =
   -149      -50     -154
    537      180      546
    -27       -9      -25
```

This is an example of a matrix whose eigenvalues are sensitive to the effects of roundoff errors introduced during their computation. The actual computed eigenvalues may vary from one machine to another, but on a typical workstation, the statements

```
format long
e = eig(A)
```

produce

```
e =
    1.00000000001122
    1.99999999999162
    2.99999999999700
```

Of course, the example was created so that its eigenvalues are actually 1, 2, and 3. Note that three or four digits have been lost to roundoff. This can be easily verified with the toolbox. The statements

```
B = sym(A);
e = eig(B)'
p = poly(B)
f = factor(p)
```

produce

```
e =
[1,  2,  3]

p =
x^3-6*x^2+11*x-6

f =
(x-1)*(x-2)*(x-3)
```

Are the eigenvalues sensitive to the perturbations caused by roundoff error because they are "close together"? Ordinarily, the values 1, 2, and 3 would be regarded as "well separated." But, in this case, the separation should be viewed on the scale of the original matrix. If `A` were replaced by `A/1000`, the eigenvalues, which would be .001, .002, .003, would "seem" to be closer together.

But eigenvalue sensitivity is more subtle than just "closeness." With a carefully chosen perturbation of the matrix, it is possible to make two of its eigenvalues coalesce into an actual double root that is extremely sensitive to roundoff and other errors.

One good perturbation direction can be obtained from the outer product of the left and right eigenvectors associated with the most sensitive eigenvalue. The following statement creates

```
E = [130,-390,0;43,-129,0;133,-399,0]
```

the perturbation matrix

```
E =
130   -390      0
 43   -129      0
133   -399      0
```

The perturbation can now be expressed in terms of a single, scalar parameter t. The statements

```
syms x t
A = A+t*E
```

replace A with the symbolic representation of its perturbation:

```
A =
[-149+130*t, -50-390*t, -154]
[  537+43*t, 180-129*t,  546]
[ -27+133*t,   -9-399*t,  -25]
```

Computing the characteristic polynomial of this new A

```
p = poly(A)
```

gives

```
p =
x^3-6*x^2+11*x-t*x^2+492512*t*x-6-1221271*t
```

Prettyprinting

```
pretty(collect(p,x))
```

shows more clearly that p is a cubic in x whose coefficients vary linearly with t.

```
  3                 2
 x  + (- t - 6) x  + (492512 t + 11) x - 6 - 1221271 t
```

It turns out that when `t` is varied over a very small interval, from 0 to 1.0e-6, the desired double root appears. This can best be seen graphically. The first figure shows plots of `p`, considered as a function of `x`, for three different values of `t`: `t` = 0, `t` = 0.5e-6, and `t` = 1.0e-6. For each value, the eigenvalues are computed numerically and also plotted:

```
x = .8:.01:3.2;
for k = 0:2
  c = sym2poly(subs(p,t,k*0.5e-6));
  y = polyval(c,x);
  lambda = eig(double(subs(A,t,k*0.5e-6)));
  subplot(3,1,3-k)
  plot(x,y,'-',x,0*x,':',lambda,0*lambda,'o')
  axis([.8 3.2 -.5 .5])
  text(2.25,.35,['t = ' num2str( k*0.5e-6 )]);
end
```

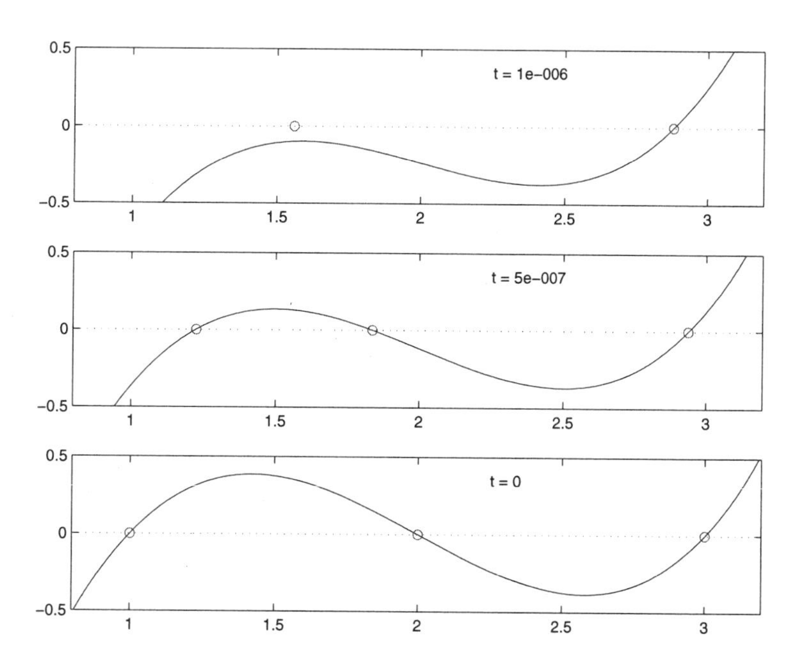

The bottom subplot shows the unperturbed polynomial, with its three roots at 1, 2, and 3. The middle subplot shows the first two roots approaching each other. In the top subplot, these two roots have become complex and only one real root remains.

The next statements compute and display the actual eigenvalues

```
e = eig(A);
pretty(e)
```

showing that `e(2)` and `e(3)` form a complex conjugate pair:

```
[                                                  2           ]
[        1/3       492508/3 t - 1/3 - 1/9 t                    ]
[1/3 %1      - 3 ------------------------ + 1/3 t + 2]
[                                      1/3                     ]
[                                    %1                        ]

[                                                  2
[          1/3       492508/3 t - 1/3 - 1/9 t
[- 1/6 %1      + 3/2 ------------------------ + 1/3 t + 2
[                                      1/3
[                                    %1

                 /                                         2\]
            1/2 |        1/3      492508/3 t - 1/3 - 1/9 t |]
 + 1/2 I 3      |1/3 %1      + 3 ------------------------|]
                |                                  1/3      |]
                \                                %1         /]

[                                                  2
[          1/3       492508/3 t - 1/3 - 1/9 t
[- 1/6 %1      + 3/2 ------------------------ + 1/3 t + 2
[                                      1/3
[                                    %1

                 /                                         2\]
            1/2 |        1/3      492508/3 t - 1/3 - 1/9 t |]
 - 1/2 I 3      |1/3 %1      + 3 ------------------------|]
                |                                  1/3      |]
                \                                %1         /]
```

```
                            2                     3                          3
%1 := -2216286 t  + 3189393 t + t  + 3 (358392752910068940 t

                                  2                    4                    1/2
       - 1052829647418 t  - 181922388795 t  + 4432572 t - 3)
```

Next, the symbolic representations of the three eigenvalues are evaluated at many values of t

```
tvals = (2:-.02:0)' * 1.e-6;
r = size(tvals,1);
c = size(e,1);
lambda = zeros(r,c);
for k = 1:c
   lambda(:,k) = double(subs(e(k),t,tvals));
end
plot(lambda,tvals)
xlabel('\lambda'); ylabel('t');
title('Eigenvalue Transition')
```

to produce a plot of their trajectories.

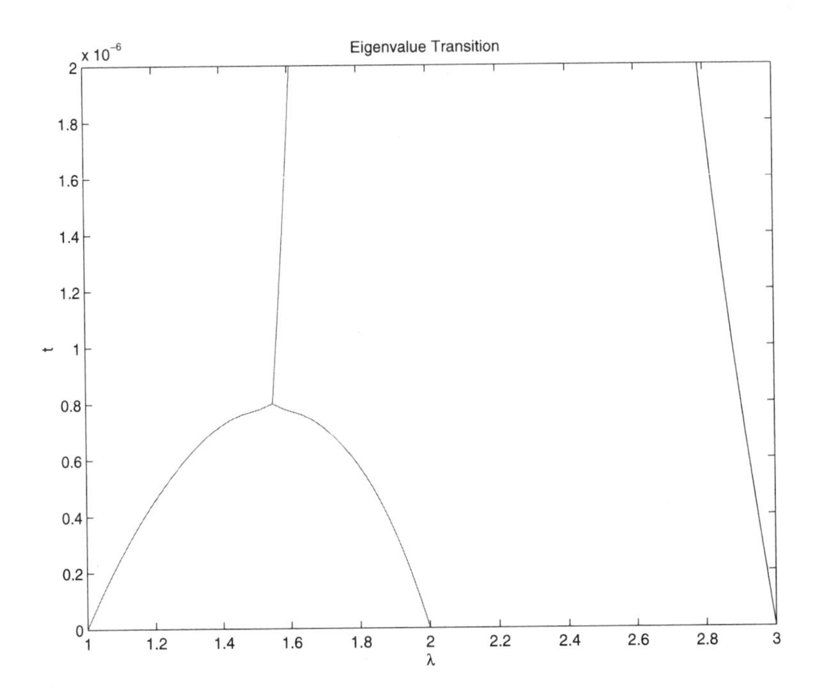

Above `t = 0.8e`$^{-6}$, the graphs of two of the eigenvalues intersect, while below `t` = 0.8e^{-6}, two real roots become a complex conjugate pair. What is the precise value of `t` that marks this transition? Let τ denote this value of `t`.

One way to find τ is based on the fact that, at a double root, both the function and its derivative must vanish. This results in two polynomial equations to be solved for two unknowns. The statement

```
sol = solve(p,diff(p,'x'))
```

solves the pair of algebraic equations `p = 0` and `dp/dx = 0` and produces

```
sol =
    t: [4x1 sym]
    x: [4x1 sym]
```

Find τ now by

```
format short
tau = double(sol.t(2))
```

which reveals that the second element of `sol.t` is the desired value of τ:

```
tau =
   7.8379e-07
```

Therefore, the second element of `sol.x`

```
sigma = double(sol.x(2))
```

is the double eigenvalue

```
sigma =
   1.5476
```

To verify that this value of τ does indeed produce a double eigenvalue at $\sigma = 1.5476$, substitute τ for t in the perturbed matrix $A(t) = A + tE$ and find the eigenvalues of $A(t)$. That is,

```
e = eig(double(subs(A,t,tau)))

e =
   1.5476 + 0.0000i
   1.5476 - 0.0000i
   2.9048
```

confirms that $\sigma = 1.5476$ is a double eigenvalue of $A(t)$ for t = 7.8379e-07.

Solving Equations

Solving Algebraic Equations

If `S` is a symbolic expression,

```
solve(S)
```

attempts to find values of the symbolic variable in `S` (as determined by `findsym`) for which `S` is zero. For example,

```
syms a b c x
S = a*x^2 + b*x + c;
solve(S)
```

uses the familiar quadratic formula to produce

```
ans =
[1/2/a*(-b+(b^2-4*a*c)^(1/2))]
[1/2/a*(-b-(b^2-4*a*c)^(1/2))]
```

This is a symbolic vector whose elements are the two solutions.

If you want to solve for a specific variable, you must specify that variable as an additional argument. For example, if you want to solve `S` for `b`, use the command

```
b = solve(S,b)
```

which returns

```
b =
-(a*x^2+c)/x
```

Note that these examples assume equations of the form $f(x) = 0$. If you need to solve equations of the form $f(x) = q(x)$, you must use quoted strings. In particular, the command

```
s = solve('cos(2*x)+sin(x)=1')
```

returns a vector with four solutions.

```
s =
[       0]
[      pi]
[ 1/6*pi]
[ 5/6*pi]
```

Several Algebraic Equations

This section explains how to solve systems of equations using the Symbolic Math Toolbox. As an example, suppose you have the system

$$x^2y^2 = 0$$

$$x - \frac{y}{2} = \alpha$$

and you want to solve for x and y. First create the necessary symbolic objects.

```
syms x y alpha
```

There are several ways to address the output of solve. One is to use a two-output call

```
[x,y] = solve(x^2*y^2, x-y/2-alpha)
```

which returns

```
x =
[     0]
[     0]
[ alpha]
[ alpha]

y =
[ -2*alpha]
[ -2*alpha]
[        0]
[        0]
```

Consequently, the solution vector

```
v = [x, y]
```

appears to have redundant components. This is due to the first equation $x^2y^2 = 0$, which has two solutions in x and y: $x = \pm 0$, $y = \pm 0$. Changing the equations to

```
eqs1 = 'x^2*y^2=1, x-y/2-alpha'
[x,y] = solve(eqs1)
```

produces four distinct solutions:

```
x =
[ 1/2*alpha+1/2*(alpha^2+2)^(1/2)]
[ 1/2*alpha-1/2*(alpha^2+2)^(1/2)]
[ 1/2*alpha+1/2*(alpha^2-2)^(1/2)]
[ 1/2*alpha-1/2*(alpha^2-2)^(1/2)]


y =
[ -alpha+(alpha^2+2)^(1/2)]
[ -alpha-(alpha^2+2)^(1/2)]
[ -alpha+(alpha^2-2)^(1/2)]
[ -alpha-(alpha^2-2)^(1/2)]
```

Since you did not specify the dependent variables, `solve` uses `findsym` to determine the variables.

This way of assigning output from `solve` is quite successful for "small" systems. Plainly, if you had, say, a 10-by-10 system of equations, typing

```
[x1,x2,x3,x4,x5,x6,x7,x8,x9,x10] = solve(...)
```

is both awkward and time consuming. To circumvent this difficulty, `solve` can return a structure whose fields are the solutions. In particular, consider the system `u^2-v^2 = a^2`, `u + v = 1`, `a^2-2*a = 3`. The command

```
S = solve('u^2-v^2 = a^2','u + v = 1','a^2-2*a = 3')
```

returns

```
S =
    a: [2x1 sym]
    u: [2x1 sym]
    v: [2x1 sym]
```

The solutions for a reside in the "a-field" of S. That is,

```
S.a
```

produces

```
ans =
[  3]
[ -1]
```

Similar comments apply to the solutions for u and v. The structure S can now be manipulated by field and index to access a particular portion of the solution. For example, if you want to examine the second solution, you can use the following statement

```
s2 = [S.a(2), S.u(2), S.v(2)]
```

to extract the second component of each field.

```
s2 =
[ -1,  1,  0]
```

The following statement

```
M = [S.a, S.u, S.v]
```

creates the solution matrix M

```
M =
[  3,  5, -4]
[ -1,  1,  0]
```

whose rows comprise the distinct solutions of the system.

Linear systems of simultaneous equations can also be solved using matrix division. For example,

```
clear u v x y
syms u v x y
S = solve(x+2*y-u, 4*x+5*y-v);
sol = [S.x;S.y]
```

and

```
A = [1 2; 4 5];
b = [u; v];
z = A\b
```

result in

```
sol =

[ -5/3*u+2/3*v]
[  4/3*u-1/3*v]

z =
[ -5/3*u+2/3*v]
[  4/3*u-1/3*v]
```

Thus `s` and `z` produce the same solution, although the results are assigned to different variables.

Single Differential Equation

The function `dsolve` computes symbolic solutions to ordinary differential equations. The equations are specified by symbolic expressions containing the letter `D` to denote differentiation. The symbols `D2`, `D3`, ... `DN`, correspond to the second, third, ..., Nth derivative, respectively. Thus, `D2y` is the Symbolic Math Toolbox equivalent of d^2y/dt^2. The dependent variables are those preceded by `D` and the default independent variable is `t`. Note that names of symbolic variables should not contain `D`. The independent variable can be changed from `t` to some other symbolic variable by including that variable as the last input argument.

Initial conditions can be specified by additional equations. If initial conditions are not specified, the solutions contain constants of integration, `C1`, `C2`, etc.

The output from `dsolve` parallels the output from `solve`. That is, you can call `dsolve` with the number of output variables equal to the number of dependent variables or place the output in a structure whose fields contain the solutions of the differential equations.

Example 1

The following call to `dsolve`

```
dsolve('Dy=1+y^2')
```

uses `y` as the dependent variable and `t` as the default independent variable.

The output of this command is

```
ans =
tan(t+C1)
```

To specify an initial condition, use

```
y = dsolve('Dy=1+y^2','y(0)=1')
```

This produces

```
y =
tan(t+1/4*pi)
```

Notice that `y` is in the MATLAB workspace, but the independent variable `t` is not. Thus, the command `diff(y,t)` returns an error. To place `t` in the workspace, type `syms t`.

Example 2

Nonlinear equations may have multiple solutions, even when initial conditions are given:

```
x = dsolve('(Dx)^2+x^2=1','x(0)=0')
```

results in

```
x =
[ sin(t)]
[ -sin(t)]
```

Example 3

Here is a second order differential equation with two initial conditions. The commands

```
y = dsolve('D2y=cos(2*x)-y','y(0)=1','Dy(0)=0', 'x');
simplify(y)
```

produce

```
ans =
4/3*cos(x)-2/3*cos(x)^2+1/3
```

The key issues in this example are the order of the equation and the initial conditions. To solve the ordinary differential equation

$$\frac{d^3u}{dx^3} = u$$

$$u(0) = 1, u'(0) = -1, u''(0) = \pi$$

simply type

```
u = dsolve('D3u=u','u(0)=1','Du(0)=-1','D2u(0) = pi','x')
```

Use D3u to represent d^3u/dx^3 and D2u(0) for $u''(0)$.

Several Differential Equations

The function dsolve can also handle several ordinary differential equations in several variables, with or without initial conditions. For example, here is a pair of linear, first-order equations.

```
S = dsolve('Df = 3*f+4*g', 'Dg = -4*f+3*g')
```

The computed solutions are returned in the structure S. You can determine the values of f and g by typing

```
f = S.f
f =
exp(3*t)*(C1*sin(4*t)+C2*cos(4*t))

g = S.g
g =
exp(3*t)*(C1*cos(4*t)-C2*sin(4*t))
```

If you prefer to recover f and g directly as well as include initial conditions, type

```
[f,g] = dsolve('Df=3*f+4*g, Dg =-4*f+3*g', 'f(0) = 0, g(0) = 1')
```

```
f =
exp(3*t)*sin(4*t)

g =
exp(3*t)*cos(4*t)
```

This table details some examples and Symbolic Math Toolbox syntax. Note that the final entry in the table is the Airy differential equation whose solution is referred to as the Airy function.

Differential Equation	MATLAB Command
$\frac{dy}{dt} + 4y(t) = e^{-t}$ $y(0) = 1$	`y = dsolve('Dy+4*y = exp(-t)', 'y(0) = 1')`
$\frac{d^2y}{dx^2} + 4y(x) = e^{-2x}$ $y(0) = 0, y(\pi) = 0$	`y = dsolve('D2y+4*y = exp(-2*x)', 'y(0)=0', 'y(pi) = 0', 'x')`
$\frac{d^2y}{dx^2} = xy(x)$ $y(0) = 0, y(3) = \frac{1}{\pi}K_{\frac{1}{3}}(2\sqrt{3})$ (The Airy equation)	`y = dsolve('D2y = x*y','y(0) = 0', 'y(3) = besselk(1/3, 2*sqrt(3))/pi', 'x')`

The Airy function plays an important role in the mathematical modeling of the dispersion of water waves.

Index

Symbols

A

B

C

D

E

Q

R

S

T

V

W

X